Free DVD   Free DVD

Essential Test Tips DVD from Trivium Test Prep

Dear Customer,

Thank you for purchasing from Trivium Test Prep! Whether you're looking to join the military, get into college, or advance your career, we're honored to be a part of your journey.

To show our appreciation (and to help you relieve a little of that test-prep stress), we're offering a **FREE NACE Essential Test Tips DVD** by Trivium Test Prep. Our DVD includes 35 test preparation strategies that will help keep you calm and collected before and during your big exam. All we ask is that you email us your feedback and describe your experience with our product. Amazing, awful, or just so-so: we want to hear what you have to say!

To receive your **FREE NACE Essential Test Tips DVD**, please email us at 5star@triviumtestprep.com. Include "Free 5 Star" in the subject line and the following information in your email:

1. The title of the product you purchased.
2. Your rating from 1 – 5 (with 5 being the best).
3. Your feedback about the product, including how our materials helped you meet your goals and ways in which we can improve our products.
4. Your full name and shipping address so we can send your **FREE NACE Essential Test Tips DVD**.

If you have any questions or concerns please feel free to contact us directly at 5star@triviumtestprep.com.

Thank you, and good luck with your studies!

NURSING ACCELERATION CHALLENGE EXAM RNBSN PRACTICE TEST BOOK:

Exam Prep with 600+ Practice Questions for the NACE II

E. M. Falgout

Copyright © 2021 by Ascencia Test Prep

ISBN-13: 9781637980064

ALL RIGHTS RESERVED. By purchase of this book, you have been licensed one copy for personal use only. No part of this work may be reproduced, redistributed, or used in any form or by any means without prior written permission of the publisher and copyright owner. Ascencia Test Prep; Trivium Test Prep; Accepted, Inc.; and Cirrus Test Prep are all imprints of Trivium Test Prep, LLC.

Ascencia is not affiliated with or endorsed by any testing organization and does not own or claim ownership of any trademarks, specifically for the Nursing Acceleration Challenge Examination (NACE). All test names (and their acronyms) are trademarks of their respective owners. This study guide is for general information only and does not claim endorsement by any third party.

Image(s) used under license from Shutterstock.com

About the Authors

Roma Lightsey, MSN, BSN, RN has been a registered nurse since 2003 and specializes in critical care. She has written content for online nursing programs, NCLEX preparation materials, and peer-reviewed nursing journals. Lightsey has also worked as a national clinical nurse educator.

Rochelle Santopoalo, PhD, RN has been a registered nurse since 1977. She has more than four decades of experience in both nursing and higher education. Santopoalo has served in leadership roles at multiple rehabilitation-focused health care organizations and has taught at several universities.

Table of Contents

Introduction i

Practice Test One 1
PRACTICE TEST ONE ANSWER KEY 43

Practice Test Two 71
PRACTICE TEST TWO ANSWER KEY 112

Practice Test Three 137
PRACTICE TEST THREE ANSWER KEY 178

INTRODUCTION

What is the NACE?

The Nursing Acceleration Challenge Examination (NACE) was developed by the National League for Nursing (NLN) for use by nursing educators. The exam evaluates candidates' nursing knowledge and experience so they can be accurately placed in nursing education programs. The NACE is usually taken by licensed nurses, but allied professionals may also be asked to take the exam as part of a placement evaluation.

The NACE series include seven tests:
- NACE I: Nursing Care of Child
- NACE II: Nursing Care of Child
- NACE I: Nursing Care of Childbearing Family
- NACE II: Nursing Care of Childbearing Family
- NACE I: Foundations of Nursing
- NACE II: Nursing Care of the Adult Client
- NACE II: Nursing Care of the Client with Mental Disorder

What is the Format of the NACE?

The NACE uses the same question format as the NCLEX exams. Most of the questions on the NACE are multiple choice, with four to six answer choices. However, some questions follow *alternate formats*.

Hot-spot questions ask you to move your cursor to label a place on a diagram or figure (for instance, an injection point on an image of a muscle). Fill-in-the-blank questions ask you to answer a question in your own words or to complete a calculation. Ordered-response questions may ask you to arrange a list of steps in a process, for example.

The NACE has no guess penalty. That is, if you answer a question incorrectly, no points are deducted from your score; you simply do not get credit for that question. Therefore, you should always guess if you do not know the answer to a question.

What's on the NACE II: Nursing Care of the Adult Client?

The NACE II: Nursing Care of the Adult Client includes 200 questions on drug administration, nutrition and diet therapies, and nursing interventions for care of patients with the following conditions:

- A. Cardiac
    1. Angina pectoris
    2. Myocardial infarction
    3. Congestive heart failure
    4. Rheumatic heart disease
    5. Mitral stenosis
    6. Heart block
- B. Vascular
    1. Aneurysms
    2. Thrombophlebitis
    3. Embolism
    4. Cerebrovascular accident
    5. Varicose veins
    6. Buerger's disease
    7. Raynaud's disease
    8. Arteriosclerosis
    9. Essential hypertension
- C. Pulmonary
    1. Chronic pulmonary disease
    2. Neoplasms
    3. Tuberculosis
    4. Asthma
    5. Acute respiratory infections

- D. Upper GI System
    1. Hiatus Hernia
    2. Peptic Ulcer
    3. Food Poisoning
    4. Regional Ileitis
    5. Gallbladder Disease
- E. Large Bowel
    1. Appendicitis
    2. Diverticulitis
    3. Ulcerative colitis
    4. Cancer of the colon
    5. Hemorrhoids
    6. Anal abscess
    7. Anal fistula
    8. Pilonidal cyst
- F. Liver and Pancreas
    1. Cancer of the liver
    2. Hepatitis
    3. Pancreatitis
    4. Cirrhosis
- G. Metabolic Regulation
    1. Diabetes mellitus
    2. Hyperthyroidism
    3. Hypothyroidism
    4. Addison's disease
- H. Blood
    1. Pernicious anemia
    2. Nutritional anemia
    3. Sickle cell anemia
    4. Leukemia
    5. Hodgkin's disease
    6. Ruptured spleen
- I. Integumentary Conditions
    1. Herpes zoster
    2. Contact dermatitis
    3. Burns

How is the NACE Administered and Scored?

The NACE is a computer-based test. You will have three and a half hours to take the exam, but you should expect to spend additional time signing in and doing a computer orientation.

The exam is administered by the faculty of the nursing school where the candidate will be placed. Each individual nursing school or program will determine how the exam is administered and whether students will be allowed to retake the exam.

Your NACE score report will show a scaled score from 0 – 100 as well as a subscore for each diagnostic area. Again, each nursing school or program determines how it will use NACE scores as part of its larger candidate placement process. Thus, there is no set score to "pass" the test. Instead, you should speak with your advisor or test administrator about how the results will be used.

Ascencia Test Prep

With health care fields such as nursing, pharmacy, emergency care, and physical therapy becoming the fastest-growing industries in the United States, individuals looking to enter the health care industry or rise in their field need high quality, reliable resources. Ascencia Test Prep's study guides and test preparation materials are developed by credentialed industry professionals with years of experience in their respective fields. Ascencia recognizes that health care professionals nurture bodies and spirits, and save lives. Ascencia Test Prep's mission is to help health care workers grow.

ONE: Practice Test One

READ THE QUESTION, AND THEN CHOOSE THE MOST CORRECT ANSWER.

1. A nurse is preparing a client scheduled for a right mastectomy. Which statement indicates the need for further intervention?
    1. The client refuses to sign the blood consent since she is a Jehovah's Witness.
    2. The client identifies the right breast as the surgical site for a right mastectomy.
    3. The client signs the consent form with an X, which is witnessed by two licensed personnel.
    4. The client expresses doubt over her decision and asks the nurse to explain more about the procedure.

2. The nurse is preparing to transfer a client from the ICU to the floor. Which of the following ensures continuity of care for the client? Select all that apply.
    1. using approved abbreviations in documenting care
    2. providing report on the client using standard hand-off reports
    3. informing the receiving nurse of pending lab results and when they are expected
    4. informing the receiving nurse of any care that needs to be done, such as bathing
    5. telling the receiving nurse that the family is demanding and asks too many questions

3. The nurse has assessed the assigned group of clients. Which client would the nurse identify as being at the greatest risk for alterations in sensory perception?
    1. a client in a halo vest following an automobile accident
    2. a child with severe autism who is having a tonsillectomy
    3. a teenager who broke her leg during cheerleader practice
    4. a schoolteacher who was hospitalized for shortness of breath

4. The nurse is caring for a client with deep vein thrombosis (DVT). Which should be included in the plan of care?
    1. bed rest with the affected extremity elevated
    2. bed rest with the bed in reverse Trendelenburg
    3. walking slowly in the hall with assistance to prevent pneumonia
    4. sitting up in the chair for all meals and during visitation time

5. The nurse is caring for a client who is sedated and on the ventilator in ICU. The family expresses concern about controlling the client's pain when he cannot speak. The nurse explains that assessing pain in a nonverbal client involves watching for which of the following signs? Select all that apply.
    1. grabbing at the bed rails
    2. biting the ventilator tubing
    3. facial grimacing
    4. stiffness or rigidity of the body
    5. decreased urinary output
    6. increased blood pressure and heart rate as shown on the cardiac monitor

6. The nurse is caring for a client with breast cancer who has an order for doxorubicin IV. The nurse anticipates which common side effect of this medication?
    1. permanent hair loss
    2. halos around objects and blurred vision
    3. red urine for 1 – 2 days after administration
    4. facial flushing and red streaking along the vein

7. A nurse in intensive coronary care is caring for a client with an endotracheal tube who underwent coronary bypass surgery. The client awakens and attempts to communicate. Which nursing interventions should the nurse perform? Select all that apply.
    1. offer a communication board
    2. ask simple yes/no questions
    3. ask open-ended questions
    4. offer an electrolarynx

8. The nurse is assessing a client with Addison's disease. The nurse expects to note which of the following?
    1. craving of salty foods
    2. weight gain
    3. craving of sweet foods
    4. hyperactivity

9. An elderly man is admitted to the ED during the night shift. He reports slipping and hitting his forehead on the bathtub several hours earlier. The nurse is assessing the client's frontal lobe function. Which of the following questions/statements should the nurse ask the client?
   1. "Tell me when you feel me touch your arm."
   2. "Tell me when you stop hearing the tuning fork sound."
   3. "Do you have problems with balance?"
   4. "How much is two plus four plus seven?"

10. The nurse is teaching a client about peritoneal dialysis. Which complication of this treatment would the nurse instruct the client to report?
    1. bone pain
    2. confusion
    3. muscle cramps
    4. cloudy outflow

11. The nurse is talking with a client who has been diagnosed with thyroid cancer. The client is asking about different treatment options. Which response by the nurse is most appropriate?
    1. "There are several local support groups you can join after you have completed chemo."
    2. "Don't worry about it. Your doctor will explain the best course of treatment for you."
    3. "What information has your health care provider shared about the different treatment options?"
    4. "I wouldn't take chemo if I were you. I've seen so many clients say that they wish they hadn't done it."

12. The nurse is caring for an elderly client following a total knee replacement. The client is disoriented to time and place, and has pulled out multiple IVs. The health care provider writes an order for soft wrist restraints. Which of the following are appropriate nursing actions for this client? Select all that apply.
    1. secure restraints with a double knot
    2. offer toileting and nutrition every 2 hours
    3. ask for a new restraint order every 48 hours
    4. check restraints for proper placement and check the skin every 2 hours
    5. document the type of restraint, need for continued use, and trial release results

13. The nurse is preparing to administer the first dose of IV antibiotic to the client. Halfway through the infusion, the nurse realizes that the antibiotic dosage is not the same as ordered by the health care provider. Which action should the nurse take first?
    1. stop the infusion
    2. fill out an incident form
    3. notify the health care provider
    4. only give part of the antibiotic to obtain the correct dose

14. The nurse is in the medication room drawing up insulin for a client when a code blue is called. In his haste to respond to the call, the nurse places the syringe of insulin on the counter and responds to the code. Afterward, the nurse returns to the medication room and retrieves the syringe of insulin. Which action by the nurse is correct?
    1. return the insulin to the insulin vial and draw up a new syringe
    2. administer the insulin after labeling the syringe with the date, dose, and client name
    3. dispose of the syringe in the sharps container, and draw up a new dose in a new syringe
    4. administer the insulin that was drawn up, since the syringe is still in the medication room

15. An elderly client's wife tells a nurse she is concerned because her husband insists on talking about past events. The nurse assesses the client and finds him alert, oriented, and responsive to questions. Which statement should the nurse make to the client's wife?
    1. "Your husband is choosing to live in a happier time in his life."
    2. "Redirect your husband to speak about current events when he begins regressing into the past."
    3. "If he were my husband, I would call our minister to speak to him."
    4. "Your husband is reflecting on his life. This is normal at his age."

16. A client who is postmenopausal asks the nurse how to prevent osteoporosis. Which statement should the nurse make to the client?
    1. "Eat 2 ounces of cheese each day and walk a mile a day."
    2. "There are no known ways to prevent osteoporosis."
    3. "Do weight-bearing exercises regularly and take hormones as ordered by your physician."
    4. "Take potassium supplements daily."

17. The nurse is caring for a client who is HIV-positive. The nurse understands which of the following to be true regarding HIV and AIDS?
    1. Viral load testing monitors disease progression and evaluates effectiveness of treatment.
    2. The Western blot test is positive if antibodies to at least three major HIV antigens are present.
    3. Patients with AIDS present with a white blood cell (WBC) count between 5,000 and 10,000 cells/mm3.
    4. An enzyme-linked immunosorbent assay (ELISA) test can detect the presence of antibodies within 2 weeks of exposure.

18. The nurse is performing hemodialysis on a client, with the understanding that air embolus is a complication of this treatment. Which assessment findings by the nurse indicate an air embolus?
    1. cold intolerance
    2. chest pain and anxiety
    3. decreased respirations
    4. hypertension and widening pulse pressure

19. The nurse is caring for a client who recently experienced a massive stroke. Which of the following statements by the spouse indicates a need for further teaching by the nurse?
    1. "My spouse may not return to normal for some time."
    2. "I plan on returning to work full time as soon as my spouse returns home."
    3. "Home health care will help us once my spouse is discharged."
    4. "You will provide me with support during this difficult time."

20. A client who is Muslim is refusing to eat food served to him by a nursing assistant. The nurse should do which of the following? Select all that apply.
    1. arrange a mealtime that will avoid prayer times
    2. remove farm-raised catfish from the food tray
    3. arrange with the family for halal food to be brought from home
    4. deliver food by a nursing assistant of the same sex

21. The nurse is taking care of a 12-year-old male who sustained 30% full-thickness burns on his chest and arms 20 hours ago. To maintain optimal fluid and electrolyte balance, the nurse expects to administer which of the following?
    1. lactated Ringer's
    2. D10W
    3. plasma
    4. normal saline

22. The nurse working in an outpatient pain clinic has the opportunity to teach a client with chronic back pain about nonpharmacological pain management. Which of the following would be most appropriate for the nurse to include when teaching? Select all that apply.
    1. music
    2. therapeutic massage
    3. stretching exercises
    4. relaxation

23. The nurse working in an outpatient clinic has the opportunity to teach a client recently diagnosed with irritable bowel syndrome (IBS). Which of the following topics would be most appropriate for the nurse to include? Select all that apply.
    1. daily iced tea intake
    2. stress reduction techniques
    3. limit fluids
    4. daily probiotic

24. The nurse is caring for an elderly female client in an extended-care facility who has dry age-related macular degeneration (AMD). Which nursing intervention would be the most appropriate?
    1. provide written materials to explain medications
    2. stand in front of the client when addressing her
    3. limit room lighting to create a relaxed environment
    4. encourage use of radio and CDs

25. The nurse working in an outpatient clinic is preparing to teach insulin injection to an elderly male client who is hard of hearing yet refuses to wear prescribed hearing aids. Which of the following communication strategies would be most appropriate for the nurse to use?
    1. speak in a high-pitched voice
    2. use sign language
    3. ensure the room is well lit
    4. refrain from touching the client

26. The nurse is caring for a group of clients in an infectious disease unit. The nurse understands that which of the conditions listed are required to be reported by the CDC? Select all that apply.
    1. tetanus
    2. scarlet fever
    3. chlamydia
    4. Lyme disease
    5. group B streptococcal infection

27. The nurse administers ciproflaxin to a client and then realizes that the client is allergic to the medication. What nursing action is the priority for this client?
    1. induce vomiting
    2. obtain the client's vital signs
    3. complete an incident report
    4. notify the health care provider

28. The nurse is monitoring a client taking chlordiazepoxide hydrochloride (Librium). Which adverse effect would be of greatest concern?
    1. hiccups
    2. lethargy
    3. drowsiness
    4. respiratory depression

29. The nurse has an order to give 1,000 mL of 0.9% NS with 20 meQ of potassium chloride over 8 hours. The IV set has a drop factor of 15. How many gtts/min should the client receive?

    _____

30. The nurse is monitoring the labs of a client admitted with viral hepatitis. Which of the following lab findings would the nurse expect for this client? Select all that apply.
    1. decreased ALT levels
    2. increased AST levels
    3. elevated ammonia levels
    4. low serum albumin levels
    5. shortened prothrombin time

31. The nurse is talking to a client and his family about hepatitis. Which of the following statements by a family member indicate understanding of the nurse's teaching? Select all that apply.
    1. "Hepatitis D only occurs with hepatitis B."
    2. "Hepatitis A can occur at any time of the year."
    3. "Hepatitis D is transmitted through contaminated drinking water."
    4. "Hepatitis A can be spread by uncooked shellfish and contaminated water or milk."
    5. "Hepatitis B is spread by contact with blood or body fluids, sexual contact, or sharing dirty needles."

32. The nurse is caring for a client who just had a supratentorial craniotomy to remove a tumor. The nurse will implement which of the following in the client's plan of care? Select all that apply.
    1. check the dressing every 8 hours for excessive drainage
    2. assess the pupils for signs of increased intracranial pressure
    3. position the client flat with the head rotated away from the surgical site
    4. monitor the client's respiratory status, including rate and pattern of breathing
    5. notify the health care provider if the dressing is saturated or the client has more than 50 mL of drainage in 8 hours

33. The nurse is caring for a client who presents to the ED with the following arterial blood gas (ABG) results:

    pH 7.32
    PaCO2 47 mm Hg
    HCO3 24 mEq/L
    PaO2 91 mm Hg

    Which clinical manifestation would the nurse anticipate, based on these findings?
    1. confusion
    2. nausea and vomiting
    3. deep, rapid respirations
    4. hypoventilation with hypoxia

34. The nurse is caring for a client with abdominal aortic aneurysm. Which observation by the nurse indicates the need for immediate intervention?
    1. complaints of yellow-tinted vision
    2. sudden onset of frothy, pink sputum
    3. urinary output of 75 mL/hr. per urinary catheter
    4. complaints of sudden and severe back pain and shortness of breath

35. A nursing student is assigned to a client with an endotracheal tube on a ventilator. Upon entering the client's room the primary care nurse is alerted by observing which of the following?
    1. The head of the bed is elevated 45 degrees.
    2. The cuff on the endotracheal tube is inflated.
    3. Normal saline is present at the bedside table.
    4. The client is wearing an intermittent compression device on each leg.

36. The nurse is assessing a client at home who is receiving outpatient hemodialysis 12 hours a week. The nurse knows the client needs further instruction about proper diet when he states which of the following?
    1. "I drink prune juice when I'm constipated."
    2. "I drink ginger ale with lunch."
    3. "I drink 1 cup of milk with my dinner."
    4. "My bread choice is white rather than whole grain."

37. The nurse is teaching a female client who is experiencing urge incontinence how to manage her condition at home. Which statement by the client indicates a need for further explanation by the nurse?
    1. "I will be cured in four weeks if I follow the bladder retraining instructions."
    2. "I will perform the pelvic muscle exercises daily."
    3. "I will wait five minutes once I get the urge to urinate to go to the bathroom."
    4. "I will empty my bladder when I first get up in the morning."

38. A nurse has received report on the day's clients. In planning morning rounds, which client is the priority to see?
    1. a new admission with a UTI and fever
    2. a client who is NPO for surgery later in the morning
    3. a client complaining of nausea after eating breakfast
    4. a client recently complaining of shortness of breath

39. A client has signed the consent form for a right radical mastectomy. Shortly before the client is to be taken to surgery, she tells the nurse, "I'm not really sure that this is what I want to do. Everything was so sudden." Which response by the nurse is most appropriate?
    1. "You will be glad you did it once it's over."
    2. "What are your thoughts right now on this procedure?"
    3. "I will notify the surgeon and let her know you have concerns about having the surgery."
    4. "The OR has been prepared for you, and the doctor will be mad if you mess up the surgery schedule."

40. A client is on contact and airborne precautions. In which order should the nurse don personal protective equipment (PPE) before entering the room?
    1. perform hand hygiene, don the gown, don the mask, don eye protection, apply gloves
    2. don the gown, perform hand hygiene, don the mask, apply gloves, don eye protection
    3. don the mask, don eye protection, perform hand hygiene, don the gown, apply gloves
    4. don eye protection, don the mask, perform hand hygiene, apply gloves, don the gown
    5. perform hand hygiene, apply gloves, don the gown, don the mask, don eye protection

41. The nurse is caring for a client on airborne precautions. Which of the following would the nurse expect to see in the client's medical record?
    1. measles
    2. influenza
    3. Lyme disease
    4. herpes simplex

42. The nurse is preparing to pull a thin, frail client up in the bed. No one responds to the nurse's call for lifting assistance. Which is the best action by the nurse?
    1. call again and apologize to the client for the wait
    2. stand behind the bed at the client's head, and pull her up gently from her armpits
    3. since the client is small, pull her up in the bed by pulling on the draw sheet, alternating sides
    4. if the client is able to roll and bend her knees, lower the head of the bed and place it in Trendelenburg's position while helping the client bend her knees and push up

43. A client asks what diabetes mellitus does to the body over time. Which condition should the nurse include in teaching as a common chronic complication of diabetes mellitus?
    1. hyperglycemia
    2. diabetic ketoacidosis
    3. hyperglycemia
    4. retinopathy

44. A client has recently lost her best friend to cancer. The client tells the nurse, "I'm very sad about the loss of my friend." Which of the following responses by the nurse is the most appropriate?
    1. "I lost my best friend two years ago, but I feel better now."
    2. "It's important for you to keep busy."
    3. "Why do you feel this way?"
    4. "It's normal to feel loss. Tell me about your friend."

45. The nurse is caring for a client in the intensive care unit. The nurse recognizes that to prevent sensory alteration in a client, the nurse needs to do which of the following interventions? Select all that apply.
    1. orient the client to person, place, and time during every contact
    2. limit visitors to one 15-minute visit per 8-hour shift
    3. explain all nursing care
    4. keep the lighting level consistent throughout the day

46. An 88-year-old client fractured a hip after a fall in her home. Because of her peripheral vascular disease and asthma, surgery is not an option. The client tells the nurse she does not know how she is going to get better. Which response by the nurse is best?
    1. "You'll do just fine."
    2. "You can't live alone anymore."
    3. "What are you most worried about?"
    4. "You should get a second opinion."

47. The nurse is caring for a client with hypoparathyroidism. The nurse understands that this client is at risk for which problem?

1. hypercalcemia
2. hypermagnesemia
3. decreased phosphorus levels
4. low parathyroid hormone levels

48. The nurse is performing an admission assessment on a client with thrombocytopenia. Which signs and symptoms and lab findings would the nurse expect to see in this client? Select all that apply.

1. epistaxis
2. petechiae
3. vomiting blood
4. elevated hematocrit
5. increased platelet count

49. The nurse is taking a history from a client in an outpatient clinic. The client has been taking duloxetine (Cymbalta) for fibromyalgia. Which of the following over-the-counter medications would cause the nurse some concern if the client says she is taking it?

1. aspirin
2. garlic supplements
3. vitamin B6
4. cough medicine with dextromethorphan

50. The nurse is caring for a client with Crohn's disease. How should the nurse educate the client regarding nutrition and hydration?

1. Drink coffee each morning, as this can help stimulate the appetite.
2. Avoid enteral supplements, as they may decrease the appetite for solid foods.
3. Select high-calorie, low-fiber, high-protein, and high-vitamin foods for each meal.
4. Drink clear liquids as soon as they are tolerated, and then progress the diet rapidly in order to obtain needed nutrients.

51. The nurse is caring for a client who is at risk for altered fluid balance. Which signs and symptoms of dehydration would the nurse expect to find in this client? Select all that apply.

1. bounding pulses
2. increased hematocrit
3. orthostatic hypotension
4. diminished bowel sounds
5. decreased urine specific gravity

52. The nurse is caring for a client who has stage 3 lung cancer and is in renal failure. The client indicates that he does not wish to have life-sustaining treatment and wants to die a natural death. What document does the nurse anticipate this client completing? Fill in the blank.

   _____

53. The nurse is caring for a client post-op day 1 for a bowel resection. The client is receiving pain medication via a patient-controlled analgesic pump (PCA) but states that her pain is severe and the pain pump is not providing adequate relief. Which is the priority nursing action for this client?

    1. assess vital signs and pain for location, quality, and intensity
    2. reposition the client with the head of bed elevated 30 degrees
    3. offer nonpharmacologic pain relief measures since the medication dose cannot be increased
    4. press the PCA button to deliver a bolus and ask family members to press the button for the client if she is asleep

54. The nurse is caring for a client receiving IV heparin therapy for a pulmonary embolism. Which lab values would the nurse expect to order on this client?

    1. hematocrit
    2. HDL and LDL
    3. PT, PTT, INR
    4. troponin level

55. The nurse on a physical rehabilitation unit is assigned a 63-year-old male client post-amputation of his left lower limb above the knee two weeks prior. The client has a history of peripheral vascular disease due to diabetes mellitus. Which statement by the client indicates a need for further teaching?

    1. "I had my leg removed because of diabetes."
    2. "My exercises are going well."
    3. "My left leg hurts after I wrap my stump."
    4. "I use canes to walk to the bathroom."

56. The nurse is caring for a client diagnosed with a cerebral aneurysm. Which precautions would the nurse put in place for this client? Select all that apply.

    1. keep the room dark and avoid direct, bright lights
    2. allow frequent visitors to provide social interaction to the client
    3. administer deep vein thrombosis (DVT) prophylaxis as ordered
    4. encourage the client to breathe deep and cough to clear secretions
    5. keep the client on bed rest in a side-lying or semi-Fowler's position

57. The nurse is caring for a client who has been diagnosed with pulseless electrical activity (PEA). Following effective CPR and administration of epinephrine, which is the next priority nursing action?

1. check for a pulse
2. insert a urinary catheter
3. prepare to shock the client
4. administer a bolus of sodium bicarbonate

58. The nurse is caring for a client with cardiogenic shock. The nurse expects which signs present with this client? Select all that apply.

1. hypertension; slow, labored breathing
2. decreased urine output; warm, pink skin
3. increased urine output; cool, clammy skin
4. hypotension; weak pulse; cool, clammy skin

59. The nurse is caring for a client who fractured her leg in a motor vehicle accident. A cast is applied. The nurse will assess which of the following? Select all that apply.

1. pulses
2. capillary refill
3. skin temperature
4. squeeze the cast every hour to check for firmness
5. assess for pain, numbness, tingling, or inability to move the toes

60. The nurse is providing post-op education to a client who had a splenectomy. Which statement by the client indicates that the nurse's teaching was successful?

1. "I can resume yoga classes in two weeks."
2. "I need to eat a diet low in fiber to rest my digestive tract."
3. "I will need to be careful when I go to the NFL game next month."
4. "I need to talk to my doctor about getting influenza, pneumococcal, and meningococcal vaccines."

61. The nurse is caring for a client with dementia who has pulled out three peripheral IVs. Which intervention by the nurse is the best way to manage this client?

1. place the client in restraints or mitts
2. tell the family that they need to stay with the client
3. replace the IV and wrap it in gauze to hide it from view
4. tell the client that if she pulls another IV out, she will have to have a PICC line placed

62. The nurse is preparing a 73-year-old client for cataract surgery on the left eye. Which statement by the client indicates a need for further teaching?
    1. "I will wear glasses when going outside."
    2. "I will avoid bending below the waist."
    3. "I will stop taking Coumadin after surgery."
    4. "I will still be able to work out on weight training."

63. A client admitted for treatment of a deep venous thrombosis of the calf complains of dyspnea and chest pain. What is the best response by the nurse?
    1. administer oxygen at 2L/min as ordered prn
    2. place client in a semi-Fowler's position
    3. prepare client for diagnostic tests
    4. obtain vital signs

64. The nurse in an ambulatory care clinic is admitting a 27-year-old client with severe systemic lupus erythematosus (SLE). In assessing the client's health history, the nurse knows to question which of the following statements?
    1. "I avoid being outside on sunny days."
    2. "The medications I take make me bloated."
    3. "My work schedule is down to four hours a day."
    4. "I get an eye exam annually."

65. The nurse is reviewing labs on a client receiving IV heparin and notes an INR of 4.6. Which order by the health care provider does the nurse anticipate?
    1. an order for vitamin K IM
    2. an order for protamine sulfate
    3. an order to redraw labs in 6 hours
    4. an order to increase the infusion rate

66. The nurse is providing client education on self-administration of insulin. Which action by the client indicates the need for further education?
    1. The client gently rubs the insertion site after removing the needle.
    2. The client verifies the type of insulin and checks the expiration date.
    3. The client cleans and grasps the skin, inserting the needle at a 90-degree angle.
    4. The client cleans the rubber stopper on the bottle with an alcohol swab before drawing a dose.

67. A nurse working in ICU has a client on a propofol (Diprivan) drip while on the mechanical ventilator. The nurse needs another bottle, which must be picked up in person in the hospital pharmacy. Which is the correct action by the nurse concerning this medication?

1. ask the unit secretary to go to the pharmacy and pick it up
2. send the unlicensed assistive personnel (UAP) to pick it up since the nurse is busy
3. ask the client's health care provider to bring it when he or she rounds on the client
4. ask another nurse to watch the clients while the nurse goes to the pharmacy to get the medication

68. A 68-year-old woman newly diagnosed with diabetes is preparing for discharge. Which of the following activities best describes the nurse's role as an advocate?

1. teach the client how to test her glucose level
2. provide a short-term supply of insulin syringes
3. refer the patient to home health care follow-up
4. reinforce the follow-up visit to her primary care provider in two weeks

69. An enema is prescribed for a client with suspected appendicitis. The nurse should take which action?

1. tell the client to lie on his left side
2. explain the procedure to the client
3. compile necessary equipment
4. question the physician about the order

70. The nurse enters the client's room and smells cigarette smoke. When confronted, the client says, "I only smoked one cigarette because I was having a bad craving." Which action by the nurse is most appropriate?

1. escort the client outside to smoke
2. call the health care provider to obtain an order for a nicotine patch
3. remind the client that oxygen is in use and smoking is banned in the facility
4. tell the client that if he continues to smoke in the room, he will be discharged from the hospital

71. The nurse is providing education at a senior center. Which of the following measures will the nurse say is most effective in attaining normal blood pressure in a client with hypertension?

1. eating red meat daily
2. increasing potassium and calcium intake
3. increasing fluid intake
4. decreasing sodium intake

72. A 92-year-old male client with Alzheimer's frequently experiences urinary incontinence. Which intervention should the nurse do first?
    1. apply a condom catheter
    2. insert an indwelling catheter
    3. apply a diaper
    4. offer the urinal every 2 hours

73. The nurse is caring for a client newly diagnosed with diabetes type 2. The health care provider plans to start the client on a rapid-acting insulin. Which insulin does the nurse anticipate noting on the order?
    1. Lantus
    2. Levemir
    3. Humalog
    4. Humulin 70/30

74. A community center is having a health fair. Which of the following main food courses should the nurse recommend as most healthful for a 20-year-old adult whose total cholesterol level is 300 mg/dL?
    1. fettuccine alfredo
    2. fried chicken
    3. grilled cheese sandwich with bacon
    4. natural peanut butter and banana sandwich on whole wheat bread

75. A student nurse is precepting on the unit and caring for a client with a Dobbhoff nasoenteric tube. Which statement by the student nurse indicates the need for further teaching on caring for a client with this tube? Select all that apply.
    1. "I should wait for X-ray confirmation before using the tube."
    2. "I can confirm placement by auscultating over the epigastric area."
    3. "I can mix liquid medications in with the tube feeding for administration."
    4. "I will flush the tube with 20 to 30 mL of water every 4 hours during continuous tube feeding."
    5. "I will observe the client for diarrhea, abdominal distention, nausea and vomiting, and tube dislodgement."

76. The nurse is reviewing morning labs for a client. Which lab value requires immediate intervention by the nurse?
    1. calcium 9.8 mg/dL
    2. sodium 137 mEq/L
    3. chloride 104 mEq/L
    4. potassium 3.1 mEq/L

77. A client recently diagnosed with atrial fibrillation is being discharged home on digoxin (Lanoxin). The nurse is providing education to the client and family. Which client statement indicates the need for further teaching?

1. "I should take my medicine at the same time each day."
2. "If I miss a dose, I can take it as soon as I remember it."
3. "I need to call my doctor if my heart rate goes below 60 or above 110."
4. "Changes in my vision could be toxicity and should be reported immediately."

78. The nurse is caring for a client who just arrived in the PACU following a colonoscopy with polyp removal. The client's level of sedation is assessed using the Ramsay Sedation Scale (RSS). The client responds quickly, but only to commands. What Ramsay score would the nurse chart for this client?

1. RSS 1
2. RSS 2
3. RSS 3
4. RSS 4
5. RSS 5
6. RSS 6

79. The nurse is caring for a client receiving hemodialysis. During hemodialysis, the client becomes anxious, experiencing tachypnea and hypotension. The nurse suspects which complication of hemodialysis?

1. air embolism
2. clotting of the graft site
3. dialysis encephalopathy
4. disequilibrium syndrome

80. The nurse is seeing a client in the clinic who has shingles (herpes zoster). The client is concerned about spreading the disease to others. How should the nurse respond?

1. It is only possible to have one episode of the disease.
2. Persons with leukemia are at higher risk.
3. Persons of all ages should receive the zoster vaccine (Zostavax).
4. Persons between 30 and 40 years old are at high risk.

81. The nurse is caring for a client after he experienced a seizure (postictal). Which intervention would the nurse expect not to perform?

1. return client to pre-seizure activity
2. administer medications as appropriate
3. reorient as necessary
4. assess neurologic and vital signs

82. The nurse is teaching feeding protocol to the spouse of a client who experienced a severe stroke. Which statement by the spouse indicates a need for further explanation by the nurse?
    1. "I will not let him use a straw."
    2. "I will turn on the television during meals."
    3. "Instead of whole pills, I will crush the pill and place it in custard."
    4. "He will sit up for a half hour after eating."

83. The nurse is reviewing arterial blood gases (ABGs) on a client. Which finding would prompt the nurse to notify the health care provider?
    1. pH 7.42
    2. pH 7.67
    3. hCO3 24 mEq/L
    4. paCO2 41 mmHg
    5. paCO2 44 mmHg

84. The nurse is caring for a client receiving warfarin therapy for atrial fibrillation. Laboratory results show an INR of 3.9. The nurse would expect which order from the health care provider?
    1. an order to increase the warfarin dose
    2. an order to decrease the warfarin dose
    3. an order for protamine sulfate
    4. no new order; the INR is therapeutic

85. A client scheduled for a cardiac catheterization tells the nurse, "My mother died during this same procedure 10 years ago. I'm afraid the same thing will happen to me." Which of the following responses by the nurse is the most appropriate?
    1. "It's normal to be scared. You are safe here. Let's discuss the procedure."
    2. "I'll ask the cardiologist to come and speak with you about your concerns."
    3. "We have the best outcomes of any facility in the area for this procedure."
    4. "Don't worry. The procedure has improved a lot in the last 10 years."

86. A young male client who has recently become a quadriplegic makes a sexually inappropriate comment to the nurse. Which of the following statements by the nurse would be most appropriate?
    1. "It is inappropriate to speak me or any nurse that way."
    2. "While you're attractive, I'm married."
    3. "Don't you have a fiancé?"
    4. "I'm old enough to be your parent."

87. The nurse is infusing total parenteral nutrition (TPN) through a peripherally inserted central catheter. The client's TPN was turned off for 1 hour for an MRI. Which action by the nurse is most appropriate for this client?
    1. notify the health care provider for further orders
    2. discard the volume of the TPN that should have been administered and make a note in the chart
    3. double the flow rate on the infusion for 1 hour to keep the TPN on schedule, and then resume the normal flow rate
    4. increase the flow rate on the infusion for two hours to keep the TPN on schedule, and then resume the normal flow rate

88. The nurse is providing discharge teaching to a client newly diagnosed with heart failure. Which statement by the client indicates an understanding of the side effects of furosemide (Lasix)?
    1. "I should eat bananas, dried dates, or peaches every day."
    2. "I should check my heart rate before taking this medicine."
    3. "I will avoid foods containing tyramine while on this medicine."
    4. "I will not take the medicine when I have to go on a long car trip."

89. The nurse is preparing to deliver an infusion of vancomycin through a client's peripherally inserted central catheter (PICC). Shortly after the infusion begins the IV pumps beeps, indicating a blockage. How should the nurse proceed? Select all that apply.
    1. start a peripheral IV in the opposite limb
    2. notify the PICC nurse if unable to clear the blockage
    3. use a 5 mL syringe to flush the PICC with sterile saline
    4. ask the client to raise and lower the arm or cough
    5. attempt to flush the line by aggressively pushing heparin to clear the blockage
    6. use a 10 mL syringe to gently flush the PICC with sterile saline or tPA as ordered

90. The nurse is caring for a client taking vancomycin. The nurse anticipates drawing a peak and trough on this client. Which statement regarding peak and trough levels is correct?
    1. The peak is drawn 1 hour after the infusion, and the trough is drawn right before the next scheduled dose.
    2. The peak is drawn 2 hours after the infusion, and the trough is drawn 1 hour before the next scheduled dose.
    3. The peak should be drawn immediately after infusion, and the trough is drawn right before the next scheduled dose.
    4. The peak should be drawn 30 minutes before the next scheduled dose, and the trough drawn immediately after the infusion.

91. The nurse is caring for a client receiving IV vancomycin. The trough level is 14 mcg/mL. The next dose is now due. What is the correct response by the nurse?
    1. give the next dose as ordered
    2. wait 2 hours and redraw the trough
    3. wait 30 minutes and redraw the trough
    4. hold the dose and notify the health care provider

92. The nurse is preparing to discharge a client diagnosed with gout. Which statement by the client indicates understanding of dietary restrictions while managing gout?
    1. "I should avoid beer, anchovies, and liver."
    2. "I should avoid bananas, grapefruit, and oranges."
    3. "I should avoid dairy products such as milk and ice cream."
    4. "I should avoid red wine, dark chocolate, and aged cheeses."

93. The nurse is assessing a client who has a sacral pressure ulcer. The wound has partial thickness, loss of dermis and a red-pink wound bed. No slough is present. How would the nurse chart this wound?
    1. Stage I
    2. Stage II
    3. Stage III
    4. Stage IV
    5. unstageable

94. A child who ingested 18 500-mg acetaminophen tablets 30 minutes ago is seen in the ED. Which of these orders should the nurse do first?
    1. activated charcoal per pharmacy
    2. start an IV with D5W to keep the vein open
    3. gastric lavage PRN
    4. acetylcysteine (Mucomyst) for age per pharmacy

95. The nurse is caring for a client with a stage II sacral ulcer. Which nursing intervention would be most effective in promoting healing?
    1. a heat lamp positioned 12 inches from the skin for 10 minutes twice a day
    2. antibiotic therapy as ordered
    3. increasing the client's nutritional intake of protein and calories
    4. wet to dry dressings once every shift

96. The nurse is teaching a client about dietary modifications to control hypertension. Which statement by the client indicates a need for further teaching?

1. "I can have a cup of fresh fruit as a snack."
2. "Baked ham is a good dinner choice for me."
3. "I need to check the label for sodium in ketchup."
4. "I need to cut out frozen pizza as a fast meal option."

97. The nurse is caring for a client who has shortness of breath, +2 pitting edema bilaterally of the lower extremities, crackles in the bases of the lungs, and a weight gain of 7 pounds in 1 week. The nurse administers furosemide 40 mg IV as ordered. Which would the nurse anticipate to indicate that the furosemide was effective? Select all that apply.

1. pitting edema of +3
2. pitting edema of +1
3. less shortness of breath
4. an increase in urine output of 250 mL/hr
5. a decrease or absence of crackles in the lungs

98. The nurse is caring for a client with left-sided heart failure. Which assessment findings does the nurse anticipate for this client? Select all that apply.

1. dyspnea
2. engorged spleen
3. dependent edema
4. jugular vein distention
5. weak peripheral pulses
6. crackles or wheezes in the lungs

99. The nurse is admitting a client directly from a health provider's office. The client has a rash and has been diagnosed with measles. Which room assignment by the nurse indicates an understanding of the disease process of measles?

1. a private negative-pressure room
2. a semiprivate room with a client who has a broken femur
3. a semiprivate room with a client diagnosed with type 1 diabetes
4. a private room at the end of the hall away from the nurses' station

100. The nurse is caring for a group of clients who are experiencing pain. Which client is the priority for the nurse to see first?

1. a client with dull abdominal pain and constipation
2. a client complaining of pain 6/10 due to sickle cell crisis
3. a client with severe chest pain experiencing an acute myocardial infarction (MI)
4. a client who had a laparoscopic appendectomy yesterday with mild incision pain

101. The nurse is caring for a client diagnosed with C. diff. The client has soiled the bed and the nurse is preparing to change it. Which action by the nurse is correct in regard to handling soiled linens that have been exposed to C. diff?
    1. throw the linens in the trash can in the soiled utility room
    2. leave the dirty linens in a bag in the client's room until he is discharged
    3. place the items in a red biohazard bag and place them in the soiled utility room
    4. place the soiled linen in a regular dirty linen bag and place in the soiled utility room

102. A nurse is planning care for a client with human immunodeficiency virus. The nurse knows to wear gloves under the following circumstance(s). Select all that apply.
    1. when there is an open wound
    2. during all client contact
    3. when starting an IV
    4. when drawing blood for a specimen

103. The nurse is caring for a client admitted with chest pain and atrial fibrillation. The nurse accidentally gives the client the wrong dose of digoxin. The client is monitored throughout the shift and no ill effects are noted. Which actions by the nurse are correct? Select all that apply.
    1. fill out an incident report and make a note of it in the nurse's notes
    2. print out rhythm strips every 2 hours and place on the client's chart
    3. fill out an incident report and notify the health care provider for further orders
    4. notify the health care provider at the end of the shift, since no ill effects were observed
    5. notify the pharmacy that they loaded the wrong dose in the automatic medication dispensing system

104. The nurse is preparing her client for an MRI to evaluate intracranial hemorrhage. Which finding in the client history would prompt the nurse to notify the health care provider?
    1. vertigo
    2. atrial fibrillation
    3. allergy to contrast dye
    4. past military duty in Iraq

105. The nurse finds a client crying after she was told hemodialysis is needed due to the development of acute renal failure. Which intervention is best?
    1. refer the client to the chaplain
    2. quietly sit with the client
    3. arrange for a hemodialysis client to speak with her
    4. leave the client alone

106. The nurse is caring for a middle-aged woman who walks 3 miles every morning. The nurse notes that during her morning walk, the client called her son and stated that she thought she was having a heart attack. Which symptom, identified by the client, is the most common and consistent with a myocardial infarction (MI)?
    1. palpitations
    2. lower extremity edema
    3. uncomfortable feeling of pressure in the chest
    4. nausea

107. A client undergoes total shoulder replacement on the left shoulder. Which statements by the client indicates he requires further teaching? Select all that apply.
    1. "I look forward to soaking in my hot tub when I get home from surgery."
    2. "The surgery will eliminate my pain within 24 hours."
    3. "I will receive therapy for several weeks after my surgery."
    4. "Walking is an exercise I'll be able to do after surgery."

108. While terminating the therapeutic nurse-client relationship, which action should be avoided?
    1. raise a new issue with the client
    2. review accomplishments of the relationship
    3. refer the client to a community support group
    4. allow the client to express his feelings about ending the relationship

109. A 53-year-old client had a colostomy 2 days ago due to colon cancer and is having trouble adjusting to it. Following this procedure, which condition is most common?
    1. disturbed body image
    2. panic attacks
    3. impaired mobility
    4. acute pain

110. The oncology nurse is caring for a 24-year-old male client with testicular cancer. Cisplatin IV has been ordered. Which lab value would the nurse notify the health care provider about before administering this medication?
    1. iron 129 mcg/dL
    2. ammonia level 52 mcg/dL
    3. creatinine clearance 23 mL/minute
    4. brain natriuretic peptides (BNP) 36 pg/mL

111. The nurse is preparing to administer streptomycin 0.25 g. The directions say to reconstitute with 9 mL of sterile water for a concentration of 400 mg/2 mL. How many mLs will the nurse give? Fill in the blank.

    _____

112. A client has orders for ampicillin 350 mg IM daily. The directions state to reconstitute with 3.5 mL of sterile water for a concentration of 500 mg/mL. How much will the nurse give?

    _____

113. The nurse is caring for a client with a wound that presents with full-thickness tissue loss and eschar covering the wound bed. The nurse would record this wound as which stage?

    1. Stage I
    2. Stage II
    3. Stage III
    4. Stage IV
    5. unstageable

114. The nurse is monitoring the labs of a client admitted with viral hepatitis. Which of the following lab findings would the nurse expect for this client? Select all that apply.

    1. decreased ALT levels
    2. increased AST levels
    3. elevated ammonia levels
    4. low serum albumin levels
    5. shortened prothrombin time

115. A nurse is floated to oncology from the postsurgical floor. The assigned client is almost finished with an infusion of doxorubicin for breast cancer. The floated nurse is not chemotherapy certified. Which nursing action is the priority in this situation?

    1. assess the client's pain
    2. ask another nurse about side effects of the drug
    3. assess the IV site, including the date on the tubing and IV site
    4. inform the charge nurse that she is not chemotherapy certified and ask for another assignment

116. A client is scheduled for a CT with and without contrast to rule out diverticulitis. Which medication on the client's medication list would be of concern to the nurse?

    1. paroxetine (Paxil)
    2. gabapentin (Neurontin)
    3. metformin (Glucophage)
    4. methocarbamol (Robaxin)

117. The nurse is teaching a newly diagnosed client about Crohn's disease but discovers that the client has several barriers to learning. The nurse understands that socioeconomic barriers to learning include which factors? Select all that apply.
    1. cognitive delays
    2. low level of literacy
    3. adequate health insurance
    4. lack of access to health resources
    5. lack of interest in learning about disease

118. A client has orders for a heparin drip with 20,000 units in a 250 mL bag. The heparin must be delivered at 750 units per hour. What rate will the nurse set for the IV?

    _____

119. The nurse is caring for a client taking levothyroxine (Synthroid) for hypothyroidism. Which finding indicates a side effect of this medication?
    1. weight loss
    2. weight gain
    3. light sensitivity
    4. excessive sleepiness

120. Mix and Match: Match the therapeutic position with a reason for assuming the position.

	Position	Reason
1.	Fowler's	prevent pulmonary aspiration
2.	lithotomy	nasogastric tube in place
3.	prone	administering an enema
4.	reverse Trendelenburg's	gynecological procedures
5.	Sim's	post neck surgery

121. A client admitted with hepatic encephalopathy continues to attempt ambulation without assistance despite repeated instruction. Which intervention should the nurse take to promote safety?
    1. administer Xanax 6 mg PO
    2. apply a vest restraint device
    3. request a family member stay with the client around the clock
    4. move the client closer to the nurses' station

122. The nurse has orders for dopamine at 20 mcg/kg/min. The bag has 500 mg of dopamine in 500 mL. The client weighs 60 kg. What rate will the nurse set?

    _____

123. The nurse is teaching a client with limited mobility about preventing blood clots. Which statement by the nurse is correct?
    1. "Do not cross your legs when sitting."
    2. "Avoid riding in a car for more than two hours."
    3. "Put a pillow under your knees when lying in bed."
    4. "You should ask your doctor to give you a blood thinner."

124. A client is scheduled for a hypophysectomy following the discovery of a pituitary gland tumor. The nurse is teaching the client about the procedure. Which statement by the client indicates effective learning? Select all that apply.
    1. "I should brush my teeth with a soft toothbrush."
    2. "I can remove the pad under my nose the next morning."
    3. "I will avoid bending my head down or bending forward."
    4. "I will not blow my nose until cleared by my health care provider."
    5. "I will need to breathe through my mouth due to the nasal packing."

125. A client presents to the emergency room with severe pain in the upper right abdomen. The client is nauseated and has a temperature of 102.2°F. Which nursing action would be a priority at this time?
    1. relieve pain
    2. obtain vital signs
    3. administer IV fluids
    4. prepare for surgery

126. The nurse is preparing to administer cefazolin to a client who is allergic to penicillin. The client states that penicillin causes him to itch and be slightly short of breath. Which response by the nurse is correct?
    1. administer the cefazolin as ordered
    2. call the pharmacy to substitute another medication
    3. hold the medication and notify the health care provider
    4. give the client diphenhydramine and then administer the cefazolin

127. The oncoming nurse receives report on a group of clients. Which client should have priority during the nurse's rounds?
    1. a client who just returned from surgery for an open appendectomy
    2. a client with a blood pressure of 184/86 who has not received the morning dose of lisinopril
    3. a client who is on a 100% non-rebreather mask with an oxygen saturation level of 96%
    4. a client with COPD who is on 2L of oxygen via nasal cannula with an oxygen saturation level of 90%

128. The ED nurse admits a client with second-degree burns to the arms and third-degree burns to the legs. Based on the Parkland formula, which IV fluid would the nurse anticipate for this client during the first 24 hours?

1. D5W
2. colloid solutions
3. crystalloid solutions
4. 5% albumin in isotonic saline

129. A client with suspected vitamin C toxicity presents to the ED. Which manifestations of toxicity would the nurse expect in this client? Select all that apply.

1. muscle weakness
2. halos around objects
3. occult rectal bleeding
4. dry mucous membranes
5. increased estrogen levels

130. An external weather disaster has flooded the emergency department with several new clients. Which client should the nurse see first?

1. the client complaining of chest pain and nausea who is diaphoretic
2. the client with a simple fracture of the radius from a fall on a staircase
3. the client complaining of slight redness and itching at the IV site in his hand
4. the client presenting with a sprained ankle from a tree branch falling on him

131. The nurse is caring for a client experiencing an acute flare-up of diverticular disease. Which interventions by the nurse are appropriate for this client? Select all that apply.

1. encourage a diet high in fiber
2. insert a nasogastric (NG) tube
3. administer enemas as ordered
4. administer IV fluids as ordered
5. encourage coughing and deep breathing
6. check stools for frank or occult bleeding

132. The nurse has rounded on all the assigned clients. While rounding, several health care providers have written orders on the nurse's clients. Which order would be the priority for the nurse to address?

1. furosemide (Lasix) 80 mg IV push STAT for a client with fluid overload
2. a new insulin sliding scale for a client with a glucose level of 242
3. perform a dressing change on a client with a stage 2 diabetic foot ulcer
4. discharge a client who was admitted for removal of an abdominal abscess

133. The nurse is precepting a student nurse on the postsurgical floor. The student nurse needs to draw a potassium level. Which of the following statements by the student nurse is correct regarding blood draws from venous catheters?

1. "I can obtain the sample from the short peripheral catheter if I flush it well."
2. "I should flush with 10 to 20 mL of sterile normal saline after drawing blood from any catheter."
3. "Drawing blood from a central venous line is less risky than sticking the client if he is afraid of needles."
4. "I should use a syringe with a large needle to transfer blood into the test tube to avoid hemolyzing the sample."

134. The nurse is educating a client who has been ordered to wear a Holter monitor. Which statement by the client indicates a need for further education by the nurse?

1. "I can wear the monitor while I shower."
2. "I should keep the monitor on when I sleep."
3. "I should avoid metal detectors and electric razors while wearing the monitor."
4. "I should keep a log of any chest pain, shortness of breath, or skipped beats while wearing the monitor."

135. The nurse is caring for a client who just had an arteriovenous (AV) fistula placed for dialysis. The nurse is providing home care instructions to the client. Which statement by the client indicates a need for further teaching by the nurse?

1. "I should avoid wearing a watch on my arm with the fistula."
2. "It may take several weeks before the fistula is ready to use."
3. "I should not have my blood pressure taken in my access arm."
4. "I should wear tight sleeves to protect and support the fistula so I don't bend it."

136. A client in restraints is assigned to a newly graduated nurse. The nurse understands that which of the following are true regarding restraints? Select all that apply.

1. Restraints can be chemical, mechanical, or physical.
2. Children under 9 years of age have a 30-minute time limit in restraints.
3. Bed rails are a form of restraint if used to prevent the client from leaving the bed.
4. Restraints must be assessed every 2 hours for proper application and continued need.
5. Once released, the client may be placed back in restraints for up to 24 hours if needed.
6. Active listening, diversionary techniques, and reducing stimulation are alternatives to restraints.

137. The nurse is preparing to teach about poisonous snake bites to community members at the local recreational department. What information should the nurse provide regarding prehospital care? Select all that apply.

1. Attempt to kill or capture the snake for identification purposes.
2. Apply ice to the wound and elevate the affected extremity to the level of the heart.
3. Immobilize the affected extremity with a splint and maintain the extremity at the level of the heart.
4. Move the person to a safe area away from the snake and encourage rest to decrease venous circulation.
5. Apply ice to the wound and place a tourniquet before elevating the affected extremity to the level of the heart.

138. Nurses are expected to understand the principles of triage when caring for multiple clients. The ICU charge nurse is reviewing assignments. Based on the principles of triage, to which client would the charge nurse give priority for treatment? Select all that apply.

1. a client on a ventilator who has an alarm sounding
2. a client who has just returned from an open appendectomy
3. a client ready to transfer to the floor after the nurse calls report
4. a client who has been talking with family and is now unresponsive
5. a client receiving a new antibiotic who complains of tingling in the mouth
6. a client who has not eaten yet and is a type 2 diabetic with a morning blood sugar of 90

139. The RN is precepting a nursing student in the surgical ICU. The client is diabetic and asks the student nurse about insulin. Which response by the RN is best?

1. ask the family to step out of the room to ensure client privacy
2. tell the client that he should ask the health care provider when she rounds
3. inform the client that the student nurse cannot answer questions regarding medication
4. allow the nursing student to answer the client's question while the RN is present and can provide additional information if needed

140. The nurse is performing a neurological assessment on a client. She asks the client to smile, close both eyes, and frown. Which cranial nerve (CN) is the nurse testing?

1. CN V
2. CN VII
3. CN VIII
4. CN XI

141. The wife of a client with colorectal cancer (CRC) is talking to the nurse about prevention and screening of the disease. Which statement should the nurse make to the wife?
1. "A diet low in fat and high in fiber can help lower the risk, along with eating more fruit such as oranges."
2. "When an adult turns 40 years of age, a colonoscopy should be done to screen for CRC, regardless of family history."
3. "Those with average risk at age 50 and up should have a colonoscopy and fecal occult blood test every five years."
4. "Those with average risk at age 50 and up should have a colonoscopy and fecal occult blood test every 10 years."

142. A client is admitted with possible appendicitis. Which finding by the nurse would be expected in assessment of this client?
1. a positive psoas sign
2. a positive Murphy's sign
3. a positive Homan's sign
4. a positive Chadwick's sign

143. The nurse is caring for a client after an open reduction to the left ulna. The client's left arm is in a plaster cast with an Ace wrap for reinforcement. Which intervention by the nurse can offer nonpharmacological comfort to this client?
1. elevate the left arm on a pillow and apply an ice pack over the approximate location of the surgical incision
2. call the physician and obtain an order for acetaminophen (Tylenol) 650 mg PO PRN q6 hours as needed for pain
3. advise the client that if he starts to itch under the cast, he can use a wire coat hanger or an ink pen to gently scratch up under the cast
4. perform range-of-motion exercises twice a shift, including bending the fingers, opening and closing the hand, and lifting the arm up to shoulder level

144. A client is on bed rest following surgery for a fractured femur. The nurse is teaching the client about what to expect while on bed rest. Which dietary choice would the nurse advise the client to avoid while on bed rest?
1. high-fiber fruits
2. grapefruit juice
3. goods high in fat
4. milk or milk-based products

145. The nurse is caring for a client who is intubated and on the ventilator. The client is alert but cannot talk while intubated. Which method of communication would be the best choice for this client?

1. a clipboard with pen and paper
2. a picture board that the client could point to
3. asking the client to mouth words while a family member interprets the meaning
4. telling the client to blink once for yes and twice for no while asking close-ended questions

146. The nurse is caring for a client with a Foley catheter. While rounding on the client, the nurse notices that the client's urinary output has suddenly stopped over the last 2 hours. The client's kidney function is within normal limits. Which intervention would the nurse expect to perform? Select all that apply.

1. check the tubing for any kinks or to see if it is under the client
2. attempt to gently flush the Foley with 30 cc of sterile saline
3. perform a bladder scan, record the results, and notify the health care provider
4. pull back on the catheter about 6 inches, then reinsert it to see if urine flow begins
5. assess the client for bladder distention and discomfort if the client is alert and oriented

147. The nurse is preparing a client with type 2 diabetes for a CT with contrast to evaluate diverticulitis with a possible mass. Which of the following medications on the client's medication list would be of concern to the nurse?

1. fish oil
2. warfarin (Coumadin)
3. fluoxetine (Prozac)
4. metformin (Glucophage)

148. The nurse is teaching a client on the proper technique to use an inhaler with a spacer for asthma management. Which action by the client would require intervention by the nurse?

1. The client shakes the unit vigorously 3 or 4 times.
2. The client places the inhaler over his tongue and seals his lips tightly around it.
3. The client administers the next puff immediately after exhaling.
4. After administering the dose, the client keeps his lips closed and holds his breath for at least 10 seconds before exhaling.

149. The nurse is preparing to administer blood to a client with anemia. Which signs and symptoms of transfusion reaction should the nurse monitor for during the first 30 minutes? Select all that apply.
    1. The client has a respiratory rate of 18 breaths/minute.
    2. The client's blood pressure increases from 104/56 to 164/92.
    3. The client has an oxygen saturation level of 97% on 2L of oxygen.
    4. The client becomes restless and confused with distended jugular veins.
    5. The client complains of low back pain and a sense of impending doom.

150. The nurse is reviewing medication orders for his clients. Which order would necessitate contacting the health care provider?
    1. Paxil (paroxetine) 20 mg PO daily for a 57-year-old client with social anxiety disorder
    2. Phenergan (promethazine hydrochloride) 12.5 mg PR q12h prn for a child with Reye's syndrome
    3. Diflucan (fluconazole) 150 mg × 1 dose PO for a 24-year-old client with vaginal candidiasis
    4. Lopressor (metoprolol tartrate) 50 mg PO daily for a 48-year-old client with hypertension

151. Which statement by the client regarding sickle cell disease indicates a need for further teaching?
    1. "I should avoid strenuous exercise."
    2. "I can enjoy one glass of red wine per day."
    3. "I will avoid cigarettes and all tobacco products."
    4. "I should avoid traveling to places at high altitudes such as Denver."

152. A client with hyperkalemia is admitted to the telemetry unit. Which of the following would require notification of the health care provider? Select all that apply.
    1. The telemetry strip shows spiked T waves.
    2. The client has a heart rate of 53 beats per minute.
    3. The client has a heart rate of 84 beats per minute.
    4. The client does not eat the cantaloupe on his meal tray.
    5. The client's urinary output is 30 cc per hour via urinary catheterization.

153. The nurse receives an order from blood cultures and sensitivity for a client. Which statement is correct concerning this test?
    1. Preliminary test results are available 36 hours to allow the organisms time to grow.
    2. Growth and identification of the organism often takes 48 to 72 hours to complete.
    3. If the client has IV antibiotics infusing, stop the infusion before drawing blood cultures.
    4. If catheter sepsis is suspected, culturing the catheter tip is more accurate for identification.

154. The nurse is caring for a client with a small-bowel obstruction. A Salem sump nasogastric tube (NGT) is in place. Which finding by the nurse requires corrective action? Select all that apply.

1. There is a sudden decrease in output.
2. The NGT is set to low continuous suction.
3. The NGT is set to medium intermittent suction.
4. The patient is positioned in the semi-Fowler's position.
5. The client dislodges the tube and the nurse replaces it, confirming placement by X-ray before use.

155. The nurse is caring for a client with suspected meningitis who will be having a lumbar puncture. Which statement regarding aftercare is correct?

1. Specimen jars should be labeled and numbered and taken to the laboratory immediately and refrigerated.
2. The nurse should position the client with the head of the bed up 20 degrees so the client can drink fluids to replace CSF removed during the procedure.
3. The nurse should put the client in the low semi-Fowler's position with a pillow under her abdomen to increase intraabdominal pressure.
4. The nurse should assess for numbness, tingling, pain at injection site, movement of the extremities, any drainage at the site, and the ability to void.

156. The nurse is teaching the parents of a client with iron deficiency anemia about administering a liquid oral iron supplement. Which statement by the parents indicates that teaching was successful?

1. "We will give the iron through a straw."
2. "The iron should be given just before breakfast."
3. "We will give it with food to decrease stomach upset."
4. "We will mix the iron with a milkshake so it will taste better."

157. A nurse is caring for a client with Parkinson's disease who takes an MAOI as part of the medication regimen. Which item on the lunch tray would the nurse remove?

1. cheese
2. an apple
3. bread with butter
4. a cup of whole milk

158. The nurse is caring for a client with a long history of taking magnesium hydroxide for managing symptoms of peptic ulcer disease. Which finding in the client's medical history would be of concern to the nurse?

1. asthma
2. arthritis
3. heart failure
4. enlarged prostate

159. The nurse is caring for a client with a digitalis level of 2.1 ng/mL. Which signs would the nurse be alert for in this client?
    1. tinnitus
    2. flushed skin
    3. easy bruising
    4. anorexia, nausea, or diarrhea

160. The nurse is providing instruction to a client's family regarding home safety with thrombocytopenia. Which statement by the client's family indicates a need for further education?
    1. "He should use an electric razor for shaving instead of a razor."
    2. "We will use soft-bristled toothbrushes or tooth sponges for oral care."
    3. "He can no longer take aspirin or aspirin-containing products for a headache."
    4. "We should put rugs down on the hardwood floors to prevent his feet from getting cold."

161. At the scene of an accident, which intervention applies to a client with a suspected neck injury?
    1. administer CPR
    2. keep the person warm
    3. do not move the client
    4. ask the client to state her name and birthday

162. The nurse is teaching a smoking cessation program. He will state that which of the following benefits of quitting appear within one year?
    1. risk of coronary heart disease is the same as that of a nonsmoker
    2. carbon monoxide level in blood drops to normal
    3. risk of dying from lung cancer is about half that of a smoker's
    4. risk of having a stroke is reduced to that of a nonsmoker's

163. The nurse is preparing to admit a client from the emergency department with tuberculosis. Which of the following should the nurse anticipate in caring for this client? Select all that apply.
    1. fall precautions
    2. droplet precautions
    3. airborne precautions
    4. standard precautions
    5. placement in a negative airflow room
    6. use of PPE, including an N95 mask or powered air purifying respirators (PAPRs)

164. The nurse is caring for a client who is a Jehovah's Witness and is scheduled for hip replacement surgery. The client refuses to sign consent for blood due to religious reasons. The client's daughter has the power of attorney in case the client is unable to state his wishes regarding health care. The daughter tells the nurse, "I'm afraid if something goes wrong, dad might need blood. I want to sign a blood consent form since I'm his power of attorney." The daughter is not a Jehovah's Witness. Which action by the nurse is the best in this situation?

1. notify the charge nurse so that she can ask the night shift nurse to handle the situation
2. go and get a blood consent form for the daughter to sign, noting that she has power of attorney over the client
3. notify the surgeon that the client's daughter has power of attorney and will be signing a blood consent form so that an order may be obtained for a type and cross
4. remind the daughter that the client clearly does not wish to receive blood, and that a power of attorney cannot override client wishes that have been clearly stated when he was able to give or refuse consent

165. The nurse is preparing to administer a calcium channel blocker to a client with hypertension. The nurse understands that the mechanism of action of these drugs is to

1. cause vasodilation and increase total peripheral resistance.
2. cause vasodilation and decrease total peripheral resistance.
3. cause vasoconstriction and decrease total peripheral resistance.
4. cause vasoconstriction and increase total peripheral resistance.

166. The charge nurse is working with a student nurse who reports that her assigned client has severe flushing of the upper body following an IV antibiotic infusion. The charge nurse understands that the antibiotic likely responsible for this "red man syndrome" is which medication?

1. cephalexin
2. amoxicillin
3. gentamicin
4. vancomycin

167. The nurse is performing discharge teaching to a client newly diagnosed with hypertension and high cholesterol. Which statement by the client indicates that the nurse's teaching was effective?

1. "I need to buy canned foods that are low in sodium."
2. "I can substitute lean sirloin for my homemade fried chicken."
3. "I will take a can of soup to work for lunch instead of eating a burger."
4. "Frozen dinners are better for me than eating in the cafeteria at work."

168. The nurse is caring for a client with end-stage kidney disease and multiple organ failure. Which action by the nurse indicates an understanding of end-of-life care? Select all that apply.
    1. The nurse explains signs and symptoms that indicate death is near.
    2. The nurse explains to the client and family what to expect during the final phase of the illness.
    3. Cultural beliefs are acknowledged, but priority is placed on life-lengthening treatment options.
    4. The nurse avoids talking to the client about impending death to avoid upsetting him and the family.
    5. The nurse asks the client and family what their goals and wishes are regarding care, pain management, and emergency resuscitation.

169. The nurse is talking in the lounge with other nurses about grief and loss. The nurse understands which to be true regarding grief and loss? Select all that apply.
    1. The process of grief is detrimental to physical and emotional health.
    2. Age, gender, and culture are a few factors that influence the grieving process.
    3. The nurse must explore his own feelings about death before he may effectively help others.
    4. The nurse should discourage expression of grief and loss because it may upset other clients nearby.
    5. The nurse can help the family develop ways to relieve loneliness and depression following the death of a loved one.

170. The nursing assistant is taking vitals for a client on mechanical ventilation. Which of the following findings should the nursing assistant report to the nurse immediately?
    1. respiratory rate 26 breaths/minute
    2. heart rate 82 beats/minute
    3. blood pressure 152/86 mmHg
    4. temperature 102.1°F

171. A 32-year-old male client has just undergone a liver biopsy and is released to the post-op floor for observation. The nurse should have the client lie in what position?
    1. semi-Fowler's
    2. on his right side
    3. supine
    4. on his left side

172. The nurse is caring for a client who has just been diagnosed with ovarian cancer. The nurse is using silence as an effective therapeutic response. How is silence an effective therapeutic response?
    1. It is not therapeutic; it implies that the nurse is not listening.
    2. It encourages the client to keep her feelings to herself.
    3. It allows the client time to think and reflect and lead the conversation.
    4. It allows the nurse to think about other tasks she needs to tackle to provide efficient care to all of her clients.

173. The nurse is caring for an adult who had an appendectomy 6 hours ago. Which intervention would the nurse expect to perform to promote rest and sleep? Select all that apply.
    1. provide a substantial meal of meatloaf, mashed potatoes, corn, and milk
    2. offer Ambien 5 mg as ordered
    3. lower the temperature of the room
    4. change bed linen

174. The nurse is taking care of an elderly client with congestive heart failure. Which of the following are the most appropriate nursing interventions to reduce the workload of the heart and to promote comfort and rest? Select all that apply.
    1. obtain daily weight
    2. provide assistance with self-care activities
    3. provide sensory stimulation
    4. check vital signs after activity

175. The nurse is preparing an adult male for a transurethral resection of the prostate (TURP). Which statement by the client indicates a need for further teaching by the nurse?
    1. "My urine may change color because of bleeding."
    2. "I will need to drink water frequently."
    3. "I will have a dressing where the surgeon cuts."
    4. "I will have a catheter in place after surgery."

176. The nurse is assisting a client who has experienced a left-sided cerebral vascular accident. The client requires assistance with personal hygiene. Which intervention should the nurse do initially?
    1. provide positive feedback
    2. place hygiene items on the client's left side
    3. provide assistive devices
    4. assess abilities and level of deficit

177. The nurse is preparing a middle-aged female for a total knee replacement (TKR) surgery on her left leg tomorrow. Which statement by the nurse is incorrect?
    1. "Have you had a cold within the past 2 weeks?"
    2. "You will receive a dose of an antibiotic before surgery."
    3. "When you need to urinate the first night you'll need to use a fracture pan."
    4. "You should ask for medication when you are in pain."

178. The nurse is preparing to administer levofloxacin (Levaquin) 400 mg orally to a client with a urinary tract infection. Which statement by the client requires further teaching by the nurse?
    1. "I will need to wear sunscreen if I am outdoors."
    2. "I need to finish all the medication, even if my symptoms go away."
    3. "I should take my antacid right before my pill so I don't get heartburn."
    4. "I need to check my pulse twice daily and call my doctor if I have new-onset irregular heartbeats."

179. The nurse is reviewing a new client's medication orders. Which order would prompt the nurse to notify the health care provider?
    1. allopurinol 300 mg PO daily
    2. potassium chloride 20 mEq PO daily
    3. warfarin (Coumadin) 50 mg PO daily
    4. metoprolol (Lopressor) 50 mg PO daily

180. The nurse is caring for a client with congestive heart failure who is scheduled for the morning dose of digoxin 0.125 mg PO. The client's apical pulse is 54. Which is the priority nursing action?
    1. place the client on 2L of oxygen via nasal cannula
    2. hold the drug and notify the health care provider
    3. wait an hour and recheck the pulse; then administer the drug
    4. administer the drug and ask the unlicensed assistive personnel (UAP) to recheck the pulse in 30 minutes

181. The nurse is caring for a client who has an order for Diuril. Directions say to reconstitute with 20 mL of sterile water. This will provide a concentration of _____ mg/mL.

182. A 34-year-old client is receiving an IM injection of ceftriaxone (Rocephin) for a urinary tract infection. Which is correct regarding IM injections?
    1. A 1-inch-long 25-gauge needle should be used.
    2. The injection should be given at a 45-degree angle.
    3. The injection should be given at a 90-degree angle.
    4. A bleb should form on the skin's surface following injection.

183. A client with an upper GI bleed is about to undergo gastric lavage by the nurse. Which action by the nurse is correct in performing this procedure?
    1. instill 200 to 300 mL of a prewarmed solution
    2. instill 400 to 600 mL of a room-temperature solution
    3. position the client on the right side during the procedure
    4. manually withdraw the solution until clear or light pink with no clots

184. The nurse is educating a client who is newly diagnosed with angina about his newly prescribed nitroglycerin. The nurse understands that teaching is effective when the client makes which statement?
    1. "It is safe to take one dose of nitroglycerin if I am taking sildenafil."
    2. "I should chew up three tablets at once, and then call 9-1-1 if I still have chest pain in 15 minutes."
    3. "I can take up to three tablets, 5 minutes apart, under my tongue as needed for chest pain."
    4. "I can keep the pills in a glass cup on my nightstand so I can reach them easily in an emergency."

185. A client is ordered to receive 1,000 ml of D5W over 6 hours. The infusion set administers 10 gtt/mL. At what rate (gtt/min) should the nurse set the flow?
    1. 24 gtt/min
    2. 26 gtt/min
    3. 28 gtt/min
    4. 30 gtt/min

186. The nurse is caring for a client with a wound with purulent, foul-smelling drainage. A wound culture is ordered. Which describes the correct collection technique?
    1. clean the wound with normal saline before obtaining specimen
    2. allow 24 hours for antibiotic therapy to take effect before sampling
    3. obtain the specimen from the drainage at the bottom of the wound
    4. culture the outer surface around the wound before collecting exudate

187. In caring for a critically ill client with a nasogastric tube (NGT) for enteral feeding, which action by the nurse demonstrates competency in NGT care? Select all that apply.
    1. The nurse checks gastric residual every 4 hours for continuous feedings.
    2. The nurse maintains the client in a low Fowler's position during feeding.
    3. The nurse checks gastric residual before each bolus or intermittent feeding.
    4. The tubing is changed every 48 hours or when the bag appears visibly soiled.
    5. The nurse returns the residual to the stomach unless the volume is greater than 250 mL.

188. A client has orders for placing a small-bore nasoenteric tube. Which finding in the health history would prompt the nurse to notify the prescriber before placing tube?
    1. small-bowel lesion
    2. basilar skull fracture
    3. acute coronary syndrome
    4. use of diabetic insulin pump

189. The nurse is assigned a male client with a long-term in-dwelling catheter for incontinence. The nurse plans on performing which of the following to prevent complications?
    1. perform perineal care using sterile technique
    2. irrigate daily with 60 cc normal saline
    3. restrict fluids to 1,500 cc/day
    4. stabilize the catheter on the abdomen

190. The ED nurse is working in triage on a summer weekend. The following clients present at the same time. Which client does the nurse anticipate being seen first?
    1. a 58-year-old man with abdominal pain and nausea
    2. an infant with fever, a shrill cry, diarrhea, and nuchal rigidity
    3. a 38-year-old jogger who twisted her ankle, has a good pedal pulse, and has no deformity
    4. a 46-year-old client who was working outside and has tachypnea, diaphoresis, and fatigue
    5. an ambulatory child who fell off a bicycle and hit his head on grass while wearing a helmet

191. The charge nurse in the medical unit is preparing a bed assignment for a stable client diagnosed with necrotizing fasciitis. The client has a history of diabetes and hepatitis. There are four beds available. The nurse knows that the best roommate for this client is which of the following?
    1. a client with gout in the large toe
    2. a client with fever, vomiting, and diarrhea
    3. a client with MRSA
    4. a client with severe dementia with a tendency to wander

192. The nurse is auscultating the apical pulse over the PMI (point of maximum impact). Which heart sounds would be audible?
    1. S2 and S3
    2. S3 and S4
    3. S4 and S1
    4. S1 and S2

193. A 54-year-old female is brought into the ED by her spouse. The client's spouse tells the nurse the client has been experiencing muscle stiffness, increased perspiration, and anxiety. The nurse obtains bloodwork as ordered by the physician, including a complete blood count and a comprehensive metabolic panel. For which result should the nurse immediately notify the physician?

1. calcium 7.2 mg/dL
2. alkaline phosphatase 120 IU/L
3. sodium 143 mEq/L
4. creatinine 0.8 mg/dL

194. The nurse is caring for a client in intensive care with a diagnosis of traumatic brain injury. The client is found to be restless, complains of extreme nausea, and is weak on the left arm and leg. Which is the best response by the nurse?

1. check the blood pressure
2. elevate the client's head to 30 degrees
3. administer oxygen
4. increase the IV rate

195. The nurse has received report on the day's assigned clients. Which of the following clients should the nurse see first?

1. a client who is post-op day 2 from a spinal fusion at L3-4 with a pain level of 4 on a scale of 1 – 10
2. a client with a peripheral IV on a 6-hour infusion with 42 cc remaining
3. a client who is 6 hours post–atrial fibrillation ablation, is agitated, has a HR of 130 with B/P at 90/50, and has a urine output of 30 cc in the last 2 hours
4. a client with a nasogastric tube in place who is complaining of gastric distress

196. The nurse is caring for a 27-year-old female who presents to the ED with a fractured arm along with multiple bruises in various stages of healing around her left eye and chest. The client implies an intimate domestic partner inflicted her injuries. Which statement by the nurse is most appropriate?

1. "Why do you stay with a person like that?
2. "Are you in need of an immediate place for safety?"
3. "Why did he hit you?"
4. "You need to report your partner to the police."

197. The nurse is caring for a client with documented severe allergies to latex. Which item on the client's meal tray should the nurse remove?

1. a banana
2. a bowl of beef broth
3. a vanilla pudding cup
4. a cup of strawberries

198. The nurse is precepting a student nurse on an orthopedic floor. The student nurse needs to insert an indwelling catheter into a male client. Which of the following statements by the student nurse are correct regarding insertion of the catheter? Select all that apply.

   1. "I need to establish an aseptic field."
   2. "I will place the client in the supine position."
   3. "I will lubricate the tip of the catheter with sterile lubricant included in the tray."
   4. "I will inflate the catheter balloon with 5 cc of sterile water."

199. A client is provided instructions for a low-sodium diet. Which statement by the client indicates an understanding of the diet?

   1. "I'll miss eating tomatoes."
   2. "I'll enjoy eating take-out more frequently."
   3. "I'll avoid potato chips and cheese."
   4. "I'll miss eating celery."

200. During assessment of a client, the nurse notes crackles in the lung bases and bilateral pedal edema. A common cause of fluid volume excess is which factor?

   1. excessive IV infusion
   2. short-term corticosteroid administration
   3. prolonged diarrhea
   4. high fever

PRACTICE TEST ONE ANSWER KEY

1. Number 4 is correct.

   Rationale: Expressing doubt and asking further questions of the nurse indicates that the client may not be fully informed and should confer further with the health care provider. The nurse may clarify facts, but it is the health care provider's responsibility to give detailed information about the surgical procedure. The nurse is responsible for ensuring that the client has been adequately informed. A client may refuse to sign a blood consent due to religious beliefs prior to surgery. The client has correctly identified the surgical site, which is to be expected. The client who cannot write may sign with an X as long as it is witnessed by two people.

2. Numbers 1, 2, 3, and 4 are correct.

   Rationale: Ensuring continuity of care is especially important when the client is being transferred to another area of the hospital. Options 1, 2, 3, and 4 are guidelines that ensure continuity of care. Addressing pending lab results, listing client requests that the nurse was unable to do, and informing the receiving nurse of upcoming medications or glucose checks that will need to be done shortly after the client arrives make it easier for the receiving nurse to be sure that upcoming tests or medications are not missed. Complaining about the family is unprofessional and takes the focus away from client needs. A smooth transition is essential to ensure that no orders are overlooked. The nurse should be prepared to answer questions from the receiving nurse if needed for clarification after the client is transferred.

3. Number 2 is correct.

   Rationale: A child with severe autism who is having a tonsillectomy is at greatest risk for alterations in sensory perception. Clients with severe autism experience altered thought processes. Adding an unfamiliar environment (the hospital) with pain from a surgical procedure compounds the risk of altered sensory perception. The client in the halo vest may have pain and restricted mobility, but he does not have as great a risk for altered perception as the child with severe autism. A teenager who broke her leg during cheerleader practice is more likely to have a large social group and be less isolated. A schoolteacher is more likely to work in a stimulating environment and have many social contacts. Risk factors for altered perception include emotional disorders, a non-stimulating environment, acute illness, limited mobility, pain, decreased cognitive ability, and impaired hearing or vision.

4. Number 1 is correct.

   Rationale: Clients with DVT should be on bed rest to prevent movement of the DVT and pressure changes that occur with walking and other weight-bearing activities. The affected extremity should be elevated. Placing the bed in reverse Trendelenburg will increase pressure on the affected extremity. Walking is contraindicated for clients with DVT; while preventing hospital-acquired pneumonia is important, client safety takes priority over pneumonia prevention at this time. The client may still use an incentive spirometer and practice coughing and deep breathing to clear the lungs without ambulating. Sitting up in a chair is also contraindicated until the DVT has resolved and the health care provider has prescribed activity for the client.

5. Numbers 1, 2, 3, 4, and 6 are correct.

   Rationale: Grabbing at the bed rails and general restlessness may indicate pain. Biting the ventilator tubing and breathing over the vent due to increased respiratory rate are other indicators of pain. Facial grimacing and frowning is another pain indicator. Guarding an area of the body during the "sedation vacation" or stiffness or rigidity can indicate a pain response. Blood pressure and heart rate generally increase when experiencing pain. Decreased urinary output is not an indicator of pain. Based on the client's injury, disease process, or surgical procedures, the nurse should be able to anticipate what type and intensity of pain the client may experience. When multiple indicators suggest pain, the nurse should administer pain medications as ordered. It is important to remember that just because a client is sedated does not mean he is not experiencing pain.

6. Number 3 is correct.

Rationale: Doxorubicin causes red urine for 1 – 2 days after administration. Hair loss is temporary; regrowth begins 2 – 3 months after treatment is completed. Visual changes are not a side effect of this medication. Facial flushing and red streaking along the vein only occur when infused too rapidly; therefore, this should not be an expected side effect.

7. Numbers 1 and 2 are correct.

Rationale: Communication boards are highly effective in allowing clients to express their needs. Similarly, yes/no questions allow ease in communicating needs with minimal frustration. Open-ended questions require oral communication the client with an endotracheal tube cannot perform. An electrolarynx, a battery-powered handheld device that transmits sound when pressed against the oropharyngeal cavity, is used for clients with a tracheostomy.

8. Number 1 is correct.

Rationale: The impaired ability of the adrenal gland to produce the hormone aldosterone (a mineralocorticoid), which helps the kidney retain sodium, results in a craving for salty foods. Weight loss is associated with the disease. Loss of appetite, rather than craving for sweet foods, is consistent with Addison's disease. Fatigue and muscle weakness are typically seen with Addison's disease.

9. Number 4 is correct.

Rationale: Asking the client to add a simple series of numbers tests problem solving, a function of the frontal lobe. Tactile sensation is a parietal lobe function. Hearing function is a temporal lobe function. Balance is a function of the cerebrum.

10. Number 4 is correct.

Rationale: Cloudy outflow is a sign of peritonitis, which is life-threatening if left untreated. Other signs include distention, pain, fever, and tenderness. The classic sign is a rigid, boardlike abdomen. Bone pain is a sign of dialysis encephalopathy. Confusion and muscle cramps occur with disequilibrium syndrome.

11. Number 3 is correct.

Rationale: Before launching a discussion, the nurse must be aware of the client's knowledge and understanding of the different treatments. Understanding the client's background will guide the nurse in what information to reinforce to the client, or highlight areas the client may want to explore further with the health care provider. Telling the client about local support groups is helpful, but the nurse's response implies that the client will choose chemo. Telling the client not to worry because the doctor will select the best course of treatment is belittling and also implies that the decision will be made for her, not with her. Telling the client not to take chemo is offering the nurse's opinion, giving advice, and shuts down the opportunity for further discussion.

12. Numbers 2, 4, and 5 are correct.

Rationale: Clients in restraints must be offered toileting and nutrition every 2 hours. Restraints should be checked every 2 hours for proper placement, and the skin assessed. Documentation of restraints includes type of restraint, the need for continued use, and the results of a trial release. Many facilities require that a trial release be performed on clients with restraints at least once per shift. Restraints should be tied with a quick-release knot in case of emergency. Restraint orders must be renewed every 24 hours, and they may not be written on a PRN basis. Follow facility guidelines when caring for restrained clients.

13. Number 1 is correct.

Rationale: The first step after discovering any medication error is to stop the infusion. The nurse should also notify the health care provider for further orders and complete an incident report. The nurse should observe the client for any signs of allergic reaction or overdose and be prepared to report to the health care provider exactly how much of the medication infused. If the wrong dose of a medication is hung, the nurse should never try to give the ordered amount by adjusting the amount to infuse. This can cause an error and may lead to serious side effects if the client is overdosed.

14. Number 3 is correct.

    Rationale: Since the medication was left out, there is no way to be sure that it was not tampered with or contaminated; therefore, the nurse should dispose of the syringe in the sharps container and draw up a new dose of insulin. Returning the insulin to the vial increases the risk of cross-contamination, since the contents of the syringe may be contaminated. Administering the insulin after labeling it still leaves the client vulnerable, since the medication was left unattended. Option 4 is risky because the insulin in the syringe may have been contaminated or replaced by something else. Nurses should never give medications that were drawn up and then out of their sight for any period of time. If a medication error or adverse reaction occurs, the nurse is responsible due to negligence.

15. Number 4 is correct.

    Rationale: Reminiscing is a common occurrence by the elderly. The nurse should confirm this behavior with the client's wife. Redirecting the husband to speak on current events interferes with the normal pattern of reminiscing. Stating what you would do is contraindicated when interacting with the client's wife. Additionally, this statement assumes the client's wife is involved in organized religion.

16. Number 3 is correct.

    Rationale: Hormone replacement therapy and weight-bearing exercises (such as walking) are recommended to prevent osteoporosis. A therapeutic dose of calcium to influence bone density for women 51 and older is 1,200 mg/day. Two ounces of hard cheese contains 500 mg of calcium, which is suboptimal. Potassium supplements are not effective in preventing osteoporosis.

17. Number 1 is correct.

    Rationale: Viral load testing measures the level of HIV RNA or other viral proteins and monitors disease progression and evaluates effectiveness of treatment. The Western blot test is positive if antibodies to at least two major HIV antigens are present. Clients with AIDS are frequently leukopenic, with a WBC less than 3,500 cells/mm3. The ELISA test cannot detect antibodies before 3 weeks to 3 months. The client can test negative although HIV infection is present until sufficient antibodies are made.

18. Number 2 is correct.

    Rationale: Signs of air embolus include chest pain, anxiety, changes in sensorium, and decreased oxygen saturation. Cold intolerance is not an indication of air embolus. Tachypnea, dyspnea, and hypotension are other findings.

19. Number 2 is correct.

    Rationale: The spouse will likely need to limit her work hours at least initially to remain available to the client upon discharge. The goal of hospitalization is to return the client to maximum independence, although he may not return to normal for some time, if at all. Home health care will assist the client at home upon discharge. Nursing care involves the family as well as the client. Providing support to the client and family are within the scope of nursing practice.

20. Numbers 1, 3, and 4 are correct.

    Rationale: From an Islamic perspective, prayer time is sacred and other activities should be avoided. Food brought by family members from home is beneficial as it is prepared using Islamic traditions. Modesty and privacy are honored in the Muslim tradition where care by a staff member of the same sex is preferable. Fish killed by removal from water are considered halal (lawful) and may be eaten.

21. Number 1 is correct.

    Rationale: Lactated Ringer's is typically administered in the first 24 hours because its composition is similar to the extracellular fluid that has shifted from damage to the skin. D10W is less ideal than Lactated Ringer's at this time post-burn as it lacks sodium, chloride, lactate, potassium, and calcium. Plasma would be administered in the next 24 hours. Normal saline will not meet the fluid and electrolyte requirements for the client at this stage in his recovery.

22. Numbers 1, 2, and 4 are correct.

    Rationale: Music, stretching exercises, and relaxation are proven nonpharmacological pain management techniques that the nurse is able to teach the client. Therapeutic massage for the purpose of pain management is performed by a licensed massage therapist.

23. Numbers 2 and 4 are correct.

    Rationale: Anxiety increases sympathetic stimulation to the bowels, thereby increasing symptoms. Reducing anxiety will lessen the incidence of IBS episodes. The precise mechanism on how probiotics aid in IBS symptoms is not known, but it is thought to alter the bacteria found in the intestines. Ingestion of cold liquids will increase intestinal mobility that is contraindicated in IBS. Further, caffeine is considered a trigger food for symptoms of IBS. Fluid intake should be increased to compensate for fluid loss associated with frequent bowel elimination.

24. Number 4 is correct.

    Rationale: Auditory diversional activities, such as radios and CDs, should be encouraged. Regular-size printed material will not be readable. Instead, provide the client with large-size printed instructions. Stand to the side of the client when addressing her as central vision is impaired with AMD. Adequate lighting, such as natural or halogen, is preferred to improve vision for patients with limited acuity.

25. Number 3 is correct.

    Rationale: Proper lighting allows the client to see your face, improving communication. In many types of hearing loss, the ability to hear higher-pitched tones is lost. Unless you know the client knows sign language, this communication form will frustrate the client. Gentle touching allows the client to know where you are located.

26. Numbers 1, 3, and 4 are correct.

    Rationale: Tetanus, chlamydia, and Lyme disease are designated as reportable diseases by the CDC. Reportable diseases are considered to be a national concern due to their seriousness, the risk of death, or the ease with which they spread. Untreated tetanus can lead to laryngospasm, pneumonia, pulmonary embolism, and difficulty breathing. Chlamydia can cause permanent damage to a woman's reproductive system and may cause a potentially fatal ectopic pregnancy. Lyme disease can spread to any organ in the body and may cause permanent damage to the brain, heart, and neurological system. Scarlet fever and group B streptococcal infection are not reportable under current CDC guidelines.

27. Number 4 is correct.

    Rationale: The first action is to notify the health care provider for further orders. The nurse should never induce vomiting, as this may cause more harm to the client. Obtaining vital signs is important but can be done after the health care provider is notified. An incident report should be completed following the facility guidelines once the situation is under control and the client has been stabilized.

28. Number 4 is correct.

    Rationale: Respiratory depression can become life-threatening if not treated early. Hiccups are not life-threatening. Lethargy and drowsiness are common side effects with anxiolytic and benzodiazepine medications.

29. The client should receive 32 gtts/min.

$\frac{\text{volume (mL)} \times \text{drop factor (gtts)}}{\text{time (min)}}$ = flow rate in gtts/min	Solve using the formula.
8 × 60 = 480 min	Convert hours to minutes.
$\frac{1,000 \text{ mL} \times 15 \text{ gtts}}{480 \text{ min}}$	Input into formula and solve.
$\frac{15,000}{480}$ = 31.25	
= 32 gtts/min	Round up to find gtts/min.

30. Numbers 2, 3, and 4 are correct.

Rationale: With viral hepatitis, lab findings include increased AST and ammonia levels. Serum albumin and ALT levels decrease. Prothrombin time is prolonged in viral hepatitis.

31. Numbers 1, 2, 4, and 5 are correct.

Rationale: Hepatitis D coexists with hepatitis B and intensifies the acute symptoms. Hepatitis A can occur at any time of the year and is spread via uncooked shellfish, contaminated water or milk, and contaminated fruits and vegetables. Hepatitis B is spread by contact with blood or body fluids, sexual contact, sharing dirty needles, and contact with infected semen or saliva. Hepatitis A is seasonal and tends to occur mainly during the fall and early winter. Hepatitis D is spread by contact with blood and blood products.

32. Numbers 2, 4, and 5 are correct.

Rationale: Following a craniotomy, the nurse should monitor the pupils for signs of increased intracranial pressure. Report dilated or pinpoint pupils or pupils that are slow to react or nonreactive to light to the health care provider. Respiratory status is monitored closely, as even minor hypoxia can increase cerebral ischemia. Notify the surgeon immediately if the dressing is saturated or if the client has more than 50 mL drainage in 8 hours, as this can cause hypovolemic shock. Immediately post-op the nurse should check the dressing every 1 or 2 hours. The drainage area can be marked once a shift to obtain a baseline. Clients with supratentorial craniotomies should be positioned with the head elevated 30 degrees in a neutral, midline position. Avoid extreme hip or neck flexion, which can cause increased intracranial pressure.

33. Number 4 is correct.

Rationale: These ABGs indicate acute respiratory acidosis. Common signs of respiratory acidosis include hypoventilation with hypoxia, disorientation, and dizziness. Untreated respiratory acidosis can progress to ventricular fibrillation, low blood pressure, seizures, and coma. The other options are signs of metabolic acidosis. If metabolic acidosis is severe, it can cause nausea and vomiting.

34. Number 4 is correct.

Rationale: Sudden back pain and shortness of breath indicate rupture of the aneurysm, which is an emergency. The nurse should notify the health care provider, monitor neurological and vital signs, and remain with the client. Yellow-tinted vision is a finding of digitalis toxicity. Frothy, pink sputum is a sign of pulmonary edema. Urinary output of 75 mL/hr. is a normal urinary output.

35. Number 3 is correct.

Rationale: The presence of normal saline is of concern as it should not be used in the endotracheal tube to promote secretion removal. The head of the bed should be elevated 30 – 45 degrees at all times to prevent ventilator-associated pneumonia. The cuff on the endotracheal tube should be sufficiently inflated to ensure the patient receives proper ventilator parameters. Wearing an intermittent compression device on both legs provides deep vein thrombosis prophylaxis, an appropriate measure.

36. Number 1 is correct.

Rationale: Potassium will accumulate in the blood with renal disease. As a potassium-rich food, prune juice should be avoided. Phosphorous can accumulate with renal disease. Because soft drinks contain phosphorous, only clear ones, such as ginger ale, are allowed. Dairy foods contain phosphorous, so milk intake is limited to 1 cup/day. White bread has less phosphorous than whole-grain bread and is preferred over whole-grain bread.

37. Number 1 is correct.

Rationale: The standard time for a bladder-retraining program to be successful is 6 to 12 weeks. The other statements are consistent with bladder retraining instructions.

38. Number 4 is correct.

Rationale: Shortness of breath is a medical emergency and can be life-threatening, so this client should be seen first. A client with a UTI and fever may be uncomfortable, but is not in any immediate danger. The client who is NPO awaiting surgery is stable and can wait to be seen. The client with nausea can be seen after attending to the client who is short of breath.

39. Number 3 is correct.

Rationale: The nurse should notify the surgeon and ask her to come talk to the client and address her concerns, even if it means the client withdraws consent and decides not to have surgery. The client may withdraw consent at any time. Telling the client she will be glad she had the surgery fails to acknowledge the client's feelings and assumes that she will proceed with surgery. Asking the client what her thoughts are will only delay the discussion with the surgeon; the client has already expressed sufficient doubt about the procedure. Telling the client that the doctor will be mad because the OR has been prepared may make the client feel guilty and possibly coerce her into having surgery she does not want. If the surgery is performed anyway, the client has a case for a lawsuit.

40. Number 1 is correct.

Rationale: Hand hygiene is the first step in performing client care. Hand hygiene is done first to minimize contamination risk. The gown is donned and securely tied in the back. The mask is applied to fully cover the nose and mouth, forming a secure seal. Eye goggles or a face shield are donned once the mask is in place. Gloves are applied, making sure they cover the wrist of the gown.

41. Number 1 is correct.

Rationale: Measles requires airborne precautions. Droplet precautions apply to influenza. There are no special precautions for Lyme disease other than universal precautions (hand washing, avoid touching areas with a rash unless gloves are used). Lyme disease is caused by a tick bite and cannot be transmitted from one person to another. Contact precautions would be used for herpes simplex.

42. Number 1 is correct.

Rationale: The nurse should never attempt to pull a client up in bed without assistance, no matter how small the client is. The nurse risks injuring her back by doing so. The nurse should call again and wait a few moments for help. Pulling the client up by the armpits increases the risk of skin shear or a skin tear to the client. Trying to pull the client up by pulling on one side of the draw sheet at a time is ineffective and may result in skin shear on the client. If other help is not available, a lifting assistive device should be used for the client. With a client who can self-position, option 4 may be used if no other help is available and if the client can tolerate the position with the head down; however, another person or a lifting device should be used whenever possible to avoid injury to the nurse and client.

43. Number 4 is correct.

Rationale: Retinopathy, an eye complication due to breakdown of blood vessels in the back of the eye, is a chronic complication of diabetes mellitus. Hyperglycemia, diabetic ketoacidosis, and hyperglycemia are short-term complications of diabetes mellitus.

44. Number 4 is correct.

Rationale: Confirming how the client feels confirms the client's experience. Allowing verbalization of the loss is consistent with therapeutic communication. The first response places the need of the nurse above the client's. The second response fails to listen to the client. The third response implies disapproval of what the client is saying.

45. Numbers 1 and 3 are correct.

Rationale: Manage the therapeutic environment to provide an appropriate level of stimuli to the client. Orienting the client and explaining interventions actively engages the client in normal cognitive activities. Limiting visitors to one 15-minute visit per 8-hour shift will produce a nonstimulating environment. The level of lighting should be varied throughout the day to provide the client with a sense of normalcy.

46. Number 3 is correct.

Rationale: Asking an open-ended question allows the client to verbalize her feelings and discuss health care options. Telling the client she is fine allows no opportunity to discuss her feelings. Telling the client she cannot live alone or that she should get a second opinion closes communication channels.

47. Number 4 is correct.

Rationale: Clients with hypoparathyroidism have low parathyroid hormone levels on blood tests. Hypocalcemia, not hypercalcemia, is also present. Magnesium levels are decreased, while phosphorus levels are increased.

48. Numbers 1, 2, and 3 are correct.

Rationale: Clients with thrombocytopenia have decreased platelets. The nurse would expect to see signs of bleeding such as epistaxis, petechiae, and vomiting blood. Hematocrit and platelet count would both be decreased in this client.

49. Number 4 is correct.

Rationale: Cymbalta increases the body's serotonin level. A rare but life-threatening condition called serotonin syndrome may occur when someone takes two or more medications that increase the body's serotonin levels. Cough medicines that contain dextromethorphan may interact with Cymbalta and cause serotonin syndrome. The other over-the-counter medications have no known interaction with Cymbalta.

50. Number 3 is correct.

Rationale: Clients with Crohn's must have adequate nutrition to promote wound and fistula healing and prevent loss of lean muscle mass. High-calorie, low-fiber, high-protein, and high-vitamin foods should be available at every meal to maximize nutritional benefits. Coffee should be avoided, since clients with Crohn's should avoid caffeine. Enteral supplements may be given through a gastrostomy tube to supplement solid foods eaten by the client and should not cause a decrease in appetite. The diet should progress slowly, not rapidly.

51. Numbers 2, 3, and 4 are correct.

Rationale: Clients with dehydration experience increased hematocrit, orthostatic (postural) hypotension, and diminished bowel sounds. Thready pulses are a sign of dehydration. Bounding pulses would be found in clients with fluid volume excess. Urine specific gravity increases in clients with dehydration.

52. The correct response is DNR form.

Rationale: A DNR, or do not resuscitate order, allows the client to make his wishes known regarding care and treatments desired should he be unable to speak for himself. A DNR covers specific life-prolonging treatments such as tube feedings, artificial hydration, and code status. A DNR is a legally binding document; if a client requests to be a no-code and a code is run on him and he survives, the family or client may bring legal action against the health care provider and the facility. DNR status should be determined as soon as possible following client admission.

53. Number 1 is correct.

Rationale: The first priority is to evaluate pain, including vital signs. Clients on a PCA must have vital signs monitored regularly due to the risk of respiratory depression from oversedation. The nurse can contact the health care provider with this information for further orders. Repositioning the client may increase comfort but is not the first priority for this client with severe pain. Nonpharmacologic measures are not likely to offer much relief to this client, and the nurse should not assume that dosages cannot be adjusted. In teaching the client and family proper use of the PCA, emphasis should be placed on the client being the only one to administer pain medication in order to avoid oversedation. If the client is unable to use the PCA, other means of pain relief should be considered.

54. Number 3 is correct.

Rationale: PT, PTT, and INR are blood tests that monitor effectiveness of anticoagulant therapy. Hematocrit measures packed red blood cells and is not a specific study of anticoagulant effectiveness. HDL and LDL are components of cholesterol measurement. Troponin levels measure myocardial muscle injury.

55. Number 3 is correct.

Rationale: Pain in the residual limb indicates the wrapping is too tight and should be reapplied. Peripheral vascular disease due to diabetes mellitus is a common reason for surgical removal of a lower limb. Range-of-motion exercises are standard after an amputation. Use of adaptive devices such as canes to ambulate is standard post-amputation.

56. Numbers 1, 3, and 5 are correct.

Rationale: Clients with a cerebral aneurysm need a quiet, non-stimulating environment. This client is at risk for DVT, so the appropriate DVT prophylaxis should be administered as prescribed. The client should be on bed rest in a side-lying or semi-Fowler's position. Visitors should be limited to avoid overstimulation. The client should not be encouraged to cough or perform other activities that mimic the Valsalva maneuver. Stool softeners should be given to avoid straining with bowel movements.

57. Number 1 is correct.

Rationale: Following CPR, the most important priority is to check the client for a pulse. Often the cardiac monitor may display normal sinus rhythm when there is no pulse present. A urinary catheter would not be the first priority. PEA is never shocked. Once airway is established, the client should be monitored for a pulse, regardless whether the monitor displays an organized rhythm or not.

58. Number 4 is correct.

Rationale: Classic signs of cardiogenic shock include a rapid pulse that weakens; cool, clammy skin; and decreased urine output. Hypotension is another classic sign.

59. Numbers 1, 2, 3, and 5 are correct.

Rationale: Pulses and capillary refill are assessed and compared to the unaffected limb. Pulses should be equal in both feet, with brisk capillary refill. The skin should be warm. The nurse should assess the client's pain and ask her to report numbness, tingling, or inability to move the toes. Decreased pulses or capillary refill, cool skin, and changes in sensation and movement indicate a possible complication. The client is at risk of necrosis if unusual findings are not reported immediately. The nurse should not squeeze the cast for any reason. The cast can take 24 – 48 hours to completely harden, and squeezing it can create pressure points inside that can damage the skin.

60. Number 4 is correct.

Rationale: Clients without a spleen are at increased risk of infection. The spleen manufactures many antibodies, so clients should consult their health care provider about receiving vaccinations two weeks following surgery. Regular activity cannot be resumed for a period of 4 – 8 weeks after surgery. Two weeks is too soon to return to yoga. There is no need to eat a low-fiber diet to rest the digestive tract following a splenectomy. Large crowds should be avoided due to the risk of infection, so the client should not attend a sporting event within a month of surgery.

61. Number 3 is correct.

Rationale: Many clients with dementia pull out an IV because they see it and know that they don't normally have one. Placing the IV in an inconspicuous place, such as where it can be covered by the gown or wrapped up in gauze, prevents the client from pulling it out, because he cannot see it. Restraints should not be the first-line intervention for this client, as this may increase confusion and agitation. If the family can stay with the client, they can help watch, but many clients do not have family close by that can stay with them around the clock. Threatening the client with a more invasive procedure should never be used as a means of obtaining cooperation.

62. Number 4 is correct.

Rationale: Lifting heavy objects is contraindicated after cataract surgery as this will increase intraocular pressure on the newly operated eye. Wearing glasses outside is recommended after surgery to protect from infectious agents. Bending below the waist increases intraocular pressure on the newly operated eye and is contraindicated. Anticoagulants should be stopped as this predisposes the patient to hemorrhage.

63. Number 2 is correct.

Rationale: The client is experiencing symptoms of a pulmonary embolism. The best action by the nurse is to place the client in a semi-Fowler's position to enable a clear airway. Obtaining vital signs would be action number 2, to compare to established baseline data. Administering oxygen as ordered would be the third response to provide adequate oxygenation of the client. Last, prepare the client for diagnostic tests such as blood gases, ventilation-perfusion lung scan, and pulmonary angiography.

64. Number 4 is correct.

Rationale: SLE is a chronic autoimmune disorder treated with a variety of medications. One such drug is an antimalarial drug that produces retinal toxicity. Eye exams every six months, rather than annually, are advised to monitor ocular changes. Avoidance of sunlight prevents the skin rash that occurs with SLE. Also, sensitivity to light is seen in persons with lupus. High-dose prednisone, commonly prescribed with severe SLE, will result in water retention and the appearance of being bloated. Due to fatigue, the work schedule is limited for persons with lupus.

65. Number 2 is correct.

Rationale: An INR of 4.6 indicates that the client is at risk for bleeding. Protamine sulfate is the antidote for heparin. Vitamin K is the antidote for warfarin. Redrawing labs in 6 hours is only ordered when INR is therapeutic and no changes to therapy must be made. Increasing the infusion rate greatly increases the risk of bleeding in this client.

66. Number 1 is correct.

Rationale: Rubbing the injection site is not advised as it can affect absorption. The client should check the vial of insulin for the correct type and expiration date. Insulin is a high-risk medication, and some clients may be on more than one type. Grasping the skin and inserting the needle at a 90-degree angle is correct injection technique. Prior to drawing up the dose, the rubber stopper should be cleaned with alcohol.

67. Number 4 is correct.

Rationale: Propofol is an anesthetic agent and therefore a controlled substance. Most hospitals require licensed nurses to pick up controlled substances. Asking the unit secretary or the UAP to pick up propofol is outside their scope of practice. The health care provider is not responsible for picking up medications from the hospital pharmacy. The nurse should ask another nurse to look after her clients while she runs the errand to the pharmacy. Before leaving the unit, the nurse should give report to the nurse who will watch the clients, as this is important for client safety.

68. Number 1 is correct.

Rationale: The focus of the nurse's role as an advocate is to teach the client the necessary skills to manage her diabetes, making number 1 correct. The other actions, while important, do not directly provide the client with the necessary skills to manage her disease.

69. Number 4 is correct.

Rationale: An enema is contraindicated for a client with suspected appendicitis as increased intestinal motility may aggravate the suspected appendicitis. When enema administration is appropriate, the other answers are correct.

70. Number 3 is correct.

Rationale: Remind the client that oxygen is highly flammable and that smoking is banned throughout the facility. If the client continues to smoke in the room, notify security so that they can intervene. There have been documented cases of explosions in facilities caused by smoking around oxygen, so this situation should be taken seriously and not dismissed. Escorting the client outside to smoke places the client at risk for falling, especially if he has an IV pole. It also encourages behavior that is not healthy and takes a staff member off the unit without good cause. To help prevent cravings, clients who smoke should be offered a nicotine patch upon admission when the smoking history is documented. The nurse should check and see if the health care provider ordered one as a PRN medication. If not, the nurse can ask the client if he would like a patch. Threatening the client with discharge if he is not compliant with the smoking ban does not address the situation in a safe manner and can escalate the situation.

71. Number 4 is correct.

Rationale: Decreasing sodium intake is an effective way to reduce blood pressure in a client with hypertension. Eating red meat daily, increasing potassium and calcium intake, and increasing fluid intake are not measures that affect blood pressure readings.

72. Number 1 is correct.

Rationale: Using a condom catheter to drain urine in the least intrusive manner is the best intervention for maintaining skin integrity and preventing infection. An indwelling catheter puts the client at risk of an infection. A diaper would allow the urine to be kept in contact with the skin thereby affecting skin integrity. Offering the urinal every 2 hours is unlikely to be effective in controlling urine output.

73. Number 3 is correct.

Rationale: Humalog, NovoLog, and Apidra are all rapid-acting insulins. Lantus and Levemir are long-acting insulins. Humulin 70/30 is an intermediate-acting insulin.

74. Number 4 is correct.

Rationale: A cholesterol level less than 200 mg/dL is desirable for an adult without heart disease. At the stated level, this client needs to consume a low-cholesterol diet. Natural peanut butter contains no cholesterol, making this sandwich the best choice. The remaining options are high in fat that will elevate the cholesterol level.

75. Numbers 2 and 3 are correct.

Rationale: The most accurate method to confirm placement is by X-ray. Auscultation may not be reliable, especially with small-bore tubes. Medications should never be mixed with the tube feeding. The student nurse should hold the feeding and flush with 20 to 30 mL of water before giving any medications. She should follow medication administration with another flush and then resume feeding. Options 1, 4, and 5 are correct tube management techniques.

76. Number 4 is correct.

Rationale: Normal potassium ranges from 3.5 to 5 mEq/L. Hypokalemia can manifest with weak peripheral pulses, orthostatic hypotension, diminished breath sounds, lethargy, confusion, and coma. EKG changes include ST depression and T wave changes. Severe hypokalemia (less than 2.5 mEq/L) can cause death without emergent treatment. The health care provider should be notified for orders. The other laboratory findings are within normal limits.

77. Number 2 is correct.

Rationale: Digoxin must be taken exactly as prescribed without skipping or doubling up on doses. It should be taken at the same time each day. Options 3 and 4 indicate potential problems that need to be addressed by the health care professional.

78. Number 3 is correct.

Rationale: The client who responds quickly, but only to commands has a Ramsay score of 3. The client with an RSS of 1 is restless, anxious, or agitated. Clients with an RSS of 2 are alert, oriented, and cooperative. Clients with an RSS of 4 respond briskly to stimulus. A client with a sluggish response to stimulus is scored as a 5. A client with an RSS of 6 is deeply sedated and does not respond to stimulus.

79. Number 1 is correct.

Rationale: This client is exhibiting signs of an air embolism, which is a complication of hemodialysis. The nurse should stop the dialysis immediately and turn the client on the left side in the Trendelenburg's position. The health care provider should be notified immediately. The nurse should administer oxygen and assess vital signs and pulse oximetry. Positioning the client in this manner helps to trap the air in the right side of the heart so it cannot travel to the lungs. Clotting at the graft site would be present when there is no thrill to palpate or a bruit to auscultate. A clotted graft site would not produce this client's signs. Dialysis encephalopathy is caused by aluminum toxicity from dialysate water that contains aluminum. Signs include mental cloudiness, speech disturbances, bone pain, and seizures. Disequilibrium syndrome is characterized by nausea and vomiting, headache, hypertension, muscle cramps, and confusion.

80. Number 2 is correct.

Rationale: Persons with suppressed or compromised immune systems, such as occurs with leukemia, are at higher risk to acquire shingles. Although rare, a second and even third episode of shingles can occur. A zoster vaccine is recommended for persons 60 years and older, the timeline for highest risk of acquiring herpes zoster.

81. Number 1 is correct.

Rationale: The client should be allowed to gradually assume normal activities at his own pace to prevent aggression or combativeness. Medications may be administered to reduce anxiety post-seizure. The client may become disoriented, confused, or anxious as a result of the seizure, making reorientation necessary. Assessment of neurologic and vital signs should occur until the client is stable to ensure complete recovery.

82. Number 2 is correct.

Rationale: The client will need to focus his attention on proper swallowing technique during meals, making television undesirable. Talking while eating should also be avoided. Unless recommended by a speech pathologist, use of a straw can increase aspiration by administering a bolus of liquid. As approved by the pharmacist, whole pills may be crushed and placed in a soft food item such as custard to allow complete administration. To prevent the chance of aspiration, the client should remain sitting upright after consuming a meal.

83. Number 2 is correct.

Rationale: The normal pH is 7.35 – 7.45. A pH of 7.67 is highly alkalotic and should be reported immediately to the health care provider. The normal range for hCO3 is 22 – 26 mEq/L. The normal range for paCO2 is 35 – 45 mmHg. ABGs are used to assess how well the lungs move oxygen into the blood and remove carbon dioxide. They are used to guide ventilator settings in clients who require mechanical ventilation.

84. Number 2 is correct.

Rationale: The therapeutic INR is generally 2.0 to 3.0, so the nurse should expect an order to decrease the warfarin dose. Increasing the warfarin dose increases the risk of bleeding. Protamine sulfate is the antidote for heparin, not warfarin. The client should be observed closely for signs of bleeding until the INR stabilizes in a therapeutic range.

85. Number 1 is correct.

Rationale: Demonstrating empathy for the client is an essential component for a therapeutic relationship, as is allowing an opportunity to verbalize feelings. Contacting the cardiologist passes responsibility for therapeutic communication on to someone else. Stating a record of good outcomes is not a component of therapeutic communication. Dismissing the client's concerns is inconsistent with establishing a therapeutic relationship.

86. Number 1 is correct.

Rationale: Setting appropriate boundaries is necessary to establish a therapeutic relationship. Confirming an attraction is contraindicated. Questioning the client's relationship status avoids the fundamental issue of establishing limits. Identifying an age difference between the client and the nurse fails to set limits.

87. Number 1 is correct.

Rationale: The health care provider should be notified so that the client's ability to tolerate an increased flow rate can be determined. If orders are given to increase the flow rate, the nurse should monitor for signs of fluid overload such as increased respirations and heart rate, and lung congestion. The TPN should not be discarded. Increasing TPN rates may result in electrolyte imbalance or osmotic diuresis, which can lead to severe dehydration and hypovolemic shock. It is outside the scope of practice for a nurse to adjust IV flow rates without a prescriber's order.

88. Number 1 is correct.

Rationale: Furosemide causes loss of potassium. Daily consumption of high-potassium foods helps prevent potassium depletion. The heart rate should be checked before taking digoxin. Foods containing tyramine should be avoided when taking MAOIs for depression. This medicine should be taken even if traveling; some patients are reluctant to take medications that cause more frequent urination while traveling. Convenience is not a reason to withhold the medication unless directed to do so by the health care provider.

89. Numbers 2, 4, and 6 are correct.

Rationale: After attempting to clear the PICC following facility protocol, the nurse should notify the PICC nurse if he is unsuccessful. The catheter may be positional, which can be corrected by having the client raise and lower the arm or cough. A 10 mL syringe should be used to flush PICCs, as smaller syringes can increase pressure within the catheter and cause it to rupture or damage the blood vessels. Starting a peripheral IV in the opposite limb would not be a first-line intervention. Depending on the IV medications the client is receiving and length of expected therapy, the health care provider will determine if the PICC can be removed and a peripheral IV placed. This should only be done with a prescriber's order. Aggressive force should never be used to try and clear a catheter, since this may cause a clot to dislodge or a fibrin tail to break off.

90. Number 1 is correct.

Rationale: Drugs requiring peak and trough levels, such as vancomycin, require precise timing in order to obtain accurate results. The peak dose should be drawn 1 – 2 hours after infusion, when drug levels are at their highest. Troughs are drawn when the drug is at its lowest level, which is right before the next dose is due. Options 2, 3, and 4 reflect inaccurate draw times.

91. Number 1 is correct.

Rationale: The nurse should give the next dose as ordered. The therapeutic range for a vancomycin trough is 10 – 20 mcg/mL, so this client is within range. There is no need to wait and redraw the trough. Since the trough level is therapeutic, there is no need to hold the medication and notify the health care provider.

92. Number 1 is correct.

Rationale: Beer, anchovies, and liver are high in purine and should be avoided in clients prone to gout. Options 2 and 3 may be included in the diet, unless there are other reasons to avoid these foods. Option 4 lists food high in tyramine, which should be avoided by clients taking certain medications, such as MAOI. Unless the client is on one of these medications, there is no need to avoid those foods.

93. Number 2 is correct.

Rationale: Stage II ulcers present with partial thickness loss of dermis and a red-pink wound bed. No slough is present. Stage I ulcers have intact skin with a red area. The area may be firm, painful, soft, or cooler or warmer compared to adjacent tissue. Stage III ulcers have full-thickness skin loss and may contain slough. The wound may have visible subcutaneous tissue, and tunneling and undermining may or may not be present. Stage IV ulcers present with full-thickness skin loss and exposed bone, muscle, or tendons. Eschar and slough may be present, and tunneling and undermining may develop. Unstageable wounds cannot be staged due to eschar or slough covering the wound. The wound bed must be visualized in order to stage the wound.

94. Number 3 is correct.

Rationale: The maximum recommended dose for acetaminophen is 4 g/day. The client ingested 9 g as a one-time dose, which is sufficient to induce liver impairment. The priority action is to remove as much of the medication from the stomach as possible. The second action would be activated charcoal. IV fluids will not affect the metabolism of acetaminophen by the liver yet may be used to maintain hydration. Acetylcysteine is effective in third-stage liver injury; given the time interval of ingestion, it would be premature to administer this pharmaceutical.

95. Number 3 is correct.

Rationale: Loss of protein in wound drainage requires high-calorie intake for proper healing. Heat directly applied to the wound will be ineffective to promote healing. Antibiotic therapy is not indicated as the ulcer is not considered infected. Wet to dry dressings are appropriate for stage III wounds.

96. Number 2 is correct.

Rationale: Processed foods such as baked ham are among the highest in sodium, along with preserved and pickled foods. Most fresh fruits and vegetables are low in sodium. Condiments tend to be high in sodium, and learning to read labels helps the client identify appropriate diet choices. Frozen pizza and many other frozen prepared foods are high in sodium because they are processed.

97. Numbers 2, 4, and 5 are correct.

    Rationale: Furosemide increases urine output, which removes excess fluid from the body. Pitting edema of +1 indicates an improvement due to the fluid loss. Urine output of 250 mL/hr is an expected finding in this client. Crackles in the lungs should be decreased or absent. Pitting edema of +3 indicates an increase in edema. Shortness of breath should be resolved, not merely decreased.

98. Numbers 1, 5, and 6 are correct.

    Rationale: Left-side heart failure manifestations include dyspnea, weak peripheral pulses, and crackles or wheezes in the lungs. Left-sided heart failure causes pulmonary congestion and decreased cardiac output. Right-sided heart failure causes systemic congestion, leading to an engorged spleen, dependent edema, and jugular vein distention.

99. Number 1 is correct.

    Rationale: Measles is highly infectious and travels via droplets in the air. Clients with measles should be isolated in negative-pressure rooms that conform to current CDC guidelines for controlling airborne infectious diseases. The client with a broken femur is just as susceptible to measles as the client with diabetes, unless he has been vaccinated, has laboratory-confirmed evidence of immunity, or was born before 1957. Optimal client safety requires the use of the negative-pressure room, regardless of the immune status of other clients. All staff and visitors entering the negative-pressure room should don appropriate personal protective equipment and follow universal precautions, in addition to airborne precautions. A private room at the end of the hall is not isolated enough to be safe without the negative-pressure room designation.

100. Number 3 is correct.

    Rationale: The client experiencing the MI should be seen first, as this is a potentially life-threatening event. The client with dull abdominal pain and constipation should be seen and his pain assessed, but this is not as urgent as the client experiencing an MI. Pain due to sickle cell crisis must be addressed as soon as possible, but the client with an MI takes priority. The client with mild incision pain from a laparoscopic appendectomy needs to be assessed, but the client with an MI takes priority. When prioritizing care for multiple clients in pain, the nurse should first consider pain caused by a potentially life-threatening event before seeing other clients.

101. Number 3 is correct.

    Rationale: C. diff is highly contagious, and soiled linens require special handling. The nurse should bag all linens in a red biohazard bag and place in the designated area for biohazard bags in the soiled utility area. Linens do not need to be thrown in the trash can, as the laundry process requires very hot water and specific detergents to kill microorganisms for hospital settings. Dirty linens should never be left in the client's room, as this increases the risk of contamination to health care givers in the client's room. The linens should never be placed in with regular dirty linen.

102. Numbers 1, 3, and 4 are correct.

    Rationale: Gloves should be worn when in contact, or potential contact, with blood, body fluids, secretions, or excretions.

103. Numbers 2 and 3 are correct.

    Rationale: When a medication error is discovered, the nurse should immediately notify the health care provider and inform her of the dose ordered, the dose actually given, follow-up vital signs, and any adverse effects noted. The client with chest pain and atrial fibrillation will be on telemetry, so the nurse should run more frequent rhythm strips to chart the client's tolerance of the dose. An incidence report should be completed, but these reports are never mentioned in the chart. The nurse should not delay notifying the health care provider, regardless of how well the client seems to tolerate the dose. The nurse should not blame the dosing error on the pharmacy, as it is up to the nurse to verify that the dose in the package is correct. Also, there is no indication that the pharmacy loaded the wrong dose in the medication dispenser. If that were the case, a diligent nurse would catch it before the medication was given and could notify the pharmacy that the loaded doses were incorrect. In that case, the nurse should wait until the proper doses are loaded before giving the medication. The nurse is the last safety point between the medication and the client and carries the ultimate responsibility for verifying any medication before administering.

104. Number 4 is correct.

Rationale: Metallic items including shrapnel cannot go into an MRI because they can become dislodged. If a client has past military duty, further questioning should be done to determine if he served in combat and was exposed to any shrapnel. Caution should also be used with anyone who may have had a gunshot wound in the past. Vertigo, atrial fibrillation, and allergy to contrast dye do not affect an MRI. Clients with allergy to contrast dye may require prophylactic treatment before undergoing a CT with contrast.

105. Number 2 is correct.

Rationale: Establishing therapeutic communication by sitting quietly with the client demonstrates compassion. A referral may be warranted, but the test question seeks the correct action to be taken by the nurse. Arranging for a hemodialysis client to speak with her does not allow the client to explore her feelings with the nurse. Leaving the client alone fails to establish a therapeutic relationship with the nurse.

106. Number 3 is correct.

Rationale: An uncomfortable feeling of pressure, squeezing, fullness, or pain in the center of the chest is the predominant symptom of an MI in women. Palpitations indicate an arrhythmia. Edema in the lower extremities is a later sign of cardiac failure. A feeling of nausea is less common when experiencing an MI.

107. Numbers 1 and 2 are correct.

Rationale: After surgery, the client should avoid getting in a pool or tub as infection may occur. Long-term pain will be reduced, hopefully eliminated. Short-term pain will require pain medication to be administered as ordered. The client should be encouraged to take pain medication as frequently as needed. Physical therapy begins soon after surgery and may continue for several weeks, until full recovery occurs. Walking is considered a low-impact activity and would be encouraged after surgery.

108. Number 1 is correct.

Rationale: Raising new issues during the ending phase of a relationship is counterproductive. The other actions are consistent with appropriate termination of a therapeutic relationship.

109. Number 1 is correct.

Rationale: A disturbed body image is most common in adjusting to a colostomy. The client should not have panic attacks, although he may not be comfortable caring for the colostomy. Mobility is not impaired after a colostomy. The client should be having less pain postoperatively.

110. Number 3 is correct.

Rationale: Cisplatin is contraindicated and should not be given to clients with a creatinine clearance below 30 mL/min. The iron level is within normal limits and is not a contraindication of administering cisplatin. The ammonia level is also within normal limits, which is important to monitor as cisplatin should be used cautiously with hepatic impairment. BNP is used to measure the severity of heart failure; this value is within the normal range.

111. The nurse will give 1.3 mL.

0.25 g × 1000 = 250 mg	Convert 0.25 g to mg.
$\dfrac{250 \text{ mg}}{400 \text{ mg}} \times 2 \text{ mL}$	Set up a proportion to solve. Recall that the concentration is 400 mg streptomycin per 2 mL of solution.
= 1.25 mL	Solve.
= 1.3 mL	Round up to find the quantity in milliliters.

113. Number 5 is correct.

    Rationale: Unstageable wounds cannot be staged due to eschar or slough covering the wound. The wound bed must be visualized in order to stage the wound. Stage I ulcers have intact skin with a red area. The area may be firm, painful, soft, or cooler or warmer compared to adjacent tissue. Stage II ulcers present with partial thickness loss of dermis and a red-pink wound bed. No slough is present. Stage III ulcers have full-thickness skin loss and may contain slough. The wound may have visible subcutaneous tissue, and tunneling and undermining may or may not be present. Stage IV ulcers present with full-thickness skin loss and exposed bone, muscle, or tendons. Eschar and slough may be present, and tunneling and undermining may develop.

114. Numbers 2, 3, and 4 are correct.

    Rationale: With viral hepatitis, lab findings include increased AST and ammonia levels. Serum albumin and ALT levels decrease. Prothrombin time is prolonged in viral hepatitis.

115. Number 4 is correct.

    Rationale: Chemotherapy administration and monitoring must be performed by nurses who have been certified in chemotherapy. This nurse is not certified and is not familiar with side effects or complications to be aware of. The nurse may care for another client who is not receiving chemotherapy. Client safety is always a priority, and though the nurse may observe other nurses administering chemotherapy as a learning moment, she is still prohibited from providing care that lies outside her area of training and expertise. Assessing pain and assessing the IV site are important, but not as important as ensuring that the nurse is familiar with chemotherapy administration. Asking about drug side effects is beneficial for the nurse who is not familiar with the drug, but does not address the fact that the nurse must be chemotherapy certified.

116. Number 3 is correct.

    Rationale: Metformin should be held before and up to 48 hours afterward when radiologic studies require the use of IV contrast dye due to the increased risk of acute renal failure or lactic acidosis. None of the other medications are contraindicated with IV contrast dye.

117. Numbers 1, 2, and 4 are correct.

    Rationale: Cognitive delays and low levels of literacy are more common in clients in the lower socioeconomic groups than in higher income groups. Lower socioeconomic groups tend to suffer from lack of access to health resources, whether it is transportation to get to the doctor or access to a computer to look up information about their condition. Having adequate health insurance is an advantage, not a barrier to learning. A lack of interest in learning about the condition is not related to income; the client may simply be in denial about the diagnosis or not be ready to learn due to pain or fatigue.

118. The infusion rate is 9 mL/hr.

$\dfrac{20{,}000 \text{ units}}{250 \text{ mL}}$	Divide the total units of heparin by milliliters (bag size).
= 80 units/mL	

$\frac{750 \text{ units}}{80 \text{ units}}$	Set up a proportion using the quotient, 80, and solve for units per hour, using the directive of 750 units.
= 9.38	Divide and solve.
9 mL/hr	Round down to find the infusion rate.

119. Number 1 is correct.

   Rationale: A side effect of levothyroxine is weight loss. Weight gain and light sensitivity are not side effects of this medication. Levothyroxine can cause insomnia, not excessive sleepiness.

120.
Position	Reason
1. Fowler's	nasogastric tube in place
2. lithotomy	gynecological procedures
3. prone	post neck surgery
4. reverse Trendelenburg's	prevent pulmonary aspiration
5. Sim's	administering an enema

121. Number 2 is correct.

   Rationale: In an effort to maintain client safety with the least restrictive method, the nurse may apply a vest restraint device to subtly remind the client to not get out of bed. As a mild sedative, Xanax dosage would begin at 0.25 mg two to three times daily. The stated dosage of 6 mg is an excessive amount of medication. Requesting a family member to stay around the clock would inappropriately relegate the responsibility for safety from the hospital to the family. Moving the client closer to the nurses' station will not promote client safety.

122. The infusion rate is 72 mL/hr.

$\frac{500 \text{ mg dopamine}}{500 \text{ mL}}$	Find the drug concentration.
= 1 mg/mL	
1 mg (1,000) = 1,000 mcg	Convert mg to mcg.
20 mcg/kg/min × 60 kg × 60 min/hr	Multiply medication amount by client's weight and time, and solve.
= 72,000	
$\frac{72,000}{1,000 \text{ mcg/mL}}$	Divide quotient by 1,000 for final drop rate.
= 72 mL/hr	

123. Number 1 is correct.

   Rationale: Crossing the legs when sitting decreases blood flow, which may lead to clot formation. If the client is bed-bound, the nurse should tell the client to avoid crossing one leg over another while lying in bed. Telling the client to avoid car rides longer than two hours may not be practical; longer car rides can be done safely if regular breaks are taken to walk around for a few minutes. Putting a pillow under the knees restricts blood flow to the lower extremities and increases the risk of a clot. Not all clients are candidates for blood thinners; the nurse should focus on actions that the client can do to prevent clots. This engages the client in managing her own care.

124. Numbers 3, 4, and 5 are correct.

Rationale: Following a hypophysectomy, the client is at increased risk of bleeding and increased intracranial pressure. To minimize the risk of increased pressure and bleeding, the client should avoid bending the head down and putting pressure on the nose. Blowing the nose should be avoided until approved by the health care provider. The client will need to mouth breathe while the nasal packing is in place. Brushing the teeth can increase intracranial pressure, which delays healing. The drip pad should remain in place for 2 or 3 days and be removed by the surgeon or by the client following the surgeon's guidelines.

125. Number 2 is correct.

Rationale: Assessment of the client is a priority in the nursing process; therefore, obtaining vital signs would be a priority. The nurse must assess before performing interventions such as relief of pain, administration of IV fluids, and preparation for surgery.

126. Number 3 is correct.

Rationale: Cefazolin can cause a reaction in clients allergic to penicillin. The nurse should hold the medication and notify the health care provider. Administering the cefazolin is likely to trigger another allergic reaction, which potentially may worsen. The pharmacy cannot change health care provider orders. The nurse should consult the health care provider before giving diphenhydramine in order to give the cefazolin, as the provider will more than likely order another medication from a different drug family.

127. Number 1 is correct.

Rationale: The client returning from surgery is the priority here, especially since an open appendectomy was performed. A client with an open procedure is at greater risk of bleeding than clients who have laparoscopic surgeries. The nurse should view the dressing and verify that it is dry and intact, or note and mark any staining. The client due for lisinopril would be expected to have a higher blood pressure; the nurse can assess the client and then administer the medication early if needed. The client on the non-rebreather mask has an expected oxygen saturation level of 96%, which is in the acceptable range. The client with COPD tends to have lower oxygen saturation levels, even on oxygen. Too much oxygen can compromise breathing, as the drive to breathe is caused by being slightly hypoxic in COPD clients.

128. Number 3 is correct.

Rationale: The Parkland formula calls for crystalloid only (Lactated Ringer's) solution for initial fluid replacement. D5W and colloid solutions are not used in the Parkland formula. The Modified Brooke formula prescribes 5% albumin in isotonic saline for the first 24 hours.

129. Numbers 3 and 5 are correct.

Rationale: Vitamin C toxicity causes occult rectal bleeding and increased estrogen levels. Muscle weakness is a sign of vitamin D toxicity. Halos around objects do not occur with vitamin C toxicity. Dry mucous membranes may occur with vitamin A toxicity.

130. Number 1 is correct.

Rationale: Triage works on the principle that clients with the highest acuity have priority over clients with injuries or conditions that are not considered life-threatening. Chest pain, nausea, and diaphoresis indicate a possible myocardial infarction, which can be life-threatening and requires immediate intervention. Fractures and sprains are nonurgent and can wait for treatment. Redness and itching at an IV site indicates a need to assess the site and remove and replace the IV, but is not immediately life-threatening.

131. Numbers 2, 4, and 6 are correct.

Rationale: An NG tube is placed to avoid complications from nausea, vomiting, and abdominal distention. IV fluids correct dehydration. Monitoring stools for bleeding is important because blood loss may lead to a drop in blood pressure or, in severe cases, progress to hypovolemic shock. A client in the acute phase of diverticular disease should have a low-fiber diet if she is able to eat. A high-fiber diet should be introduced gradually once the acute phase has resolved. Enemas are contraindicated because they cause an increase in intestinal motility. Coughing should be avoided because it increases intra-abdominal pressure.

132. Number 1 is correct.

Rationale: STAT orders should always be performed first, unless there is another eminently life-threatening event in progress. The priority is to administer the Lasix for the client in fluid overload. Untreated fluid overload can lead to crackles and other adventitious lung sounds, making breathing more laborious. Additional fluid also places strain on the heart, which must pump more effectively against the extra fluid. Edema develops, and the extra fluid to be excreted places a burden upon the kidneys. Blood pressure also increases. The next task would be to administer insulin to the client with an elevated blood sugar. It is important to get the blood sugar under control to prevent damage to the body's cells. The client should then be discharged to avoid any delay in allowing her to return home. The dressing change will be time consuming and should be performed last, after the more time-sensitive tasks have been completed.

133. Number 2 is correct.

Rationale: Flushing the catheter with 10 to 20 mL of sterile normal saline is necessary to ensure a patent line. Short peripheral catheters should not be used for routine blood sampling because manipulation can cause vein irritation and necessitate removal of the catheter. Obtaining blood samples from central venous lines carries a much greater risk of infection and may interfere with test results depending on the types of fluids that have been infused recently. Transferring blood into test tubes should be done without using exposed needles, for example, by using a vacutainer system.

134. Number 1 is correct.

Rationale: The Holter monitor cannot be worn while swimming or bathing and should be kept dry. The monitor stays in place for the entire time monitoring is performed, including sleep. Metal detectors, electric razors, microwaves, and other electrical devices may interfere with the signal and should be avoided. Cell phones should be kept at least 6 inches away from the monitor. Clients should keep a log and note any chest pain, shortness of breath, or skipped heart beats while wearing the monitor.

135. Number 4 is correct.

Rationale: Clients with AV fistulas should avoid wearing tight sleeves or jewelry over the access area because restricting the blood flow may lead to clotting. A watch should be switched to the opposite arm. Fistulas take several weeks to mature to the point where they may be used. Blood pressures should not be taken in the arm with the fistula. The client should also not have needle sticks in the access arm.

136. Numbers 1, 3, and 6 are correct.

Rationale: A restraint is any mechanical, chemical, or physical device, equipment, or material that prevents or limits movement of any part of the client's body. Bed rails are also a form of restraint, and many facilities have implemented policies barring the use of all four bed rails to keep clients in bed. Alternatives to restraints include active listening, diversionary techniques, reducing stimulation, and verbal interventions or asking the client for cooperation. Children under 9 years of age have a 1-hour time limit in restraints. Assessment of restraints and offering food, hydration, and toileting must be done regularly every 15 to 30 minutes. Many facilities mandate a trial release for clients in restraints. If restraints are removed, a new order must be obtained before replacing them. The use of restraints requires careful and complete documentation by the nurse.

137. Numbers 3 and 4 are correct.

Rationale: Immobilizing and splinting the affected extremity may help limit the spread of the venom. The extremity should be maintained at the level of the heart. Safety is the first priority, so the person should be moved to a safe area and encouraged to rest quietly to decrease venous circulation of venom. Community members should not attempt to kill or capture the snake; if feasible, a digital photograph can be taken at a safe distance for identification. Applying ice is ineffective and may worsen the person's outcome.

138. Numbers 1, 2, 4, and 5 are correct.

Rationale: Principles of triage include treating the least stable clients first. In this scenario, there are four clients requiring immediate attention. When a piece of equipment alarms, the first course of action is to check the client, and then troubleshoot the alarm. The nurse should never ignore any alarm for any reason. Clients who have just returned from surgery, especially an open surgical approach, are at risk for loss of airway due to anesthesia, bleeding from the site, and other potential surgery-specific risks. A sudden change in level of consciousness requires immediate action to determine the cause. Tingling in the mouth is a sign of a possibly serious allergic reaction and may occur if the client receives a new medication for the first time. This client is at high risk of anaphylactic shock. A client who is ready to transfer to the floor is stable and therefore not a priority situation. The client with diabetes who has a blood sugar of 90 is within a safe range and does not require emergent treatment or monitoring.

139. Number 4 is correct.

Rationale: Nursing students learn by doing, and educating clients about their medications is one of the most important skills in nursing. The student nurse should answer only when the precepting nurse is in the room. If any information is incorrect, the RN can gently offer the correct information and use it as a teaching moment for the student nurse. There is no reason to ask the family to step out of the room unless the client specifically requests it. Passing off medication questions to the health care provider is inappropriate, unless the client is receiving a medication that is unfamiliar to the nurse or is an experimental drug. It is incorrect to tell the client that the student nurse cannot answer questions about medication. A student nurse precepting in the ICU has already passed several medication tests.

140. Number 2 is correct.

Rationale: CN V is the trigeminal nerve responsible for sensory function. The nurse tests the nerve by asking the client to close his eyes and then randomly touching the client's face with a cotton ball. The client indicates whenever she feels the sensation. Motor function of CN V is tested by asking the client to clench her teeth and open and close her mouth several times. CN VII is the facial nerve and is tested by asking the client to smile, close both eyes, frown, puff cheeks, raise eyebrows, or show teeth. CN VIII is the vestibulocochlear nerve. Hearing loss or tinnitus is indicative of deficits with the cochlear branch of the nerve. Vertigo indicates a deficit of the vestibular branch. CN XI is an accessory nerve and is tested by asking the client to shrug her shoulders.

141. Number 4 is correct.

Rationale: Regular screening should begin at age 50 for those without a family history of CRC. Fecal occult blood testing and a colonoscopy should be done every 10 years or a double-contrast barium enema every 5 years. Screening should begin earlier and more frequently for those who have a personal or family history of CRC. Dietary guidelines include lowering fat and refined carbohydrates and eating high-fiber foods. At age 40, the client should discuss the need for screening with the health care provider.

142. Number 1 is correct.

Rationale: A positive psoas sign indicates inflammation of the psoas muscle associated with peritoneal inflammation or appendicitis. A positive Murphy's sign indicates cholecystitis. A positive Homan's sign may indicate a blood clot in one of the deep veins in the leg. Chadwick's sign is a normal finding in pregnancy.

143. Number 1 is correct.

Rationale: Elevating the arm and applying ice packs over the approximate location of the incision can help minimize swelling and pain. Option 2 is incorrect because the goal of the intervention is to use nonpharmacological comfort measures. Option 3 is incorrect because no foreign objects should ever be inserted into a cast. If the client is itching, suggest blowing cool air into the cast with a blow dryer. The air must be cool in order to avoid burning the skin or increasing the pain. While range-of-motion exercises are important to maintain mobility, this intervention will not promote comfort and may in fact temporarily increase client discomfort.

144. Number 4 is correct.

Rationale: Consuming large amounts of milk or milk-based products places demand on the kidneys to excrete excess calcium and can cause kidney stones. High-fiber fruits provide needed fiber to prevent constipation while immobile. There is no need to avoid grapefruit juice while on bed rest. While high-fat foods may be a poor dietary choice for health reasons, they are not contraindicated on bed rest.

145. Number 2 is correct.

Rationale: A picture board has pictures of common client needs while in the hospital. Pointing to a picture of a toilet or a pained face requires the least effort on the client's part. A clipboard with pen and paper is not the best choice because it is difficult to write lying down while trying to hold a clipboard firmly. Some clients may use one, but often the handwriting is illegible, leading to frustration for the client when the request can't be read. The client will not be able to mouth words properly while intubated, and involving the family in a guessing game is nonproductive and can increase frustration. Asking the client to blink to indicate answers is ineffective communication because the client may be tired or unable to blink on demand.

146. Numbers 1, 2, 3, and 5 are correct.

Rationale: The first step is to be sure the tubing has not become kinked or lodged under the client. The next step is to gently flush the Foley with 30 cc of sterile saline. Sometimes there may be a blood clot or sediment blocking the flow of urine. Avoid aggressive interventions in order to prevent trauma to the urethra. If the client is alert and oriented, ask the client if he feels pain or pressure or a sense of urinary urgency. The client may not show signs of discomfort, especially if mental function is impaired. A bladder scan is a noninvasive manner in which to determine how much urine is in the bladder. The results should be recorded and the health care provider notified. Joint Commission guidelines encourage minimal use of Foley catheters for the minimum time possible in order to prevent infection. Facility protocols may not allow the nurse to automatically place a new Foley, so the health care provider should be notified to obtain an order for a new Foley. The bulb of the Foley may be lodged against the urethral opening. In this case, the nurse may attempt to reinsert about 2 inches of the catheter after cleaning it with soap and water. This will move the bulb far enough to see if the bulb is blocking urine outflow. However, removing a substantial amount of the tubing and reinserting it increases the risk of infection, even if it has been cleaned.

147. Number 4 is correct.

Rationale: Metformin must be discontinued at least 24 hours before studies with contrast media because of the risk of lactic acidosis, which can be life-threatening. Hold metformin for at least 48 hours post-procedure and do not resume therapy until kidney function has been evaluated. Fish oil is a supplement and does not pose a risk for clients undergoing CT with contrast. Coumadin is an anticoagulant and does not pose a risk with contrast. Prozac is an antidepressant and does not pose a risk with contrast.

148. Number 3 is correct.

Rationale: Options 1, 2, and 4 describe the proper technique for use of an inhaler with a spacer. The client should wait at least 1 minute between puffs.

149. Numbers 2, 4, and 5 are correct.

Rationale: The respiratory rate is within normal limits. Hypertension indicates circulatory overload, which can occur when blood products are administered too quickly. The oxygen saturation level is within normal limits. Other signs of circulatory overload include restlessness, confusion, and distended jugular veins. Low back pain and a sense of impending doom indicate a hemolytic transfusion reaction caused by blood type or Rh incompatibility.

150. Number 2 is correct.

Rationale: Phenergan is contraindicated in children with Reye's syndrome. Paxil 20 mg PO daily is an appropriate dose for this client and condition. Diflucan 150 mg PO is given as a one-time dose to treat vaginal candidiasis. Lopressor 50 mg PO daily is an appropriate treatment for this client's hypertension.

151. Number 2 is correct.

Rationale: Guidelines for prevention of sickle cell crisis include avoiding strenuous exercise, avoiding alcohol and tobacco in any form, and avoiding travel to high altitude destinations.

152. Numbers 1 and 2 are correct.

Rationale: Spiked T waves are an abnormal finding. Left untreated, complete heart block or asystole can occur. Cardiovascular changes are the most serious problem in hyperkalemia. A heart rate less than 60 beats per minute is an abnormal finding and may cause cardiac compromise. The normal resting adult heart rate is 60 – 100 beats per minute. Cantaloupe is high in potassium and should not be eaten by this client. Normal urine output is 30 cc per hour.

153. Number 2 is correct.

Rationale: Cultures normally require 48 to 72 hours to complete growing. Preliminary test results are available at 24 hours. If IV antibiotics are infusing, the nurse should draw cultures just before administering the next dose in order to avoid compromising results. If catheter sepsis is suspected, drawing cultures through the catheter is more accurate than culturing the catheter tip only.

154. Numbers 1 and 3 are correct.

Rationale: A sudden decrease in output may indicate blockage. A Salem sump tube is attached to low continuous suction. Medium intermittent suction is not appropriate for this tube. The semi-Fowler's position is most appropriate for the client with an NGT. If the NGT needs to be repositioned or replaced, confirmation of proper placement is needed before use.

155. Number 4 is correct.

Rationale: After a lumbar puncture, the nurse should assess for numbness, tingling, pain at injection site, movement of the extremities, any drainage at the site, and the ability to void. Report unusual findings to the health care provider. Specimens should not be refrigerated. The client must lie in a reclining position for up to 12 hours with the head flat to avoid a spinal headache. The client may sip through a straw to replace fluids. Positioning the client prone with a pillow under the abdomen increases intraabdominal pressure, which indirectly increases the pressure in the tissues surrounding the spinal cord. This helps slow continued CSF flow from the spinal canal.

156. Number 1 is correct.

Rationale: Iron stains the teeth and should be given through a straw or by placing a medicine dropper in the back of the mouth. The child or parent should brush or wipe the teeth to prevent staining. Iron should be given on an empty stomach between meals to maximize absorption. Iron should not be mixed with food before administering.

157. Number 1 is correct.

Rationale: Clients taking MAOI should avoid foods high in tyramine, including aged or smoked foods, cheese, meats with added nitrates, and pickled foods. The other menu options are permissible for this client.

158. Number 3 is correct.

Rationale: Clients with heart failure experience decreased kidney perfusion. Magnesium hydroxide is excreted through the kidneys, leaving the client at risk for magnesium toxicity. The other conditions listed do not affect the body's ability to clear magnesium.

159. Number 4 is correct.

Rationale: The therapeutic range of digitalis is 0.5 to 2 ng/mL. This client is at the toxic level. Early signs of digitalis toxicity include anorexia, nausea, and diarrhea. Tinnitus, flushed skin, and easy bruising are not consistent with toxic digitalis levels.

160. Number 4 is correct.

Rationale: Injury prevention is important for this client. Throw rugs should be avoided because of the potential to trip and fall. Options 1, 2, and 3 are appropriate safety measures for the client with thrombocytopenia.

161. Number 3 is correct.

Rationale: Do not move a client whose neck is in an awkward position or who is unconscious. Instead, keep the client immobilized and get help immediately. In this situation, CPR is not needed for the client. Keeping the client warm is necessary but not a priority. Asking the client to state her name and birthday may be appropriate if a brain injury is suspected, not a neck injury.

162. Number 2 is correct.

Rationale: Within 12 months after quitting, the carbon monoxide level in a smoker's blood drops to normal. At 15 years after quitting, the risk of coronary heart disease is the same as that of a nonsmoker. At 10 years after quitting, the risk of dying from lung cancer is about half that of a smoker's. At 5 to 15 years after quitting, the risk of having a stroke is reduced to that of a nonsmoker's.

163. Numbers 3, 4, 5, and 6 are correct.

Rationale: Airborne precautions are used for infections caused by organisms that may remain airborne for extended periods, such as tuberculosis and measles. Standard precautions apply to all clients as all body fluids, moist membranes, and excretions are potentially infectious. Negative airflow rooms exchange air and discharge room air to the outside or through HEPA filters. N95 masks or PAPRs prevent inhalation of contaminated air. Fall precautions may or may not be needed for this client. Droplet precautions are used for infections caused by organisms that travel 3 feet but are not suspended for long periods of time, such as mumps and influenza.

164. Number 4 is correct.

Rationale: The client has made his wishes known to the nurse by refusing to sign the consent for blood. Upon admission to the facility, all clients are asked about special religious beliefs that affect care. A power of attorney completed before the client arrives at the facility allows the client to personalize what he does not wish to have done, so he may refuse blood on the power of attorney and allow his daughter to make choices regarding artificial hydration or food, for example. The nurse has an ethical duty based on the principle of client autonomy to not knowingly act against client wishes, even if she does not agree with them. Notifying the charge nurse to let the night shift nurse address the issue does not solve the problem and is irresponsible. Getting a consent for the daughter to sign goes against client wishes, which were recorded upon admission. There is no need to notify the surgeon or to order a type and cross. To give blood to the client against his wishes is considered assault and battery and may result in legal action involving the health care providers, including the surgeon, nurse, and facility. Although the client presents himself as a Jehovah's Witness, the nurse should still ask questions regarding transfusions, preferably out of the presence of friends or family members who may influence the client's true wishes. HIPAA allows the nurse to ask others to leave the room during the questioning process if the client is able to communicate, thereby preserving his privacy.

165. Number 2 is correct.

Rationale: Calcium channel blockers cause vasodilation and decrease total peripheral resistance, which leads to a decrease in blood pressure. The other options do not correctly describe the mechanism of action of calcium channel blockers. Vasoconstriction coupled with increased total peripheral resistance would raise, not lower, blood pressure. Increasing the pressure on one component results in overall blood pressure increase, even if the other component is decreased.

166. Number 4 is correct.

Rationale: Upper body flushing, often called "red man syndrome," is a side effect of vancomycin that can occur especially if the drug is infused too rapidly. Side effects of cephalexin include diarrhea, easy bruising, dark urine, and joint pain. Side effects of amoxicillin include black or "hairy" tongue, stomach pain, nausea and vomiting, and pale or yellowed skin. Side effects of gentamicin include loss of appetite, rash, increased thirst, and muscle twitching. Side effects of antibiotics may be minor, severe, or life-threatening.

167. Number 1 is correct.

Rationale: Canned foods tend to be high in sodium, so low-sodium or no-salt-added versions are a better diet choice for this client. Red meat is high in saturated fat, so it is not a better substitute than fried chicken. Red meats and fried foods should be eliminated from the diet or eaten sparingly. Canned soup is high in sodium unless labeled otherwise; the client needs to select low-sodium varieties. Frozen foods are another sodium-rich category unless otherwise labeled. The client needs to understand that processed foods (frozen foods, canned goods, and boxed items such as crackers) should be avoided as much as reasonably possible. Learning to read labels will help the client lower sodium intake.

168. Numbers 1, 2, and 5 are correct.

Rationale: In providing end-of-life care, the nurse explains to the client and family the signs and symptoms that death is approaching. Explaining what to expect during the final phase of the illness may help alleviate fear and anxiety as the family observes their loved one transitioning through the stages of death. Addressing client and family wishes regarding care, pain management, and emergency resuscitation respects their wishes and ensures that their choices are carried out as much as possible. Cultural beliefs are acknowledged, and life-lengthening treatment options may give way to maintaining comfort. The nurse should not avoid the difficult topic about end-of-life care, but ensure that open discussion is a central part of the client's care.

169. Numbers 2, 3, and 5 are correct.

Rationale: Age, gender, and culture are a few factors that influence the grieving process. The nurse must explore his own feelings about death before he may effectively help others. Nurses can help families find ways to cope with the loneliness and depression that follows the death of a loved one. The process of grief is normal following a loss, and expression of grief is essential for physical and emotional well-being. The expression of grief should never be discouraged; family members should have a quiet room in which they may express their feelings in private.

170. Number 4 is correct.

Rationale: Clients on mechanical ventilation are susceptible to infection because bacteria and viruses can enter the endotracheal tube and infect the lower respiratory system. An increased temperature could indicate a possible infection and should be reported immediately. The other vital signs are findings that would be considered within normal limits.

171. Number 2 is correct.

Rationale: The client will need to lie on his right side for several hours after the liver biopsy to reduce the chance of bleeding. The other positions increase the risk for bleeding.

172. Number 3 is correct.

Rationale: Silence allows the client time to think and reflect and lead the conversation in the desired direction. Silence does not imply that the nurse is not listening, nor does it encourage the client to keep her feelings to herself. Silence is part of listening; the nurse should be focused on the client and not thinking ahead to what else she needs to do.

173. Numbers 2, 3, and 4 are correct.

Rationale: Providing an ordered hypnotic will promote sleep. Lowering the temperature of the room will promote sleep. Fresh linens will provide comfort. A light snack rather than a large meal should be provided.

174. Numbers 1 and 2 are correct.

Rationale: Weight is the most accurate measure for volume retention that is a stress on the cardiac workload. Assistance with self-care activities should be done to avoid exertion. The environment should be comfortable and quiet to reduce stress. Vital signs should be checked before and after activity, especially if the client is taking vasodilators or diuretics.

175. Number 3 is correct.

Rationale: A TURP is done by means of a scope introduced through the urethra so there is no incision. The color of the urine will change according to how much bleeding occurs after surgery. The most common type of bleeding is from a venous source resulting in dark burgundy coloration with dark clots. This type of bleeding will typically stop on its own. Bright red urine with bright red clots is considered more aggressive and may require intervention. Drinking water will help flush the kidneys and/or bladder of bacteria and clots. A catheter is typically inserted after a TURP.

176. Number 4 is correct.

Rationale: Assessment is the first step of the nursing process and should precede all interventions. Provide positive feedback to the client when independent activity or progress occurs. Because hemiparesis typically occurs on the opposite side of the injury to the brain, hygiene items should be placed on the client's right side. As determined after assessment, assistive devices are provided for self-care activities.

177. Number 3 is correct.

Rationale: Post TKR surgery a client will be asked to ambulate the day of surgery, making a fracture pan unnecessary. Having a cold or infection of any kind up to 2 weeks prior to surgery may be a contraindication for surgery. Standard practice is to administer a preoperative antibiotic. Pain medication is routinely ordered post-op and is administered as needed by the client.

178. Number 3 is correct.

Rationale: Antacids should not be taken within 2 hours of Levaquin because they interfere with absorption of the drug, especially if they contain aluminum or magnesium. Levaquin, along with many other antibiotics, increases sun sensitivity. The client should avoid going outdoors or wear sunscreen while on therapy. Taking the complete course of medication prevents rebound infections and antibiotic resistance. Clients should be taught how to take their pulse and report any new-onset irregular heartbeats, as fluoroquinolones may cause serious dysrhythmias.

179. Number 3 is correct.

Rationale: Warfarin doses typically range from 2 to 10 mg PO daily, with dosing adjusted to maintain the PT 1.2 – 2 × the control, or an INR of 2 – 3. This is a higher-than-expected dose.

180. Number 2 is correct.

Rationale: If the client's apical pulse is below 60, the nurse should hold the medication and notify the health care provider. Placing oxygen on the client will not have any effect on the pulse. Waiting an hour to recheck the pulse means a delay in medication administration, but also allows time for the pulse to drop lower, which may worsen client outcomes. There should never be a delay when there is a need to notify the health care provider. Administering the drug may cause the client to become severely bradycardic, and the UAP is not licensed to assess the client, especially when medications have been administered. The nurse is ultimately responsible for follow-up assessments on all clients.

181. 25 mg/mL.

0.5 g = 500 mg	Convert grams to milligrams.
$\dfrac{500 \text{ mg}}{20 \text{ mL}}$	Divide milligrams of Diuril by milliliters of sterile water for reconstitution.
= 25 mg/mL	Solve the equation.

182. Number 3 is correct.

Rationale: IM injections are given at a 90-degree angle. A 25-gauge 1-inch needle is suitable for IM injections in children. A 45-degree angle is used to administer subcutaneous injections. A bleb should form only when giving intradermal injections.

183. Number 4 is correct.

Rationale: When performing gastric lavage, the solution is instilled and removed until returns are clear or light pink without clots. The volume of solution is 200 to 300 mL and should be at room temperature. The client is placed on the left side during the procedure.

184. Number 3 is correct.

Rationale: Nitroglycerin should be taken one tablet at a time, sublingually every 5 minutes up to three doses over 15 minutes as needed for chest pain. If pain relief does not occur, 9-1-1 should be called. It is not safe to take nitroglycerin if taking sildenafil unless approved by the health care provider. Nitroglycerin should be taken one tablet at a time and never chewed or crushed. The pills must be kept in a dark container to prevent loss of effectiveness of the medication.

185. Number 3 is correct.

$\dfrac{\text{amount of solution (mL)}}{\text{time (in minutes)}} \times \text{drop factor (gtt/ml)}$ = flow rate (gtt/min)	Determine flow rate by multiplying rate of infusion and number of drops per milliliter of the fluid being administered.
$\dfrac{1{,}000 \text{ ml}}{360 \text{ min}} \times 10 \text{ gtt/mL}$ = 27.7 gtt/min	Substitute and solve.
28 gtt/min	Round up to find the flow rate.

186. Number 1 is correct.

Rationale: The wound should be cleaned with normal saline before sampling in order to remove normal skin flora. Do not delay culturing the wound; if the client is not already on antibiotics, the culture results guide the health care provider in prescribing the appropriate therapy. Old drainage should never be used as a sample because resident bacterial colonies from the skin are present in the exudate and may not be the cause of infection. The outer surface of the wound should not be cultured.

187. Numbers 1, 3, and 5 are correct.

Rationale: With continuous feedings, residual should be checked every 4 hours to assess for delayed gastric emptying. In noncritical clients, residual should be checked every 4 to 6 hours or according to agency policy. Residual is also checked before each bolus or intermittent feeding. If the volume is less than 250 mL, the contents are returned to the stomach to prevent electrolyte imbalance. For volumes greater than 250 mL, the nurse should follow agency policy or prescriber's orders. Clients should be positioned in a high Fowler's position or with the head of bed elevated at least 30 (preferably 45) degrees to prevent aspiration. The tubing and bag are changed every 24 hours to prevent bacterial growth.

188. Number 2 is correct.

Rationale: A history of basilar skull fracture may contraindicate tube placement. Neurological injury can result from intracranial passage of the tube. The other history findings are not indicative of a need to notify the health care provider.

189. Number 4 is correct.

Rationale: Stabilizing the catheter for a male on the abdomen prevents meatus damage and erosion. Medical asepsis is adequate for perineal care. Routine irrigation is unnecessary. Unless medically contraindicated, fluids should be encouraged to 2,000 cc/day rather than restricted.

190. Number 2 is correct.

Rationale: Fever, a shrill cry, diarrhea, and nuchal rigidity indicate meningitis, which is a medical emergency. The infant must be placed on respiratory isolation immediately, monitored for seizures, and prepared for a lumbar puncture. Those in close contact with the infant may need prophylactic treatment as well. The client with abdominal pain and nausea is stable at this moment and can be seen later. The jogger is not the top priority because she has a good pedal pulse and no deformity in the ankle, which indicates that she is stable. The client who was working outside and presents with tachypnea, diaphoresis, and fatigue is at risk for heat syncope and should rest in a cool area and be taught to limit exposure in extreme heat, take frequent breaks, and drink plenty of water. This client is also stable. The child who fell off a bicycle onto grass while wearing a helmet is ambulatory, wore protection, and landed on a soft surface. Although he should still have an assessment to check for head injuries, he is not currently in a life-threatening situation like the infant.

191. Number 1 is correct.

Rationale: The best roommate for this client is a client with gout in the large toe. Necrotizing fasciitis is worse in immunocompromised clients, and this client has a history of diabetes and hepatitis. This leaves the client vulnerable to worsening the infection or developing a new infection on top of the necrotizing fasciitis. Gout is not a communicable illness, so this is the best roommate choice for this client. A client with fever, vomiting, and diarrhea may potentially have a contagious condition that can worsen the outcome for the client. The client with MRSA is not a good choice because there is a chance that the MRSA could infect the client with necrotizing fasciitis. The client with severe dementia and the tendency to wander is at risk of cross-contamination and further infecting the client with necrotizing fasciitis because of her inability to perform hand hygiene. Clients with necrotizing fasciitis are generally not contagious to healthy persons, but contact and universal precautions, along with hand hygiene, prevents them from further colonization by bacteria.

192. Number 4 is correct.

Rationale: Heart sounds S1 (tricuspid and mitral valves close) and S2 (aortic and pulmonic valves close) are auscultated to determine the apical pulse over the point of maximal impact. The third heart sound (S3) occurs slightly after S2. The fourth heart sound (S4) is heard slightly before S1.

193. Number 1 is correct.

Rationale: The normal lab value for calcium is 8.5 – 10.2 mg/dL. The symptoms of hypocalcemia include muscle stiffness/spasms, diaphoresis, and anxiety. The lab values stated are within normal range for alkaline phosphatase, sodium, and creatinine.

194. Number 2 is correct.

Rationale: The client's symptoms are consistent with increased intracranial pressure (ICP). The best immediate response is to elevate the client's head to 30 degrees to produce a drop in ICP. Checking the blood pressure is a secondary action. Oxygen administration will not impact the increased ICP. Increasing the IV rate would be contraindicated.

195. Number 3 is correct.

Rationale: The client who is post–atrial fibrillation ablation is experiencing symptoms of cardiac tamponade, a serious complication seen after this procedure. Cardiac tamponade occurs when the ablation penetrates the pericardium allowing fluid to collect, preventing the heart from expanding properly. Emergency intervention is required with this client, including a pericardiocentesis up to a thoracotomy to drain fluid. The other clients may be seen after assessing the client for a cardiac tamponade. While each of these needs is important to address quickly, the nurse first addresses situations that may be life-threatening for the client.

196. Number 2 is correct.

Rationale: Safety of the client is a primary concern. While domestic abuse of an adult female does not require reporting to a federal agency, the nurse is in a position to intervene with the client. Other responses are nontherapeutic communications that fail to promote a constructive relationship with the client.

197. Number 1 is correct.

Rationale: Latex allergies can cause what is known as a cross-reaction when bananas are consumed by someone with the allergy. Latex is made from rubber tree sap, which is a member of the same plant family as bananas. Certain clients may also be sensitive to kiwi, avocado, and other foods. Options 2, 3, and 4 contain foods that would not cause a cross-reaction with latex allergy.

198. Numbers 2 and 3 are correct.

Rationale: Clients need to be in the supine position to allow access to the perineal area. Sterile lubricant, part of the standard catheter kit, is applied to the tip of the catheter to ease entrance through the meatus. A sterile field is maintained when inserting an indwelling catheter. The amount of sterile water used to inflate the catheter balloon depends on the size of the balloon. Typically a 5 cc balloon will be inflated with 7 – 10 cc of sterile water (part of the catheter kit) to maintain the position of the catheter within the bladder.

199. Number 3 is correct.

Rationale: Potato chips and cheese are high in sodium and should be avoided when on a low-sodium diet. Tomatoes and celery are not high in sodium and may be consumed. Most take-out foods are high in sodium and should be avoided.

200. Number 1 is correct.

Rationale: In a compromised client, fluid volume excess can result from excessive IV infusion. Administration of corticosteroids on a short-term basis will not affect fluid volume excess. Diarrhea and fever will result in loss of body fluids rather than accumulation.

TWO: Practice Test Two

READ THE QUESTION, AND THEN CHOOSE THE MOST CORRECT ANSWER.

1. A client with diverticulitis fills out her lunch menu after instruction from the nurse on proper diet. Which selection by the client demonstrates the need for further teaching?
    1. tuna salad on tomato with crackers and a banana
    2. egg salad on whole wheat bread and a pear
    3. creamy peanut butter and grape jelly sandwich and an orange
    4. chicken salad on pita bread and a plum

2. The nurse recognizes that if eaten by a client, which food can alter results when stool is checked for occult blood?
    1. potatoes
    2. dairy products
    3. raw fruits
    4. beef

3. A client with sleep apnea complains of leg cramps that wake him from sleep. Which instruction should the nurse provide?
    1. drink a glass of water at bedtime
    2. wear compression hose at night
    3. elevate the head of the bed at night
    4. dorsiflex the foot

4. The nurse has an order to administer 100 units of regular insulin in 500 mL of 0.9% NS to infuse at 12 units per hour. The nurse should program the IV pump to deliver how many mLs per hour?

    _____

5. The nurse is caring for a client receiving theophylline for asthma. In reviewing client labs, the nurse understands that the dose is therapeutic when the drug level is at what concentration?
    1. 0.8 – 2 mcg/L
    2. 10 – 20 mg/L
    3. 10 – 20 mcg/mL
    4. 0.8 – 12 mmol/L

6. The nurse is caring for a client receiving pantoprazole. The nurse understands that long-term use of proton pump inhibitors increases the risk of which serious side effects? Select all that apply.
    1. nausea
    2. depression
    3. constipation
    4. rhabdomyolysis
    5. long bone fractures

7. The nurse is caring for a client with chronic kidney failure who is receiving Epoetin alfa. The nurse understands which statement to be true regarding this medication?
    1. Side effects include joint pain and hypotension.
    2. It stimulates the production of white blood cells.
    3. Side effects include bloody urine and headaches.
    4. It is given once a week either via the IM route or subcutaneously.

8. The nurse is working on the cardiac unit with a client scheduled to receive digitalis. The nurse understands that which finding is a contraindication for this medication? Select all that apply.
    1. AV block
    2. atrial flutter
    3. atrial fibrillation
    4. sick sinus syndrome
    5. Wolff-Parkinson-White syndrome

9. The nurse is caring for a client receiving IV vancomycin. The trough level is 14 mcg/mL. The next dose is now due. What is the correct response by the nurse?
    1. give the next dose as ordered
    2. wait 2 hours and redraw the trough
    3. wait 30 minutes and redraw the trough
    4. hold the dose and notify the health care provider

10. The nurse is preparing a community educational presentation. The topic is the leading causes of death for people ages 12 – 19. The nurse knows that which of the following should be presented?
    1. unintentional injuries
    2. cancer
    3. homicide
    4. suicide

11. The nurse is caring for a client with end-stage kidney disease and multiple organ failure. Which action by the nurse indicates an understanding of end-of-life care? Select all that apply.
    1. The nurse explains signs and symptoms that indicate death is near.
    2. The nurse explains to the client and family what to expect during the final phase of the illness.
    3. Cultural beliefs are acknowledged, but priority is placed on life-lengthening treatment options.
    4. The nurse avoids talking to the client about impending death to avoid upsetting him and the family.
    5. The nurse asks the client and family what their goals and wishes are regarding care, pain management, and emergency resuscitation.

12. A nurse assigned to a client with congestive heart failure (CHF) is providing shift report. Which nursing interventions would be appropriate to include? Select all that apply.
    1. The nurse should reduce fluid intake to less than 1,000 ml per shift.
    2. The nurse should keep the client in a supine position as much as possible.
    3. The nurse should encourage alternating activity with rest periods.
    4. The nurse should assess the ankles, legs, and feet for pitting edema.

13. The nurse is preparing to discharge a client diagnosed with gout. Which statement by the client indicates understanding of dietary restrictions while managing gout?
    1. "I should avoid beer, anchovies, and liver."
    2. "I should avoid bananas, grapefruit, and oranges."
    3. "I should avoid dairy products such as milk and ice cream."
    4. "I should avoid red wine, dark chocolate, and aged cheeses."

14. The nurse is preparing to interpret an electrocardiogram rhythm strip. Identify the order for interpreting the strip. Use all the options.
    1. measure the P-R interval
    2. determine the heart rate and rhythm
    3. analyze the P waves
    4. measure the QRS duration

15. The nurse is caring for a client with a wound that presents with full-thickness tissue loss and eschar covering the wound bed. The nurse would record this wound as which stage?
    1. Stage I
    2. Stage II
    3. Stage III
    4. Stage IV
    5. unstageable

16. The nurse is reviewing a rhythm strip of a client on the telemetry unit. There are no discernible P waves, and a sawtooth pattern of waves is present. The atrial rate is regular, and the PR interval is not measurable. The nurse would chart which rhythm for this client?
    1. atrial flutter
    2. atrial fibrillation
    3. torsades de pointes
    4. normal sinus rhythm
    5. ventricular fibrillation

17. The nurse is caring for a client with a diagnosis of fluid overload caused by congestive heart failure. Which findings would the nurse expect to find when reviewing client labs? Select all that apply.
    1. decreased BUN
    2. increased hematocrit
    3. increased sodium levels
    4. decreased sodium levels
    5. increased serum osmolality

18. The nurse is caring for an elderly client who presents to the ED with poor appetite, confusion, and weakness. Lab work is ordered for the client. The nurse should immediately notify the health care provider for which lab result?
    1. chloride 99 mEq/L
    2. calcium 9.4 mg/dL
    3. sodium 118 mEq/L
    4. potassium 4.2 mEq/L

19. The nurse is reviewing a client's PRN pain medications. There is an order for acetaminophen 1,000 mg PO q4 hours as needed for pain. How should the nurse proceed?
    1. call the health care provider to clarify the order
    2. administer the medication as ordered if needed for pain
    3. give other PRN medications for pain and ignore the order
    4. avoid giving pain medication every 4 hours and give it every 6 hours

20. The nurse is precepting a student nurse on the cardiac floor and reviewing the cardiac cycle. The nurse knows that the student nurse understands ventricular systole when the student nurse states that blood enters which vessels during ventricular systole?

   1. the aorta and vena cava
   2. the aorta and pulmonary vein
   3. the aorta and pulmonary artery
   4. the pulmonary vein and vena cava
   5. the pulmonary artery and vena cava

21. The nurse is supervising a student nurse on the oncology unit who is providing care for a client with neutropenic precautions. Which action by the student nurse requires intervention by the supervising nurse?

   1. Vital signs, including temperature, are monitored every 4 hours.
   2. The student nurse inspects the client's mouth at least every 8 hours.
   3. The student nurse delivers a potted plant to the room sent by the client's family.
   4. The student nurse washes her hands before performing client care or touching client belongings.

22. The nurse is caring for a client who is disoriented. To avoid using restraints, the nurse chooses alternative methods to help keep the client oriented. Which interventions would the nurse use for this client? Select all that apply.

   1. maintain normal toileting routines
   2. minimize visitation so that the client may rest
   3. evaluate the client's medications for side effects
   4. keep familiar items such as family pictures near the bedside
   5. use calendars and clocks to orient the client to the date and time
   6. place the client in a room near the end of the hall to minimize noise

23. The nurse has just administered morphine 4 mg IV to a client with severe pain from a kidney stone. The client then asks to get up to the toilet. Which is the correct nursing action for this client?

   1. assist the client to the toilet
   2. offer the client a bedpan or urinal
   3. obtain an order for a Foley catheter
   4. place a bedside commode in the room

24. The nurse has an order to administer a heparin drip at 12 units/kg/hr. The client weighs 178 pounds. The heparin is available as 25,000 units in 500 mL D5W. At which rate should the nurse program the pump?

   _____

25. The nurse is preparing to discharge a 60-year-old woman on warfarin (Coumadin) after mitral valve replacement. Which dietary restriction should the nurse advise the client to make?
    1. avoid green tea
    2. avoid cauliflower
    3. avoid green beans
    4. avoid asparagus

26. A client is admitted for deep vein thrombosis and is receiving 5,000 units of heparin subcutaneously every 8 hours. In case of a serious bleeding reaction, the nurse has which of the following drugs readily available?
    1. warfarin
    2. potassium chloride
    3. vitamin K
    4. protamine sulfate

27. The nurse finds that a client receiving digoxin (Lanoxin) 0.25 mg orally has an apical pulse of 54. Which of the following should the nurse do first?
    1. withhold the medicine and contact the prescribing physician
    2. ask another nurse to verify the apical pulse
    3. administer the medication and recheck the pulse in 30 minutes
    4. order a stat ECG

28. A client with pulmonary edema is ordered IV hydrocortisone (Solu-Cortef) 40 mg b.i.d. Which laboratory value would the nurse expect to see as a result of this therapy?
    1. elevated magnesium
    2. lowered magnesium
    3. elevated glucose
    4. lowered glucose

29. The nurse is preparing to teach a client about the prescribed furosemide (Lasix). The nurse should instruct the client about which adverse effect?
    1. increased appetite
    2. leg cramps
    3. anorexia
    4. dry mouth

30. A nurse assessing a client charts his blood pressure as 134/86. The pulse pressure would be
    1. 48.
    2. 86.
    3. 220.
    4. 96.

31. The nurse is talking with a client about primary and secondary prevention of cancer. Which statements are examples of primary prevention? Select all that apply.
    1. removing colon polyps to prevent colon cancer
    2. limiting alcohol to no more than 1 ounce per day
    3. colonoscopy at age 50 years and then every 10 years
    4. yearly mammogram for all women older than 40 years
    5. getting vaccinated against human papilloma virus (HPV)
    6. eating a low-fat diet high in fiber, including fruits and vegetables

32. The nurse is educating a client on meningitis. Which statements would the nurse include in the teaching? Select all that apply.
    1. The CDC recommends an initial vaccine at age 6 or upon entering first grade.
    2. Immunocompromised clients and older adults are at increased risk of meningitis.
    3. Viral meningitis is the most common type; typically, no organisms are isolated from CSF cultures.
    4. Young preschool-age children have the highest rates of infection from life-threatening meningococcal infection.
    5. A booster vaccine is given at age 11 or 12 to children living in crowded spaces, such as group homes or summer camps.

33. The nurse is caring for a female client following the removal of the parathyroid glands. The client complains of a "pins and needles" sensation and difficulty swallowing lunch. The nurse would expect which laboratory value to be abnormal?
    1. calcium
    2. potassium
    3. magnesium
    4. blood glucose

34. The nurse is reviewing labs on a group of adult clients. Which lab value would prompt the nurse to immediately notify the health care provider?
    1. hemoglobin 4.8 g/dL
    2. troponin T 0.04 ng/mL
    3. phosphorus 3.8 mg/dL
    4. bilirubin (total) 0.7 mg/dL

35. The nurse has a client complaining of chest pain. Where should the nurse place the V5 lead for a 12-lead EKG?
    1. in the left midaxillary line
    2. in the fifth intercostal right midclavicular line
    3. in the fourth intercostal space to the left of the sternum
    4. in the fourth intercostal space to the right of the sternum

36. The nurse is caring for a client who will have a pulmonary function test (PFT) performed as an outpatient following hospital discharge. Which should the nurse include in his teaching on the procedure? Select all that apply.
    1. have a driver accompany the client to the test site
    2. limit activity in the days leading up to the test
    3. remain NPO after midnight the day before the test
    4. do not smoke for at least 6 – 8 hours before the test
    5. withhold bronchodilators for 4 – 6 hours prior to the test
    6. increase aerobic activity as much as possible in the days before the test

37. The nurse is caring for a client with marked clubbing of the fingers and toes. The nurse understands which to be true regarding clubbing? Select all that apply.
    1. It is a permanent condition.
    2. Clients on dialysis often have clubbing.
    3. Sickle cell disease may cause clubbing.
    4. It is caused by acute oxygen deprivation.
    5. It can be caused by right-sided heart failure.
    6. It is common in clients with congenital heart defects.

38. On the diagram, identify the location where the client would present with acute abdominal pain for the specified diagnosis.

Diagnosis	Abdominal Location
1. acute cholecystitis	_____
2. acute appendicitis	_____
3. acute cystitis	_____
4. acute peptic ulcer	_____
5. splenic infarction	_____

39. The nurse begins administration of blood to a client on a medical unit. The nurse knows that which of the following activities is inappropriate to delegate to the unlicensed assistive personnel (UAP)?

    1. assist with bathing
    2. obtain a snack from the kitchen
    3. explain to the client the reason for the transfusion
    4. obtain the client's blood pressure

40. The nurse is preparing to do a 12-lead ECG on a client. Which of the following shows where the V1 lead should be placed?

    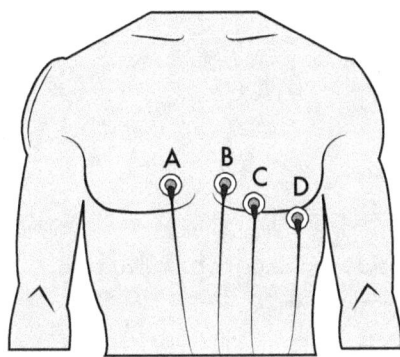

    1. site A
    2. site B
    3. site C
    4. site D

41. Upon entering the client's room the nurse discovers a dose of amoxicillin at the bedside. Which of the following should the nurse do?

    1. file an incident report and document the finding in the client's medical record
    2. document the finding in the client's medical record only
    3. report the incident to the nursing supervisor
    4. file an incident report but do not document the finding in the client's medical record

42. The nurse is reviewing labs for a client whose potassium level is 5.3 mEq/L. Which order should the nurse anticipate from the health care provider?

    1. an order for K-Dur
    2. an order for Pradaxa
    3. an order for Namenda
    4. an order for Kayexalate

43. The nurse is caring for a client with a left pneumothorax and a water-seal chest tube. Which of the following indicates a need for further action by the nurse? Select all that apply.

    1. The client is resting in a semi-Fowler's position.
    2. The client is resting in a Trendelenburg's position.
    3. The suction control chamber has constant gentle bubbling.
    4. Constant bubbling is present in the water seal after clamping off suction.
    5. Tidaling is present in the water seal chamber and corresponds to respiration.

44. The nurse is caring for a client who just returned from a supratentorial craniotomy, during which a large tumor was removed. Which of the following interventions by the nurse are appropriate for this client? Select all that apply.

    1. elevate the head of the bed 30 degrees
    2. elevate the head of the bed 90 degrees
    3. monitor neurological status every 2 hours
    4. monitor for signs of increased intracranial pressure
    5. apply antiembolism stockings to the client once he is alert
    6. turn the client every 2 hours from the operative side to the nonoperative side

45. The nurse is caring for a client diagnosed with glaucoma. The health care provider has ordered timolol maleate. Which finding in the client's history would prompt the nurse to notify the health care provider?

    1. asthma
    2. migraines
    3. atrial fibrillation
    4. urinary tract infection

46. All of the following are examples of secondary disease prevention EXCEPT

    1. leading a support group for people who suffer from depression.
    2. mammogram screenings.
    3. testing and treatment of babies born to mothers with syphilis.
    4. developing a daily exercise program to prevent a second MI.

47. A post-operative client with an abdominal wound tries to reach over and take a book off the bedside table. He immediately screams and calls for the nurse. The nurse notices serosanguineous drainage coming from the incision on the abdomen. The first action the nurse should take is to

1. cover the incision with a sterile cloth or dressing.
2. lower the head of the bed to less than 10 degrees.
3. check the client's vitals to assess for drop in blood pressure.
4. call and alert the surgeon.

48. A non-immune nurse should not be assigned a client who has which of the vaccine-preventable airborne diseases? Select all that apply.

1. tuberculosis
2. influenza
3. smallpox
4. pertussis

49. A nurse has been hired by a company to educate employees on health risks. Which of the following may suggest substance abuse by certain employees in the workplace? Select all that apply.

1. frequent call-ins and tardiness
2. taking only the allocated two 15-minute breaks per shift
3. increasingly poor performance evaluations
4. meeting coworkers for dinner after work
5. eating lunch alone at the desk instead of in the breakroom

50. The nurse is working triage in the ED when four clients present at the same time. Which client should be seen first?

1. a 45-year-old female on oral contraceptives with unusually heavy menstrual bleeding
2. a 24-year-old with a dog bite to the leg from the family dog who is current on rabies shots
3. an irritable 4-month-old with a petechial rash, nuchal rigidity, and temperature of 103.4°F
4. a 16-year-old football player with a twisted ankle who has no deformity and a pedal pulse

51. The nurse is assessing for abdominal pulsations in a client with a visible mass below the umbilicus. The nurse should use which technique?

1. light palpation
2. inspection
3. percussion
4. deep palpation

52. A physician orders 1,000 units of IV heparin to be infused over 2 hours. The pharmacy sends 10,000 units in 500 mL of 0.9% NaCl. The nurse would set the pump to administer how many mL/hr?
    1. 50 mL/hr
    2. 25 mL/hr
    3. 75 mL/hr
    4. 15 mL/hr

53. During her yearly exam, a woman's blood pressure is recorded as 146/90. She tells the nurse that her mother and grandmother had hypertension, so it likely runs in her family. Which of the following is the nurse's best response?
    1. "This indicates prehypertension and is nothing to worry about yet. Please come back in a few months and we will check it again."
    2. "Since hypertension runs in your family, this reading is within normal limits."
    3. "This shows that you have stage 2 hypertension. You will likely be prescribed medication today and will also need to see the nutritionist."
    4. "This shows that you have stage 1 hypertension. You may need to take medication and will need to make lifestyle changes as well."

54. After a cardiac catheterization procedure, the nurse should ask the client to remain in which position?
    1. on the left side, with both knees bent slightly
    2. semi-Fowler's position
    3. supine with a small pillow under the head
    4. high-Fowler's position

55. A woman comes to the clinic for a well-woman exam. The nurse charts her height as 5 feet, 3 inches and weight as 146 pounds. Her body mass index (BMI) would be
    1. 25.9.
    2. 19.6.
    3. 24.2.
    4. 28.5.

56. During a pre-op assessment, the nurse would chart which finding(s) as subjective data? Select all that apply.
    1. The client is sweating and wringing his hands.
    2. The client states, "I am having second thoughts about my surgery."
    3. The client reports he has lost 6 pounds in the last 2 months.
    4. The client's blood pressure is 128/82.
    5. The client rates his pain as a 3 on a scale of 0 – 10.

57. Which of the following would be considered a sensible type of fluid loss?

1. sweat
2. respiratory excretions
3. vomit
4. water loss in feces

58. Which of the following actions does NOT require the use of standard precautions?

1. contact with blood
2. contact with urine
3. contact with sweat
4. contact with vomit

59. A client diagnosed with gout 10 years ago admits she has never treated her gout and hoped it would just go away. The nurse knows all of the following are potential complications from untreated gout EXCEPT

1. kidney stones.
2. nodules of uric acid under the skin.
3. deformed joints.
4. peripheral neuropathy.

60. The nurse is caring for a 72-year-old female who must remain on bed rest after a hip fracture. The client has become confused and disoriented over the past 2 days. Which of the following is the best nursing intervention?

1. placing familiar objects such as family photos, a clock, and a personal calendar on the wall
2. asking the physician to order restraints so the client does not try and get up
3. asking the client's daughter to stay overnight so the client is comforted by a familiar face
4. moving the client to a better staffed floor, so she can be watched more carefully

61. Which of the following is NOT considered a risk factor for developing breast cancer?

1. early menarche
2. nulliparity
3. early menopause
4. previous history of uterine cancer

63. A student nurse is developing a care plan for a 23-year-old woman with Meniere's disease. Which of the following would NOT be an expected intervention?

1. administer narcotic pain medication PRN as ordered
2. refer client to dietician to plan meals with reduced sodium levels
3. assist client out of bed to shower and to toilet
4. encourage client to eat several, similarly sized meals throughout the day

62. A client in ICU has a chest tube, and the nurse is assessing the chest tube drainage system. The nurse notices intermittent bubbling in the water seal chamber. What action should the nurse take?
    1. clamp the chest tube and call for help
    2. document the findings in the client chart
    3. document an air leak and notify the physician
    4. call the physician to report the findings

64. A young woman experiencing a flare-up of Crohn's disease is confused about what kinds of foods she should eat and asks the nurse for a sample menu. Which of the following is the nurse's best suggestion for a breakfast meal?
    1. grits with margarine, sliced banana, and apple juice
    2. whole grain cereal with raisins, and one-half cup of coffee
    3. breakfast sandwich with bacon, fresh tomato, and onion on wheat bread, and a cup of tea
    4. bran waffles with crunchy peanut butter spread, and prune juice

65. Which laboratory finding would indicate a 62-year-old male client is at risk for ventricular dysrhythmia?
    1. magnesium 0.8 mmEq/L
    2. potassium 4.2 mmol/L
    3. creatinine 1.3 mg/dL
    4. total calcium 2.8 mmol/L

66. A client in ICU is being closely monitored after a fall. The nurse notices a slight increase in intracranial pressure (ICP). The nurse should intervene by
    1. increasing oxygen flow.
    2. elevating the head of the bed to 90 degrees.
    3. turning and repositioning the patient on his side.
    4. suctioning the patient at least hourly.

67. A patient is rushed to the emergency room after being found unconscious at home. His blood pressure is 70/35. The nurse anticipates an order for what medication?
    1. atropine sulfate (Atropine)
    2. amiodarone (Cordarone)
    3. magnesium sulfate
    4. adenosine (Adenoscan)

68. Place the steps for an abdominal assessment in the correct order.
   1. auscultation
   2. palpation
   3. inspection
   4. percussion

69. A 32-year-old woman comes into the clinic for a well-woman exam and asks for information on an intrauterine device (IUD) for contraception. The nurse should explain that all of the following are potential risks EXCEPT
   1. stroke.
   2. pelvic infections.
   3. abnormal menstrual bleeding.
   4. ectopic pregnancy.

70. Which of the following are true statements regarding peripherally inserted central catheter (PICC) lines? Select all that apply.
   1. requires sterile technique during insertion
   2. can be inserted by any LPN or RN
   3. lower risk of infection compared to other central lines
   4. increased risk of pneumothorax
   5. can be inserted at the patient bedside

71. A client taking furosemide (Lasix) comes into the clinic for routine bloodwork. Which of the following findings indicates an adverse effect of Lasix?
   1. chloride 102 mg/dL
   2. ammonia 36 µmol/L
   3. uric acid 13.5 mg/dL
   4. ferritin 176 ng/mL

72. An 82-year-old woman is being admitted to a long-term care facility. Her assigned nurse completes a full assessment, including calculating the risk for skin breakdown based on the Braden Scale. To determine a Braden Scale score, the nurse evaluates all of the following EXCEPT
   1. nutritional status.
   2. sensory perception.
   3. past history of skin breakdown.
   4. activity level.

73. A nurse receives an order to dilute ceftriaxone sodium powder in a vial prior to administration. The nurse should ensure the powder is fully diluted by
    1. shaking the vial for at least 60 seconds.
    2. rolling the vial between the palms of the hands.
    3. allowing vial to sit for at least 10 minutes before administering.
    4. asking the pharmacy to dilute the mixture.

74. A nurse is assessing a 33-year-old patient who underwent a cholecystectomy 18 hours prior. The nurse notes 500 mL of greenish-brown fluid has drained from the T-tube postoperatively. The nurse should
    1. chart these findings and reassess on the next rounding.
    2. call the physician and report the drainage.
    3. flush and irrigate the tube.
    4. chart these findings and indicate an infection is suspected.

75. All of the following are parts of the middle ear EXCEPT the
    1. pinna.
    2. incus.
    3. stapes.
    4. malleus.

76. A client has been admitted to the floor with suspected infective endocarditis. The nurse knows to look for which signs and symptoms that would indicate infective endocarditis? Select all that apply.
    1. weight gain
    2. fever
    3. Roth's spots
    4. murmur
    5. anemia

77. A 28-year-old woman with Guillain-Barre syndrome has been intubated and is on mechanical ventilation due to ascending paralysis. She has become increasingly worried and upset as the day has gone on. What would be the best response by the nurse to help the woman cope?
    1. "I am going to keep you heavily sedated so you will not have to be scared. When you wake up, you won't remember ever being sick."
    2. "I know this is overwhelming; this is a very complicated syndrome and it's too hard for you to understand. Just trust the health care providers."
    3. "I am going to hang a 'no visitors' sign on your door. You do not want your family to see you this way."
    4. "I know you are worried, and I am here to answer any questions you have. It is good to have your family here visiting to offer some distraction from being in bed."

78. The nurse is caring for a client with an internal cervical radiation implant. When performing morning care, the nurse notes the implant lying on the bed. Which nursing action should be done first?

1. notify the health care provider
2. apply gloves and attempt to reinsert the implant
3. retrieve the implant with long-handled forceps and place into a lead container
4. don a lead apron and retrieve the implant with long-handled forceps and place into a lead container

79. A nurse is preparing to start an IV on a client. Which action by the nurse increases the risk of infection in this client?

1. The nurse washes his hands and applies gloves before starting the IV.
2. After placing the IV, the nurse removes his gloves and washes his hands.
3. The nurse prepares strips of tape to secure the IV and sticks them to the tray table.
4. The nurse cleans the area with alcohol or another approved skin cleanser and allows it to dry.

80. A client with a colostomy is experiencing mild diarrhea. Which instruction should the nurse give the client?

1. drink two 8-oz glasses of water
2. eat two bananas
3. eat five prunes
4. eat a salad with vinaigrette dressing

81. The nurse reviews a 21-year-old female's bloodwork from the lab. Which result would be charted as an abnormal finding?

1. platelets 129
2. RBC 4.2
3. WBC 15.6
4. hematocrit 38%

82. A 19-year-old male was prescribed sertraline (Zoloft) 3 weeks ago for depression. He calls the clinic today and tells the nurse that he has been feeling increasingly anxious and wants to stop taking the medication because it is not working. The best response for the nurse is

1. "You can stop taking the Zoloft, but let's make another appointment with your provider so you can try a different medication."
2. "Increased anxiety is a normal side effect for the first few weeks of taking this medication. It will take several weeks to determine if it is working. Please keep taking it as prescribed."
3. "Increased anxiety is not a normal side effect of Zoloft. What day this week can you come to the clinic to discuss this with your provider?"
4. "Try taking half the prescribed dose for the next week and see if that helps the feelings of anxiety."

83. The nurse is caring for a client who is undergoing a pharmacological stress test because she cannot use the treadmill. The nurse administers the prescribed dose of adenosine. Which physiological response indicates an adverse effect of the adenosine requiring intervention by the nurse? Select all that apply.
    1. nausea
    2. RR of 18
    3. HR of 97
    4. chest pain
    5. facial flushing

84. The nurse is reviewing labs on a client with second- and third-degree burns from a house fire. Which abnormal lab value would the nurse expect to find with this client?
    1. pH of 7.41
    2. albumin of 3.9 g/dL
    3. hemoglobin of 15 g/dL
    4. potassium of 5.9 mEq/L

85. The nurse is teaching a newly diagnosed client about Guillain-Barre syndrome (GBS). What information would the nurse provide in her teaching? Select all that apply.
    1. GBS affects females more often than males.
    2. The acute period lasts several days to 2 weeks.
    3. GBS tends to be self-limiting with temporary paralysis.
    4. Common symptoms include muscle weakness and paralysis.
    5. Infections such as Epstein-Barr virus have been associated with GBS.

86. The nurse is caring for a client who was admitted with an upper respiratory infection. The client's temperature is 102.4°F, and he is confused. In the last 2 hours, systolic blood pressure has dropped from 138 to 90. The nurse should perform which intervention? Select all that apply.
    1. obtain blood cultures
    2. place the client on NPO status
    3. administer supplemental oxygen
    4. administer antipyretics as ordered
    5. encourage rest and limit physical activity
    6. provide a warming blanket to alleviate chills

87. A client is prescribed aspirin gr. V. Each aspirin tablet is 300 mg. How many tablets does the nurse administer? Fill in the blank.

    _____

88. The nurse administers 6 units of Humalog (lispro) insulin sub-q to a client at 8:30 a.m. The nurse knows to reassess the client and check for a possible hypoglycemic reaction at

    1. 8:45 a.m.
    2. 9:30 a.m.
    3. 11:30 a.m.
    4. 12:00 p.m.

89. A client is receiving gentamicin sulfate (Gentamicin) injections as part of her treatment regimen for a pseudomonas infection. The nurse knows to assess for what potential adverse reaction to this medication?

    1. orthostatic hypotension
    2. occult bleeding
    3. torsades de pointes
    4. ototoxicity

90. The nurse is caring for a client whose lab results show triglycerides of 380 and cholesterol level of 240. Which foods would the nurse educate the client about including in his diet when he is discharged? Select all that apply.

    1. wheat toast with sugar-free jelly
    2. grilled salmon seasoned with herbs
    3. an egg-white omelet with vegetables
    4. natural honey from a local farmer's market
    5. plain grilled steak prepared with pepper only

91. The nurse is preparing to discharge a client who was treated for tuberculosis. Which guidelines for home management should the nurse include in his discharge teaching? Select all that apply.

    1. The client may resume his normal activities.
    2. The family should maintain respiratory isolation at home.
    3. The medication regimen should be followed diligently as prescribed.
    4. The client may return to work when three sputum cultures are negative.
    5. The nurse should educate the client about the medication and possible side effects and their management.

92. All of the following are common symptoms seen in clients diagnosed with tuberculosis (TB) EXCEPT

    1. nail clubbing.
    2. night sweats.
    3. weight gain.
    4. fever.

93. On the oncology floor, a client has just received a bone marrow transplant. The nurse would expect to see which drug prescribed to prevent graft versus host disease?
    1. etoposide (Etopophos)
    2. cytarabine (Ara-C)
    3. metoclopramide (Reglan)
    4. sandimmune (Cyclosporine)

94. A nurse needs to draw a blood sample from a patient's central line. The line is currently infusing Ringer's lactate. In which order should the nurse take the following steps to draw the blood sample? Number the steps below.
    ___ attach the flush syringe and flush catheter with normal saline
    ___ stop the infusion and disconnect Ringer's lactate
    ___ withdraw a blood sample and discard
    ___ scrub the catheter hub
    ___ withdraw the blood sample for the lab

95. An end-of-life client receiving home hospice care states he no longer wants to eat. The nurse should
    1. speak with the health care provider about inserting a feeding tube.
    2. encourage the client to eat small, nutritious meals.
    3. accept the client's decision and work to make the client comfortable.
    4. ask the client's family to bring the client's favorite foods.

96. A 3-year-old boy is diagnosed with plumbism. Which of the following information in his chart does the nurse associate with his diagnosis?
    1. The child's family follows a strict vegetarian diet.
    2. The child lives in a 70-year-old farmhouse with his grandparents.
    3. The child was strictly bottle fed.
    4. The child required phototherapy after birth.

97. A client has been diagnosed with glossopharyngeal neuralgia. The nurse will expect the client to
    1. experience episodes of vertigo.
    2. experience difficulty moving the tongue.
    3. experience double vision.
    4. experience episodes of pain in the throat, ears, tongue, and tonsils.

98. A 20-year-old male has recently been diagnosed with schizophrenia. The nurse knows which of the following are classic signs and symptoms of this disorder? Select all that apply.
   1. social withdrawal
   2. agitation
   3. auditory hallucinations
   4. disorganized speech
   5. obsession with personal hygiene

99. The nurse is creating a discharge plan for a client with cholecystitis. The nurse should encourage the client to follow
   1. a diet low in potassium.
   2. a diet low in fat.
   3. a diet with increased vitamin B 12.
   4. a diet low in phosphorus.

100. A client's blood pressure is 132/84. What is the mean arterial pressure?
   1. 79 mmHg
   2. 48 mmHg
   3. 92 mmHg
   4. 100 mmHg

101. A client has been prescribed tetracycline (Sumycin) for Lyme disease. All of the following statements indicate successful client teaching regarding this medication EXCEPT
   1. "I may need to take an antacid to protect my stomach."
   2. "I will need to tell my doctor right away if I suspect I am pregnant."
   3. "I need to wear sunscreen at all times."
   4. "I cannot take this medicine with any dairy products."

102. A 57-year-old male with a history of vasculitis has purple discolorations on his legs, each approximately 0.3 cm to 1 cm in size. He asks the nurse what these discolorations are called, and the nurse correctly calls them
   1. ecchymosis.
   2. purpura.
   3. petechia.
   4. bruises.

103. A client pushes his call light and tells the nurse his chest is hurting. The nurse sees his oxygen saturation is 88%. The nurse's first intervention is to
    1. perform an ECG.
    2. administer oxygen.
    3. administer morphine IV.
    4. call the Rapid Response Team.

104. A nurse has delegated care of a client in wrist restraints to a nursing assistant. The nursing assistant should check the skin circulation under the restraints at least
    1. every 15 minutes.
    2. every 30 minutes.
    3. every hour.
    4. every 2 hours.

105. The nurse receives an order to administer 1,500 mL D5W IV over 12 hours. The drop factor is 15 drops/1 mL. The IV flow rate should be set at how many drops per minute? Round to the nearest whole number.

    _____

106. A home health nurse visits a 48-year-old male client who has a fear of leaving his home because the space outside is too overwhelming. He has not gone anywhere in the past 2 months. The client has likely been diagnosed with
    1. sociophobia.
    2. anthropophobia.
    3. xenophobia.
    4. agoraphobia.

107. A patient is rushed to the ER after overdosing on benzodiazepines. The nurse anticipates an order for
    1. lorazepam (Ativan).
    2. flumazenil (Romazicon).
    3. naloxone (Narcan).
    4. alprazolam (Xanax).

108. The clinical triad of abnormalities seen in serotonin syndrome includes all of the following EXCEPT
    1. cognitive effects.
    2. autonomic effects.
    3. somatic effects.
    4. behavioral effects.

109. A 19-year-old female is admitted to the psychiatric floor after a suicide attempt 3 days ago. With client safety a priority, the nurse should
    1. assign the patient to the room closest to the nursing station.
    2. assign the patient to an open room with a roommate.
    3. assign the patient to a secluded, isolated room.
    4. assign a staff member to stay with the client at all times.

110. A client has been diagnosed with renal insufficiency, which has led to pronounced fluid volume excess. The nurse would expect which of the following signs and symptoms? Select all that apply.
    1. decreased urine output
    2. hypotension
    3. jugular vein distention
    4. weak, thready pulse
    5. tachycardia

111. A nurse reviews a client's lab values and sees the BUN is 18 mg/dL and the creatinine is 0.7 mg/dL. If the physician asks the nurse for the BUN-to-creatinine ratio (rounded to the nearest whole number), the nurse would answer
    1. 25:2.
    2. 26:2.
    3. 26:1.
    4. 25:1.

112. All of the following clients are at an increased risk for aspiration pneumonia EXCEPT
    1. a client receiving nasogastric tube feeding.
    2. a client receiving total parenteral nutrition.
    3. a client on mechanical ventilation.
    4. a client with dysphagia.

113. A 35-year-old male comes into the clinic after he strains his back at work. The nurse anticipates the physician may suggest which topical anesthetic?
    1. aloe
    2. zinc oxide
    3. hydrocortisone
    4. capsaicin

114. Due to a natural progression of aging, elderly clients have the most difficulty discerning between which two colors?
    1. yellow and green
    2. red and green
    3. blue and green
    4. yellow and red

115. A nurse is caring for a client who has just undergone an ileostomy procedure. The nurse expects how much drainage from the ileostomy during the first 24 hours post-op?
    1. 650 mL
    2. 800 mL
    3. 1,500 mL
    4. 3,500 mL

116. The nurse is teaching a family about safety from poisons. The nurse would include which statements in her teaching? Select all that apply.
    1. "If someone accidentally ingests poison, try to induce vomiting unless the person is unconscious."
    2. "If the person vomits, save the vomitus in case it is requested by the Poison Control Center or emergency department."
    3. "Post the phone number of the Poison Control Center near the phone if you have small children."
    4. "If the Poison Control Center recommends going to the hospital, drive as fast as you can safely do so."
    5. "Older adults are at risk of accidentally overdosing on prescription medications due to poor eyesight or memory loss."

117. The nurse teaches a group of fire fighters about the spread of tuberculosis (TB). Which statement by a fire fighter indicates the teaching has been effective?
    1. "I could get TB if I come in contact with blood from an infected person."
    2. "I can share a cup of coffee with someone who is infected with TB."
    3. "I could get TB if I inhale infected droplets when an infected individual coughs."
    4. "I need to refrain from shaking hands with an infected person."

118. After administering the annual Mantoux tuberculin skin test to employees, the nurse instructs the staff to return within how many hours after administration to have the results determined?
    1. 12 to 24 hours
    2. 24 to 48 hours
    3. 48 to 72 hours
    4. 72 to 84 hours

119. Which client is at the greatest risk of developing colon cancer?
    1. a 83-year-old Hispanic female with a past history of cholecystectomy
    2. a 62-year-old African American male with a past history of diabetes
    3. a 70-year-old Caucasian male with a past history of cancer treated with chemotherapy
    4. a 42-year-old Asian female who follows a high-fiber diet

120. A 19-year-old male has been experiencing vomiting and diarrhea for 3 days due to food poisoning. The nurse expects a urine specific gravity of
    1. 0.850.
    2. 1.005.
    3. 1.020.
    4. 1.041.

121. A 62-year-old female with osteoarthritis asks the nurse how she can ease her pain and discomfort. The nurse should include which of the following in the discharge plan for the client? Select all that apply.
    1. maintain a healthy weight
    2. take an aspirin as needed to relieve pain
    3. incorporate high-impact exercise daily
    4. use warm compresses to relieve stiffness
    5. incorporate moderate exercise at least three times per week

122. A client diagnosed with hepatitis B asks the nurse how the virus is transmitted. Which of the following is the correct response?
    1. by infectious blood or needles
    2. by infectious blood, sexual contact, and needles, and from mother to newborn
    3. by contaminated food and water
    4. by contaminated water only

123. A 62-year-old male in septic shock suddenly develops acute respiratory arrest syndrome. The nurse immediately places the client on a non-rebreather mask, but oxygenation does not improve. The nurse anticipates which of the following?
    1. The physician will ask the nurse to place a venturi mask on the client.
    2. The physician will ask the nurse to administer 5L oxygen via a nasal cannula.
    3. The physician will ask the nurse to place a simple face mask over the client's nose and mouth.
    4. The physician will ask the nurse to prepare the client for intubation.

124. The nurse is caring for a homeless client brought to the emergency department with a diagnosis of heat stroke. Which key features of heat stroke would the nurse expect to note upon assessment? Select all that apply.

    1. a body temperature of 104.2°F
    2. heart rate of 116 and blood pressure of 78/52
    3. heart rate of 49 and blood pressure of 152/90
    4. heart rate of 120 and respiratory rate of 9 breaths per minute
    5. blood pressure of 82/48 and respiratory rate of 26 breaths per minute

125. A college student presents at the emergency department after being thrown off a horse. Head injury with increased intracranial pressure (ICP) is suspected. The nurse understands that late signs of increased ICP include which manifestations? Select all that apply.

    1. seizures
    2. irritability
    3. restlessness
    4. disorientation
    5. severe headache
    6. nausea and vomiting

126. Which of the following medication orders requires clarification before the nurse can administer the order?

    1. epinephrine (EpiPen) 0.25 mg IM STAT
    2. heparin 30 units/kg/hr IV infusion for 24 hours
    3. ampicillin (Omnipen) 500 mg PO bid
    4. lorazepam (Ativan) 1.0 mg PO prn

127. Which client is at the highest risk for a cerebrovascular accident CVA?

    1. a 67-year-old Hispanic male
    2. a 75-year-old African American female
    3. a 60-year-old Caucasian male
    4. an 82-year-old East Asian female

128. A 51-year-old client received a kidney transplant. Which of the following signs and symptoms indicates possible rejection of the kidney? Select all that apply.

    1. increased urine output
    2. increase in blood pressure
    3. weight gain
    4. pain in lower back
    5. decreased creatinine

129. The nurse is caring for a 36-year-old female recently diagnosed with Addison's disease. The nurse recognizes further teaching is needed if the client states,
    1. "I will need to limit my salt intake and use a salt substitute from now on."
    2. "I will have to take hormones for the rest of my life."
    3. "My husband is helping me pick out a medical alert bracelet to wear."
    4. "I have to watch for symptoms of adrenal failure."

130. The nurse would recognize which symptom as the most likely early indication of pneumonia in an elderly client?
    1. chest pain
    2. fever
    3. dyspnea
    4. altered mental status

131. A 19-year-old female comes into the women's clinic for an STD test. The nurse explains all of the following confirmed cases of STDs must be reported to the Centers for Disease Control (CDC) EXCEPT
    1. genital herpes.
    2. chlamydia.
    3. hepatitis B.
    4. gonorrhea.

132. The nurse is discharging a client who was prescribed prednisone. The nurse tells the client that one of the side effects may be impaired sleep. The client says, "I already have a hard time sleeping. What can I do to help with that?" Which recommendations should the nurse make? Select all that apply.
    1. avoid alcohol late in the evening
    2. keep the bedroom dark and quiet
    3. maintain the same consistent sleep schedule
    4. eat a large, heavy meal at dinner to help promote sleep
    5. read or do another quiet, noncomputer activity before bed
    6. do a vigorous exercise routine after work to help him become tired

133. The nurse is teaching a group of nursing students about proper client positioning. Which statement by a student nurse indicates an understanding of proper positioning?
    1. A client receiving an enema should be placed on the right side in the Sims' position.
    2. A client with a below-the-knee amputation should be positioned with the affected limb elevated at a 45-degree angle.
    3. Clients with pulmonary edema should be positioned upright with the legs dangling over the side of the bed.
    4. Clients with a craniotomy should be positioned with the head of bed at a 20-degree angle with the head in a neutral, midline position.

134. A client requires long-term use of corticosteroids. The nurse explains which of the following is associated with chronic corticosteroid therapy?
    1. chronic fever
    2. inability to gain weight
    3. orthostatic hypotension
    4. osteoporosis

135. The nurse is caring for a client who just had a bone marrow biopsy. The nurse understands that which statement is the nursing priority for this client?
    1. keeping the client NPO for 2 hours
    2. avoiding contact sports for 24 hours
    3. monitoring the client for excessive bleeding
    4. applying alcohol to the site every 4 hours to prevent infection

136. The nurse is caring for a client with a T-tube following a cholecystectomy. Which statement is correct regarding management of these tubes? Select all that apply.
    1. keep the drainage system at the level of the heart
    2. report foul order and purulent drainage to the health care provider
    3. remove the tube when drainage slows to less than 50 mL every 8 hours
    4. do not clamp or irrigate the T-tube without orders from the health care provider
    5. clamp the tube before meals and observe the client for abdominal distention or discomfort

137. A nurse is preparing to administer a MMR vaccine to a 35-year-old male. The nurse should
    1. swab and clean an area of skin over the dorsogluteal muscle.
    2. prepare a 25-gauge, 1 1/2-inch needle.
    3. pinch and hold the skin while injecting the needle.
    4. inject the needle at a 90-degree angle.

138. The nurse is working with a client who experiences orthostatic hypotension. Which suggestion would benefit the client?
    1. "Sleep completely flat and do not use any pillows to prop your head."
    2. "Wear your support stockings when you sleep."
    3. "Take your blood pressure medicine immediately before trying to stand up."
    4. "Do not drink any liquids after 8 p.m."

139. A 62-year-old female comes to the clinic with the complaint that her vision seems cloudy. What other signs and symptoms may the client mention that are suggestive of cataracts? Select all that apply.

1. nausea and vomiting
2. seeing double out of one eye
3. difficulty seeing at night
4. pain in eyes
5. halos seen around lights

140. A homeless client has been admitted to the hospital for observation, and he does not speak any English. The nurse does not know any of the client's medical history, but he is grimacing and looks to be in pain. The nurse should

1. use nonverbal communication such as pointing and gestures.
2. call for the hospital interpreter services.
3. give the client pen and paper and encourage him to draw.
4. wait to see if any friends or family visit the client who may be able to help.

141. The nurse recognizes all of the following as type IV hypersensitivity reactions EXCEPT

1. allergic contact dermatitis.
2. Crohn's disease.
3. graft versus host disease.
4. penicillin allergy.

142. A 34-year-old male client underwent a vasectomy one week ago and is at the clinic for a checkup. He asks the nurse how long it will be until he no longer needs to use a backup method of birth control. The nurse explains azoospermia usually occurs

1. 1 month after a vasectomy.
2. 1 year after a vasectomy.
3. 3 – 4 months after a vasectomy.
4. 6 – 8 weeks after a vasectomy.

143. A schizophrenic client has been taking haloperidol (Haldol) for 20 months and has developed moderate extrapyramidal symptoms (EPS). The nurse anticipates the physician will likely prescribe what medication for EPS?

1. flumazenil (Anexate)
2. donepezil (Aricept)
3. naloxone (Narcan)
4. benztropine (Cogentin)

144. A 52-year-old female had a hysterectomy 3 days ago and is recovering on the post-op floor. She is scheduled for an oral pain medication every 4 hours. She received her scheduled dose 1 hour ago but pushes the call light and complains of unrelenting and severe pain. The nurse should first
    1. perform a full head-to-toe assessment on the client.
    2. work with the client on alternate methods to relieve pain, such as guided imagery.
    3. explain to the client it is not time to administer more pain medication.
    4. call the physician and report the current plan for pain management is not working.

145. The nurse recognizes all of the following as part of the Cushing reflex triad EXCEPT
    1. cardiac arrhythmia.
    2. increased blood pressure.
    3. irregular respirations.
    4. decreased heart rate.

146. Cardiac muscles follow a certain order of electrical conduction in order for the heart to contract. What is the correct sequence of electrical impulse?
    1. bundle of His
    2. atrioventricular node
    3. bundle branches
    4. sinoatrial node
    5. Purkinje fibers

147. As the nurse hangs a bag of 3-in-1 total parenteral nutrition (TPN) for a client, a family member asks what is in the bag. The nurse explains a 3-in-1 TPN solution includes
    1. lipids, proteins, and amino acids.
    2. lipids, amino acids, and electrolytes.
    3. dextrose, amino acids, and lipids.
    4. dextrose, lipids, and electrolytes.

148. A client in cardiac arrest is given 40 units of vasopressin (Pitressin) IV push. The nurse knows the desired action of this medication in a cardiac arrest is to
    1. raise blood pressure.
    2. stop cardiac arrhythmia.
    3. lower blood pressure.
    4. reset the electrical cardiac conduction system.

149. A nurse is caring for an 84-year-old client who is malnourished. The nurse is concerned about all of the following complications of malnutrition EXCEPT

1. increased risk for falls.
2. poor wound healing.
3. chronic heart failure.
4. increased risk of infections.

150. An AIDS patient has developed a fungal Fusarium infection. The nurse anticipates the physician will order

1. lamivudine/zidovudine (Combivir).
2. famciclovir (Famvir).
3. ciprofloxacin (Cipro).
4. voriconazole (Vfend).

151. All of the following are modifiable risk factors for coronary artery disease (CAD) EXCEPT

1. high stress.
2. obesity.
3. smoking.
4. family history.

152. A 45-year-old female comes into the clinic for a yearly physical. The nurse calculates her body mass index (BMI) as 32. The nurse would chart this as

1. obese.
2. underweight.
3. overweight.
4. healthy weight.

153. A nurse starts an IV medication for a client. It is ordered as IV push, and she pushes the medication slowly over two minutes. The client then becomes restless, complains of chest pain, has difficulty breathing, and becomes cyanotic. The nurse recognizes this is most likely caused by

1. an allergic reaction to the drug.
2. pneumothorax.
3. septic shock.
4. pulmonary embolism.

154. An 80-year-old man with a decubitus ulcer has just been admitted to the floor. Upon assessment of the wound, the nurse notes that an area of skin under the wound extends and creates another opening in the skin 4 centimeters away. She would chart this as
    1. tunneling.
    2. dehiscence.
    3. undermining.
    4. evisceration.

155. What airborne precautions should the nurse anticipate when a client with measles is admitted to the hospital? Select all that apply.
    1. wear a surgical face mask upon entering client's room
    2. require client to wear a face mask in the hallway during transport
    3. require client to be placed in a negative pressure airflow room
    4. wear a fit-tested N-95 respirator at all times when in client's room
    5. have the client enter through the facility's dedicated isolation entrance

156. The nurse is performing an admission assessment on a client. The client states that she has been smoking two packs of cigarettes a day for 20 years. The nurse would chart how many pack years for this client?
    1. 10 pack years
    2. 20 pack years
    3. 30 pack years
    4. 40 pack years

157. A nurse on the oncology unit is preparing to care for a client newly diagnosed with small cell lung cancer. Which statements would the nurse include in client teaching? Select all that apply.
    1. "Avoid aspirin-based products to reduce the risk of bleeding."
    2. "Avoid crowds and report low-grade fever, sore throat, or chills."
    3. "Keep vaccinations current, including live vaccines, to promote wellness."
    4. "Use a soft toothbrush and electric razor to minimize the risk of bleeding."
    5. "Inspect the mouth regularly for sores and ulcers and rinse the mouth after meals."

158. The nurse is talking to a 67-year-old client who has just retired from the job he's had since age 17—the only job he's ever had. The nurse understands that the client is in which of Erikson's stages?
    1. intimacy versus isolation
    2. ego integrity versus despair
    3. identity versus role confusion
    4. generativity versus stagnation

159. The nurse is working on a discharge teaching plan for a client prescribed phenelzine (Nardil), a monoamine oxidase inhibitor (MAOI drug). The nurse knows teaching was successful if the client states,

1. "I will not be able to have wine and aged cheese anymore."
2. "I should avoid all dairy products from now on."
3. "Taking this medication with vitamin K–containing foods is dangerous."
4. "I will need to decrease my dietary fiber now."

160. A 19-year-old male is rushed to the emergency room with a GI bleed after a car accident. The priority intervention is

1. asking the client what he remembers about the accident.
2. obtaining a full set of vitals.
3. completing a full abdominal assessment.
4. administering ordered pain medication STAT.

161. A client is diagnosed with Meniere's disease. Which nursing diagnosis would take priority for this client?

1. risk for injury
2. disturbed body image
3. low self-esteem
4. impaired skin integrity

162. A community health nurse is preparing a lecture on lifestyle and risk factors for a college-age audience. The nurse understands that which causes of death are the most common among this age group?

1. HIV, suicide, unintentional injuries
2. suicide, cancer, unintentional injuries
3. suicide, unintentional injuries, homicide
4. homicide, unintentional injuries, heart disease

163. The ED nurse is caring for a female client who was just brought in following a sexual assault. Which interventions by the nurse are appropriate for this client? Select all that apply.

1. help the client bathe and change into fresh clothing before the examination begins
2. preserve any evidence, including clothing, and take photographs of injuries as appropriate
3. assure the client that surviving the assault is most important, and she did what was needed to stay alive
4. take the client to a quiet, private room for assessment to assess stress levels before beginning examination or treatments
5. tell the client that she should avoid wearing skimpy clothing in questionable areas of the city to avoid another incident

164. A woman with hypothyroidism has been taking levothyroxine (Synthroid) for 5 years. She has just been prescribed warfarin (Coumadin). The nurse immediately calls the health care provider to review these orders and anticipates the physician will

    1. order lab work.
    2. increase the dose of warfarin.
    3. discontinue the levothyroxine.
    4. decrease the dose of warfarin.

165. A woman has undergone a mastectomy of her right breast and has been brought to the recovery unit. The nurse explains that the client should

    1. keep her right arm elevated on a pillow.
    2. keep her right arm elevated above her head.
    3. keep her right arm level with the heart.
    4. keep her right arm slightly lower than her heart.

166. A client on the post-op floor underwent surgery 4 days ago. The night nurse reports to the nurse coming on to dayshift that the client complained all night of pain, even though she received every dose of prescribed pain medication. The client currently rates the pain at a 10 out of 10. The day shift nurse should first

    1. call the physician and ask her to prescribe a different medication.
    2. work with the client on alternative pain relief measures such as guided imagery.
    3. administer the next dose of pain medication, but observe the client swallow it to ensure she is really taking the medication.
    4. complete a full head-to-toe assessment on the client.

167. An operating room nurse just received a client scheduled for a laparoscopic cholecystectomy, but discovers the consent form has not been signed. What is the most appropriate action?

    1. bring the client a new consent form and have him sign it right away
    2. call the surgeon and ask how she would like to proceed
    3. inform the nursing manager there is no signed consent form
    4. ask the unit manager if the surgery can be rescheduled for later in the day

168. A woman is receiving outpatient treatment at a mental health center. She starts crying and tells the nurse her husband has filed for divorce. The best response from the nurse is

    1. "I am so sorry. I am divorced too, but it worked out for the best."
    2. "About half of marriages end in divorce these days."
    3. "You have to let him go and move on with your life."
    4. "Tell me what happened."

169. While driving, the client forgets how to get home. Which lobe could be dysfunctional?

1. temporal
2. parietal
3. occipital
4. frontal

170. A 56-year-old male with a long history of alcohol abuse is brought to the detox center per terms of his probation. He had his last drink 6 hours ago and seems confused and agitated. The nurse expects the physician to order

1. naloxone hydrochloride (Narcan).
2. chlordiazepoxide hydrochloride (Librium).
3. disulfiram (Antabuse).
4. propofol (Diprivan).

171. A nursing instructor demonstrates to several students how to wrap an amputated limb in a bandage using a figure eight technique. Which of the following correctly states the benefits of this technique? Select all that apply.

1. prevents blood clots from forming
2. reduces post-operative swelling
3. minimizes pain and discomfort
4. prevents exposure to air

172. The nurse is caring for a client who had an inguinal hernia repair. Which interventions by the nurse are appropriate for this client? Select all that apply.

1. encouraging fluid intake
2. relieving urinary retention
3. applying heat to the scrotum
4. teaching turning, coughing, and deep breathing
5. keeping the client on bed rest for the first 12 hours after surgery
6. teaching the client to avoid lifting more than 20 pounds until approved by the health care provider

173. The nurse is caring for a client experiencing an acute flare-up of diverticular disease. Which interventions by the nurse are appropriate for this client? Select all that apply.

1. encourage a diet high in fiber
2. insert a nasogastric (NG) tube
3. administer enemas as ordered
4. administer IV fluids as ordered
5. encourage coughing and deep breathing
6. check stools for frank or occult bleeding

174. A client with chronic kidney disease has just been admitted to the floor. The admitting nurse reviews a list of OTC medications the client takes at home and is concerned when he sees

1. Mylanta antacid.
2. iron supplements.
3. daily baby aspirin.
4. fish oil supplements.

175. A 49-year-old female suffered a stroke that resulted in dysphagia. The dietician orders a diet of dysphagia-pureed foods. Which of the following foods would be an appropriate choice?

1. beef stew
2. hard-boiled egg
3. custard
4. sliced peaches

176. The nurse is caring for a client with COPD who complains of poor quality of sleep. Which question should the nurse ask next?

1. "Does your partner snore heavily?"
2. "Do you get exercise during the day?"
3. "How many pillows do you sleep on?"
4. "Do you eat large meals right before bed?"

177. The nurse is caring for a client with sternal wires following a coronary artery bypass graft (CABG). The client complains of severe pain when coughing and deep breathing. What nonpharmacological measures can the nurse take to increase client comfort? Select all that apply.

1. apply hot packs to the sternum
2. give morphine PRN for pain before client coughs
3. suggest using audio books or relaxing music as a distraction
4. teach the client how to use a pillow to splint the chest when coughing
5. encourage the client to engage in prayer, meditation, or other activities
6. properly position the head of the bed to minimize pressure on the sternum

178. The physician orders 1.25 L of normal saline (NS) to infuse over 10 hours. The nurse should set the IV pump at what flow rate (mL/hr)?

1. 55 mL/hr
2. 125 mL/hr
3. 175 mL/hr
4. 200 mL/hr

179. Which of the following signs would indicate imminent death in a hospice patient?
    1. tightly clenched muscles
    2. steady, deep respirations
    3. slow pulse rate
    4. fixed, dilated pupils

180. A nurse volunteers at a health screening fair. The nurse examines a patient. Which of the following findings may be indicative of type 1 diabetes and require further investigation?
    1. stomach bloating, swollen lymph nodes, increased thirst
    2. sudden weight loss, blurry vision, muscle weakness
    3. sudden weight gain, ringing in the ears, difficulty sleeping
    4. feeling hungry all of the time, increased thirst, waking up at night to urinate

181. As serum calcium levels rise, which hormone is excreted?
    1. prolactin
    2. melatonin
    3. aldosterone
    4. parathyroid

182. A medication error has occurred, and the client has received double the ordered dosage of magnesium sulfate. The nurse anticipates the physician will order what medication STAT?
    1. chlordiazepoxide (Librium)
    2. vitamin K
    3. naloxone (Narcan)
    4. calcium gluconate

183. A client diagnosed with lung cancer asks the nurse what the term M0 refers to. The nurse says that M0 means
    1. no distant metastasis present.
    2. distant metastasis present.
    3. distant metastasis cannot be evaluated.
    4. metastasis present only in immediate lymph nodes.

184. A client comes into the emergency room after a chemical splashed into her eye at work. The priority nursing intervention is to
    1. cover the eye with a sterile cloth.
    2. determine what chemical splashed into the eye.
    3. irrigate the eye with normal saline solution.
    4. test vision in the affected eye.

185. A nurse is working with an immobile client and doing passive range-of-motion (ROM) exercises on his legs. The client states the exercise is too painful and does not want to continue. The nurse should
    1. ask the client to first rate the pain level on a scale of 0 – 10.
    2. ask the provider to order PRN pain medication to be given before exercise.
    3. continue the exercise and encourage the client to work through any pain.
    4. stop the exercise if the client complains of pain.

186. The floor nurse sees a new order in a client's chart for levothyroxine (Synthroid) 125 mcg PO every day. The pharmacy sends up Synthroid 0.1 mg tablets. How many tablets should the nurse administer? Calculate and fill in the blank.

    _____

187. The nurse is working with a nursing student to administer an enema solution to a client. The client states she feels painful cramping. The nurse should intervene by
    1. squeezing the enema bag so the flow rate is faster.
    2. explaining to the client that this is a normal feeling and continuing with the enema.
    3. clamping the tube for 1 minute and then starting the enema at a slower rate.
    4. discontinuing the enema until the provider can order a PRN pain medication.

187. A client has been diagnosed with pernicious anemia. What breakfast should the nurse suggest to increase dietary B12?
    1. banana nut muffin, bowl of grits, green tea
    2. bran waffles, grapefruit, iced coffee
    3. whole grain oatmeal with strawberry slices, orange juice
    4. scrambled eggs, beef sausage patty, milk

188. A client must take oral potassium supplements every day. The nurse explains to the client that the potassium supplements
    1. need to be stored in the refrigerator.
    2. should only be taken in the evening before bed.
    3. should be diluted in a glass of cold water or juice.
    4. need to be taken on an empty stomach.

189. A 52-year-old female with mitral valve stenosis is admitted to the floor. She asks the nurse why she got this condition because it does not run in her family. The nurse explains most cases of mitral stenosis are due to a history of
    1. right-sided heart failure.
    2. hypercholesterolemia.
    3. rheumatic fever.
    4. viral meningitis.

190. Which of the following are risk factors for developing glaucoma? Select all that apply.
    1. asthma
    2. pernicious anemia
    3. diabetes mellitus
    4. obesity
    5. hypertension

191. A client's lab results have just come in. The nurse reviews the electrolytes and contacts the health care provider regarding which result?
    1. chloride 167 mEq/L
    2. calcium 9.3 mg/dL
    3. phosphate 3.8 mg/dL
    4. sodium 141 mEq/L

192. A client in the recovery ICU is on mechanical ventilation. The nurse notices the client has frothy secretions around his mouth, and the nurse hears adventitious breath sounds with the stethoscope. The nurse should
    1. increase the oxygen level on the ventilator.
    2. suction the endotracheal tube.
    3. lower the head of the bed.
    4. call the rapid response team.

193. A nurse prepares to administer a transfusion of RBCs and takes the client's vital signs. The client's temperature is 102.7°F, but other vitals are within normal limits. The nurse should
    1. transfuse the RBC as ordered.
    2. administer an antipyretic and transfuse the RBCs.
    3. transfuse the RBCs but monitor the temperature hourly.
    4. not transfuse the RBCs and instead contact the physician.

194. A client has arterial blood gases drawn. The results are as follows: pH, 7.58; PaCO2, 48 mm Hg; HCO3, 44 mEq/L, Base Excess, +13 mEq/L. Which condition is indicated?
    1. respiratory alkalosis
    2. respiratory acidosis
    3. metabolic alkalosis
    4. metabolic acidosis

195. A 42-year-old female has thrombocytopenia with a platelet count of 75,000. The nurse should
    1. monitor for bleeding.
    2. place the client on neutropenic precautions.
    3. limit visiting hours.
    4. encourage a diet high in iron.

196. A new graduate nurse is assigned to a 30-year-old female requiring NG tube feeding. The preceptor reminds the graduate nurse to check placement of the NG tube before administering the feeding. The best way to do this is by
    1. verifying placement with an X-ray before each feeding.
    2. aspirating gastric contents and testing the contents on a pH paper.
    3. auscultating bowel sounds after administering a 30 cc air bolus.
    4. auscultating bowel sounds after administering the first 10 cc of tube feeding.

197. The nurse is caring for a client with staphylococcus epidermidis. The client is on a vancomycin IV. What nursing consideration should the nurse be aware of regarding this medication?
    1. The client should only order from the low-residue-diet menu.
    2. The nurse should assist the client to ambulate.
    3. The nurse will need to draw blood before administration to determine trough levels.
    4. The client should be monitored for cardiac arrhythmias.

198. The nurse is caring for a client who presented to the ED with a blood alcohol level of 208 mg/dL. The client states that his last drink was about 8 hours ago. He exhibits coarse tremors of the hands, anxiety, and elevated blood pressure. Which of the following would the nurse expect if his condition progresses to withdrawal delirium? Select all that apply.
    1. fever of 100°F to 103°F
    2. increased appetite, especially for sweets
    3. excessive sleeping of 14 hours or more daily
    4. onset of delirium 12 to 24 hours after the last drink
    5. onset of delirium 48 to 72 hours after the last drink
    6. disorientation and fluctuating levels of consciousness

199. The nurse suspects a client is experiencing alcohol withdrawal syndrome. Which action is most appropriate?

1. record suspicions in the medical record
2. question the family about his drinking
3. notify the physician
4. ask the client about his drinking

200. The nurse is caring for a client who received tissue plasminogen activator 2 hours ago. The nurse would be most concerned by which of the following in the client?

1. blood pressure of 134/91
2. bright red blood streaks in the stool
3. temperature of 40.1°C
4. ankle edema

PRACTICE TEST TWO ANSWER KEY

1. Number 1 is correct.

    Rationale: Clients with diverticulitis should consume low-roughage foods, avoiding nuts, seeds, popcorn, and raw celery. Seeds and tomatoes should be avoided. Consuming high-fiber foods such as fresh fruit and whole wheat bread is encouraged. Creamy peanut butter and jelly may be consumed by persons with diverticulitis. Chicken salad may be consumed by clients with diverticulitis.

2. Number 4 is correct.

    Rationale: Red meat consumption may cause false positive readings as will foods high in iron. The other foods do not cause false-positive readings.

3. Number 4 is correct.

    Rationale: Dorsiflexion of the foot is recommended to relieve a muscle spasm. Drinking a glass of water at bedtime will improve hydration but will not address the complaint. Compression hose are recommended for wearing during the day but should be removed at night. Elevating the head of the bed at night is recommended for gastric reflex disorder and in some cardiac and respiratory disorders.

4. The nurse should set the IV pump to 60 mL/hr.

$\frac{100 \text{ units}}{500 \text{ mL}} = \frac{12 \text{ units}}{x \text{ mL}}$	Set up a proportion to solve for milliliters per hour.
$100x = 500(12)$	Solve for x.
$100x = 6{,}000$	
$x = 60$ mL/hr	The IV pump should deliver 60 mL per hour.

5. Number 3 is correct.

    Rationale: The therapeutic level of theophylline is 10 – 20 mcg/mL. Option 1 represents the therapeutic level of digoxin. Option 2 represents the therapeutic level of phenytoin. Option 4 represents the therapeutic level of lithium.

6. Numbers 2, 4, and 5 are correct.

    Rationale: Serious side effects caused by long-term use of proton pump inhibitors include depression, rhabdomyolysis, and long bone fractures. Serious side effects are more likely at higher doses. Nausea and constipation are minor side effects.

7. Number 4 is correct.

    Rationale: Epoetin alfa is usually given as a weekly injection either IM or subcutaneously. Side effects include joint pain, hypertension, and headaches. Bloody urine is not a side effect of this medication.

8. Numbers 1, 4, and 5 are correct.

    Rationale: Digitalis is given to treat atrial flutter and atrial fibrillation. It is contraindicated in AV block, sick sinus syndrome, and Wolff-Parkinson-White syndrome.

9. Number 1 is correct.

    Rationale: The nurse should give the next dose as ordered. The therapeutic range for a vancomycin trough is 10 – 20 mcg/mL, so this client is within range. There is no need to wait and redraw the trough. Since the trough level is therapeutic, there is no need to hold the medication and notify the health care provider.

10. Number 1 is correct.

    Rationale: According to the Centers for Disease Control and Prevention, accidents (unintentional injuries) account for nearly one half of all teenage deaths. The other four leading causes of death among teenagers are homicide, suicide, cancer, and heart disease.

11. Numbers 1, 2, and 5 are correct.

    Rationale: In providing end-of-life care, the nurse explains to the client and family the signs and symptoms that death is approaching. Explaining what to expect during the final phase of the illness may help alleviate fear and anxiety as the family observes their loved one transitioning through the stages of death. Addressing client and family wishes regarding care, pain management, and emergency resuscitation respects their wishes and ensures that their choices are carried out as much as possible. Cultural beliefs are acknowledged, and life-lengthening treatment options may give way to maintaining comfort. The nurse should not avoid the difficult topic about end-of-life care, but ensure that open discussion is a central part of the client's care.

12. Numbers 3 and 4 are correct.

    Rationale: Inability of the myocardium to pump effectively will reduce the client's activity tolerance. Alternating activity with rest allows the client to function at her best. Assessment by the nurse is appropriate as pooling of fluid in the lower extremities results if the heart is unable to pump blood throughout the body. While clients with CHF need to be on strict intake and output, fluids do not necessarily need to be limited. Instead, the client's weight is a better assessment criteria of fluid overload. The client should be kept in a semi-Fowler's position.

13. Number 1 is correct.

    Rationale: Beer, anchovies, and liver are high in purine and should be avoided in clients prone to gout. Options 2 and 3 may be included in the diet, unless there are other reasons to avoid these foods. Option 4 lists food high in tyramine, which should be avoided by clients taking certain medications, such as MAOI. Unless the client is on one of these medications, there is no need to avoid those foods.

14. The correct order is 2, 3, 1, 4.

    Rationale: A systematic approach to interpreting each strip is needed for consistency. Rate refers to frequency, determined by spaces between R and R. Rhythm is the interval of the pattern between R waves. The P wave is produced when the left and right atria depolarize. Regular intervals vary by less than 0.06 seconds. The P wave should occur regularly; be one for every QRS complex; be smooth, rounded, and upright in appearance; and look similar. The P-R interval measures the time from the onset of atrial contraction to onset of ventricular contraction. The normal interval is 0.12 – 0.20 seconds. The QRS complex presents depolarization (contraction) of the ventricles. The normal interval is 0.06 – 0.12 seconds.

15. Number 5 is correct.

    Rationale: Unstageable wounds cannot be staged due to eschar or slough covering the wound. The wound bed must be visualized in order to stage the wound. Stage I ulcers have intact skin with a red area. The area may be firm, painful, soft, or cooler or warmer compared to adjacent tissue. Stage II ulcers present with partial thickness loss of dermis and a red-pink wound bed. No slough is present. Stage III ulcers have full-thickness skin loss and may contain slough. The wound may have visible subcutaneous tissue, and tunneling and undermining may or may not be present. Stage IV ulcers present with full-thickness skin loss and exposed bone, muscle, or tendons. Eschar and slough may be present, and tunneling and undermining may develop.

16. Number 1 is correct.

    Rationale: In atrial flutter, there are no discernible P waves, and a distinct sawtooth wave pattern is present. The atrial rate is regular, and the PR interval is not measurable. In atrial fibrillation, the rhythm would be very irregular with coarse, asynchronous waves. Torsades de pointes, or "twisting of the points," is characterized by QRS complexes that twist around the baseline and is a form of polymorphic ventricular tachycardia. It may resolve spontaneously or progress to ventricular fibrillation. Normal sinus rhythm is the rhythm of a healthy heart, originating from the sinus node. The heart rate is between 60 and 100 with a distinct P wave and regular QRS complexes. Ventricular fibrillation is life-threatening, as the ventricles are unable to pump any blood due to disorganized electrical activity. Untreated, it quickly leads to cardiac arrest.

17. Numbers 1 and 4 are correct.

    Rationale: In fluid overload, BUN and sodium levels would be decreased due to hemodilution. Hematocrit and serum osmolality would also be decreased due to extra fluid volume.

18. Number 3 is correct.

    Rationale: The normal sodium range is 135 to 145 mEq/L. Levels below 120 mEq/L are critical and may lead to death if left untreated. The values given for chloride, calcium, and potassium are within the normal range and do not require treatment.

19. Number 1 is correct.

    Rationale: The nurse should notify the health care provider and ask for another order. At this dose, the client may potentially receive 6,000 mg of acetaminophen in 24 hours, which far exceeds current FDA recommendations of a maximum dose of 4,000 mg per day. This dose can cause liver damage, especially in clients with decreased liver function. Administering the medication as ordered exposes the client to the risk of an excessive dose. Giving other PRN medications and ignoring the order may potentially harm the client if another nurse follows the order as written. Giving the medication on a different schedule than ordered places the nurse in the position of practicing medicine without a license. Client safety is always a priority in administering medication.

20. Number 3 is correct.

    Rationale: During ventricular systole, blood enters the aorta and the pulmonary artery. The other options do not correctly explain which vessels the blood enters during the ventricular systole phase of the cardiac cycle.

21. Number 3 is correct.

    Rationale: Clients on neutropenic precautions are at high risk of infection. Fresh flowers and potted plants should not be placed in the client's room. It is important to monitor vital signs, including temperature every 4 hours as increased temperature may indicate infection. Inspecting the client's mouth on a regular basis and providing oral care helps limit bacteria and allows visualization for oral changes. Strict adherence to standard precautions including hand hygiene is important with all clients, but especially those who are immunocompromised.

22. Numbers 1, 3, 4, and 5 are correct.

    Rationale: Maintaining normal toileting routines and frequent checks for toileting needs helps reassure the client that her needs are being met. Many medications cause further confusion, so the nurse should note any medications that might need to be reviewed with the health care provider. Having pictures and other familiar objects reinforces that the room belongs to the client during her stay. Clocks and calendars help orient the client and give her a sense of time and place. Family members and visitors should be encouraged, not discouraged, to visit as they can help alert the nurse to client needs. Companionship is important to the client's self-esteem and may prevent boredom, which can lead to getting up unassisted or wandering. The client should be as close to the nurses' station as possible so that frequent checks by multiple staff are quicker and easier.

23. Number 2 is correct.

    Rationale: The nurse should offer the client a bedpan or urinal. The client who has been medicated with morphine is at high risk for falls and should not get up. Assisting the client to the toilet increases the risk of falls. Foley catheters should not be used simply for client or nurse convenience, due to the risk of infection. Placing a bedside commode still allows the client to get up from the bed, and the client is unlikely to require assistance if the bedside commode is within close reach.

24. The nurse should set the IV pump to 19mL/hr.

$\frac{178 \text{ lbs}}{2.2 \text{ kg}} = 80.90 = 81$ kg	Convert the client's weight to kilograms.
12 units/kg/hr (81 kg)	Calculate the infusion rate.
= 972 units/hr	
$\frac{500 \text{ mL}}{25,000 \text{ units}} = \frac{x \text{ ml}}{972 \text{ units}}$	Set up a proportion to solve for milliliters per hour.
500(972) = 25,000x	Calculate and solve for x.
486,000 = 25,000x	
x = 19.44 mL = **19 mL/hr**	Round down to find the rate.

25. Number 1 is correct.

    Rationale: Foods high in vitamin K, including green tea, will lessen warfarin's effectiveness and should be avoided. The vegetables listed are not contraindicated when taking warfarin (Coumadin).

26. Number 4 is correct.

    Rationale: Protamine sulfate is needed to neutralize the effects of heparin. Warfarin is the generic name for Coumadin, which is used to prevent blood clot formation. Potassium chloride is used to treat or prevent low amounts of potassium. Vitamin K is the antidote in case of Coumadin overdose.

27. Number 1 is correct.

    Rationale: Unless otherwise ordered, a client's apical pulse needs to be 60 for digoxin administration. The nurse should withhold the medicine and contact the prescribing physician. Having another nurse verify the apical pulse is not the correct first action as there is no indication that the digoxin should be administered regardless or that the first nurse made an error. A stat ECG is unnecessary.

28. Number 3 is correct.

    Rationale: Solu-cortef (hydrocortisone sodium succinate) is a corticosteroid hormone (glucocorticoid) used as an anti-inflammatory agent for numerous diseases. It is known to elevate (not lower) glucose level. The effect on magnesium is insubstantial.

29. Number 4 is correct.

    Rationale: Furosemide (Lasix) is a diuretic that inhibits the absorption of sodium and chloride from the loop of Henle and distal renal tubule. This action increases renal excretion of water, sodium, chloride, magnesium, potassium, and calcium. This reduction of body fluid and electrolytes may produce a dry mouth. Appetite is not affected by furosemide. Leg cramps are an adverse effect of hypokalemia.

30. Number 1 is correct.

    Rationale: Pulse pressure is found by calculating the difference between the systolic pressure and diastolic pressure. Here, 134 − 86 = 48, so the pulse pressure is 48.

31. Numbers 1, 2, 5, and 6 are correct.

Rationale: Primary prevention is focused on using strategies to prevent the actual occurrence of cancer. Secondary prevention uses screening to detect cancer in the early stages when it is most curable.

32. Numbers 2 and 3 are correct.

Rationale: In addition to immunocompromised clients and older adults, clients with infection in the head or neck are also at increased risk. Tooth abscess, otitis media, and sinusitis have been linked to meningitis. CDC recommendations include an initial vaccine between ages 11 and 12 years with a booster at 16 years. Booster shots are recommended for adults living in cramped quarters (dorms, military barracks, group homes) or traveling to areas where outbreaks are common.

33. Number 1 is correct.

Rationale: Hypocalcemia indicates hypoparathyroidism. Symptoms include paresthesias and dysphagia. Hypoparathyroidism does not alter potassium, magnesium, or blood glucose levels.

34. Number 1 is correct.

Rationale: The normal range for hemoglobin is 14 – 18 g/dL in males and 12 – 16 g/dL in females. This client's hemoglobin value is critically low, which places him at increased risk for stroke, heart attack, congestive heart failure, and angina. The troponin, phosphorus, and bilirubin levels given are within normal limits.

35. Number 1 is correct.

Rationale: The V5 lead should be placed in the left midaxillary line. The V4 lead is placed in the fifth intercostal right midclavicular line. The V2 lead is placed in the fourth intercostal space to the left of the sternum. The V1 lead is placed in the fourth intercostal space to the right of the sternum.

36. Numbers 4 and 5 are correct.

Rationale: In preparing for a PFT, the nurse should teach the client to avoid smoking at least 6 to 8 hours before the test. Bronchodilators should be withheld for 4 to 6 hours before the test. There is no need for the client to take a driver with her because she will not be sedated. The client should maintain normal activity levels, neither limiting nor increasing activity before the test. Maintaining normal activity levels gives a truer picture of the client's lung function. There is no need to be NPO for the test.

37. Numbers 3, 5, and 6 are correct.

Rationale: Clubbing may be found in clients with sickle cell disease and right-sided heart failure. It is common in clients with congenital heart defects. Clubbing can be reversible if the underlying cause is resolved. It is caused by chronic, not acute, oxygen deprivation.

38.

Diagnosis	Abdominal Location
1. acute cholecystitis	RUQ
2. acute appendicitis	RIF
3. acute cystitis	suprapubic
4. acute peptic ulcer	epigastric
5. splenic infarction	LUQ

39. Number 3 is correct.

Rationale: Explaining the reason for the transfusion requires the knowledge base of a nurse. As such, this activity may not be delegated to a UAP. In contrast, the other stated activities are within the scope of practice of a UAP.

40. Number 1 is correct.

41. Number 1 is correct.

Rationale: Both an incident report and documentation of the finding in the client's medical record should occur. The incident report is an internal communication mechanism meant for performance and quality improvement. Reporting the incident to the nursing supervisor fails to adequately communicate a medication administration error. Filing an incident report addresses internal notification of a potential area for improvement yet fails to document a potential problem in the client's medical record.

42. Number 4 is correct.

Rationale: The nurse would anticipate an order for Kayexalate, which lowers elevated potassium levels. K-Dur is given for hypokalemia. Pradaxa is an anticoagulant given to prevent stroke in clients with nonvalvular atrial fibrillation. Namenda is used to manage moderate to severe Alzheimer's.

43. Numbers 2 and 4 are correct.

Rationale: A client with a chest tube should not be placed in a Trendelenburg's position as this will prevent drainage from going into the chest tube drainage device. Constant bubbling in the water seal after clamping off suction indicates an air leak. The nurse should check and tighten all connections and check the tubing for a leak. If a leak is noted in the tubing, replace the drainage device. Check the insertion site by removing the dressing and verifying that the chest tube eyelets are not visible. If no leaks can be seen or heard at the insertion site, the lung is the source of the leak. If the leak persists after troubleshooting, notify the health care provider. A semi-Fowler's position is appropriate and facilitates drainage into the drainage system. Constant gentle bubbling in the suction control chamber and tidaling in the water seal chamber that corresponds to respiration are expected findings.

44. Numbers 1 and 4 are correct.

Rationale: The head of the bed should be elevated 30 degrees to promote venous drainage and prevent hemorrhage caused by excessive blood flow to the brain. The client should be monitored for signs of increased intracranial pressure such as increased blood pressure with widening pulse pressure and altered level of consciousness. Elevating the head of the bed 90 degrees is incorrect as increased hip flexion should be avoided. Neurological status should be monitored more frequently in the client immediately post-op, often every 15 minutes during the first hour, then every 30 minutes for the second hour, or according to health care provider orders. Antiembolism stockings should be in place either when the client returns to the room or immediately upon arrival. The client should not be positioned on the operative side due to the risk of brain shift.

45. Number 1 is correct.

Rationale: Timolol maleate treats glaucoma by reducing intraocular pressure. It should be used with caution in clients with asthma because the beta-adrenergic effects can worsen asthma exacerbations. Migraines, atrial fibrillation, and urinary tract infection are not contraindications to prescribing timolol maleate.

46. Number 1 is correct.

Rationale: The goal of primary prevention is to prevent illness and disease before they occur, such as immunizing against disease. Secondary preventions reduce the impact and harm from an injury or disease that has already occurred. Mammogram screenings, testing and treating babies born to mothers with syphilis, and developing exercise programs to prevent MI are all examples of secondary prevention. A support group for depression is a tertiary prevention; it attempts to reduce the harmful impact of an ongoing illness or disease.

47. Number 1 is correct.

Rationale: The client likely inadvertently opened the sutures and caused the wound area to separate (wound dehiscence). The nurse's first priority is to immediately cover and protect the open wound. Then the nurse should call for help and make any other necessary interventions.

48. Numbers 2, 3, and 4 are correct.

Rationale: A nonimmune nurse should refrain from being assigned to care for a client with a vaccine-preventable airborne disease such as measles, chicken pox, smallpox, influenza, and pertussis. While tuberculosis is an airborne disease, the vaccine for prevention is rarely used in the United States.

49. Numbers 1, 3, and 5 are correct.

Rationale: Some possible signs of substance abuse in the workplace include frequent absenteeism, poor performance at work, and isolation. Other signs may include increased workplace accidents and frequent breaks.

50. Number 3 is correct.

Rationale: Petechial rash, nuchal rigidity, and fever are signs of meningitis, which is a medical emergency, especially in an infant. The client with heavy menstrual bleeding is not as urgent as the infant. Dog bites from a known pet current on rabies shots are less urgent than bites from a dog with an unknown rabies status. A twisted ankle with a pedal pulse and no deformity is not life-threatening and can be seen after more urgent clients.

51. Number 1 is correct.

Rationale: The nurse should use light palpation when assessing for pain, possible mass, or pulsations in the abdomen. Deep palpation is used for assessing organs such as liver and spleen. Inspection is a visual assessment, and percussion may be used to determine if abdominal fluid or organ enlargement is present.

52. Number 2 is correct.

$\dfrac{\text{order}}{\text{units available}} \times \dfrac{\text{amount of fluid in bag}}{\text{number of hours}}$	To determine the amount of mL per hour, use the formula.
$= \dfrac{1{,}000 \text{ units}}{10{,}000 \text{ units}} \times \dfrac{500 \text{ mL}}{2 \text{ hrs}}$	Substitute values and solve.
$= 0.1 \times 250 \text{ mL/hr}$	
$= \mathbf{25 \text{ mL/hr}}$	

53. Number 4 is correct.

Rationale: Stage 1 hypertension is defined by a systolic level between 140 and 159 mmHg or a diastolic level between 90 and 99 mmHg. A blood pressure reading of 146/90 would be considered stage 1 hypertension and would require further blood pressure monitoring and probable lifestyle changes or medication management. Prehypertension is defined by a systolic reading between 120 and 139 mmHg or diastolic reading between 80 and 89 mmHg. Stage 2 hypertension is noted when systolic pressure is over 160 mmHg and a diastolic level is over 100 mmHg. Even if hypertension runs in the patient's family, the reading indicates she must address the issue through lifestyle changes and/or medication.

54. Number 3 is correct.

Rationale: After a cardiac catheterization, the client should remain flat on his back to avoid any pressure or tension on the femoral artery, which could cause bleeding from the site where the catheter was inserted. Lying on the side with knees bent places tension on the femoral artery. In the semi-Fowler's position, the client is not fully supine. In the high-Fowler's position, the client is sitting up.

55. Number 1 is correct.

Rationale: BMI is calculated by dividing the weight in kilograms by height in meters squared.

$\frac{146 \text{ lbs}}{2.2} = 66.4 \text{ kg}$	Convert pounds to kilograms by dividing pounds by 2.2.
meters = $\frac{\text{number of inches}}{39.37}$ $\frac{63 \text{ in.}}{39.37} = 1.6 \text{ m}$ $1.6^2 = 2.56$	Convert inches (63) into meters and square.
$\frac{\text{kg}}{\text{m}^2}$ $\frac{66.4 \text{ kg}}{2.56 \text{ m}^2}$ $= 25.9$ **BMI = 25.9 (overweight)**	Calculate BMI.

56. Numbers 2, 3, and 5 are correct.

Rationale: Subjective data is information or symptoms provided by the client: his opinions, feelings, or statements. Objective data is something nurses can measure or observe by their own senses.

57. Number 3 is correct.

Rationale: Sensible fluid loss can be measured as daily output and includes gastric drainage, urine, and vomit. Insensible fluid loss from the lungs, feces, skin, and respiratory tract cannot be accurately measured as output.

58. Number 3 is correct.

Rationale: Standard precautions are recommended whenever the nurse comes in contact with blood or body fluids that could transmit blood-borne pathogens. Contact with sweat or intact skin does not require use of standard precautions.

59. Number 4 is correct.

Rationale: Untreated gout is associated with health risks such as kidney stones, nodules of hardened uric acid under the skin, and deformed joints. Other complications include heart disease and bone damage. Neuropathy is nerve damage often associated with uncontrolled diabetes.

60. Number 1 is correct.

Rationale: It is common for some patients (especially the elderly) to become disoriented during a hospital stay. The nurse's best intervention is to provide cues around the room that can reorient the client, such as familiar personal objects. Restraints are a measure of last resort, and it is inappropriate to ask the client's family to stay so the staff does not have to intervene. Transferring the client to another floor before other interventions have been attempted is also inappropriate and abdicates professional responsibility.

61. Number 3 is correct.

Rationale: Possible risks for breast cancer include early menarche, nulliparity, and previous history of breast, ovarian, or uterine cancer. Other risk factors include late menopause (not early menopause), family history of breast cancer, and having the first child after age 30.

62. Number 1 is correct.

Rationale: Meniere's disease is a condition of the inner ear that causes episodes of vertigo. The client will likely require dietary changes, such as reduction in sodium. Eating smaller, evenly sized meals throughout the day may help regulate body fluids. Since the client could become dizzy or lose her balance, it would be important to assist her in ambulation to avoid a potential fall. Narcotic pain management is not typically associated with Meniere's disease.

63. Number 2 is correct.

Rationale: Intermittent bubbling in the water seal chamber is an expected finding that indicates the system is working correctly and that air is being successfully removed from the pleural space. The nurse should document and reassess again later. Constant bubbling is indicative of an air leak, and the nurse would immediately report this to the physician so it can be corrected.

64. Number 1 is correct.

Rationale: A client experiencing a Crohn's disease flare-up should follow a low-residue diet. The client should avoid foods that are difficult to digest, such as whole-grain breads and cereals, nuts, most raw fruits and vegetables, dried fruits, and seeds. Cooked cereals such as grits, peeled fruits (banana or melon), and non-pulp juices would be examples of low-residue foods.

65. Number 1 is correct.

Rationale: Abnormalities in magnesium levels may put the client at risk for ventricular dysrhythmia. A hypomagnesemia level of 0.8 mEq/L would be of concern (normal range is 1.5 – 2.5 mEq/L). The other values listed are normal lab values.

66. Number 1 is correct.

Rationale: Increasing ICP requires nursing intervention; the nurse should increase the rate of oxygen because hypoxia can worsen ICP. Elevating the head of the bed, repositioning the patient, and suctioning the patient are not recommended interventions for patients experiencing (or at risk for) ICP because they can actually increase the pressure.

67. Number 1 is correct.

Rationale: Atropine is used for patients with pronounced bradycardia to regulate heart rate. Amiodarone and adenosine are used with tachycardic patients, and magnesium sulfate is used for ventricular tachycardia or ventricular fibrillation.

68. Abdominal inspections should be done in the following order:
   1. inspection
   2. auscultation
   3. percussion
   4. palpation

69. Number 1 is correct.

Rationale: Potential risks for IUD include pelvic infections, abnormal bleeding, and increased risk of ectopic pregnancy. Other potential risks include sepsis, perforation, and expulsion. Increased risk of stroke is associated with oral contraceptives.

70. Numbers 1, 3, and 5 are correct.

Rationale: Inserting a PICC line does require sterile technique, but it can be done at the bedside and carries a lower risk of infection compared to other central lines. RNs must have special training to intersect a PICC line. There is no risk of pneumothorax during insertion because of the placement method.

71. Number 3 is correct.

Rationale: An elevated uric acid level (hyperuricemia) is an adverse effect of furosemide (Lasix). A uric acid level of 13.5 mg/dL is high above normal range (0.18 – 0.48 mmol/L). Hypokalemia is also an adverse effect of Lasix.

72. Number 3 is correct.

Rationale: The Braden Scale assesses nutritional status, sensory perception, activity level, moisture, mobility, and friction/shear. It does not consider past history of skin breakdown.

73. Number 2 is correct.

Rationale: Rolling the vial between the palms of the hands will produce enough heat to aid in the dissolution of the powder. The rolling movement itself will also help dissolve the powder. Shaking the vial could break it, and leaving the vial to sit does not ensure the powder will dissolve. There is no need for the pharmacy to be involved in dissolving the powder.

74. Number 1 is correct.

Rationale: Normal post-operative drainage after a cholecystectomy is 500 – 1,000 mL/day. Immediately after surgery, the drainage will be sanguineous, but then turn to a greenish-brown color. The nurse's assessments of the patient's drainage are normal, expected findings. There is no need to call the physician, and an infection would not be suspected. Here, the tube does not need to be flushed.

75. Number 1 is correct.

Rationale: The middle ear is composed of the incus, stapes, malleus, and tympanic membrane. The pinna is also known as the ear flap and is part of the outer ear.

76. Numbers 2, 3, 4, and 5 are correct.

Rationale: Infective endocarditis is an inflammation of the inner tissues of the heart caused by an infective organism. A common mnemonic for signs and symptoms is FROM JANE, which stands for fever, Roth's spots, Osler's nodes, murmur, Janeway lesions, anemia, nail hemorrhage, and embolism. Other possible signs and symptoms include night sweats, weight loss, and an enlarged spleen. Weight gain is not a known indicator.

77. Number 4 is correct.

Rationale: The nurse should use therapeutic communication to alleviate worry by providing factual information and encouraging distraction and relaxation. Answering any questions honestly and allowing the client to visit with family will help her feel more comfortable. Sedation is not appropriate in this situation. Nurses should not assume patients of sound mind are unable to understand their health status or address them in a patronizing manner.

78. Number 3 is correct.

Rationale: The nurse caring for the client with a radioactive implant should don a lead gown before performing any client care; therefore, the nurse only needs to retrieve the implant with long-handled forceps and place it into a lead container. Clients with implants should have a lead container and long-handled forceps available in the room in case of dislodgement. Once the implant is retrieved, the health care provider should be notified. Attempting to reinsert the implant is beyond the scope of nursing practice and should be performed only by the health care provider.

79. Number 3 is correct.

Rationale: Securing pieces of tape to a tray table or bed rail introduces pathogens from contaminated surfaces to the client's skin when applied. This increases the risk of pathogens entering the puncture site and causing infection in the client. If additional tape needs to be applied after the clear dressing, it should be removed from the roll just prior to application, without touching it to other surfaces. Washing the hands before and after placing an IV helps minimize the risk of infection. Use of alcohol or other approved skin cleanser helps remove pathogens and minimize the risk of infection. These products should dry completely before attempting to place the IV.

80. Number 2 is correct.

    Rationale: Bananas help to bind the stool thereby reducing diarrhea. Drinking additional fluids should be encouraged but will not reduce the diarrhea. Prunes promote peristalsis thereby increasing diarrhea. A salad has fiber that will increase diarrhea.

81. Number 3 is correct.

    Rationale: A normal white blood cell count in an adult is between 3.5 and 10.5. A high result such as 15.6 may indicate infection or inflammation. The other values listed are normal, expected values in an adult female.

82. Number 2 is correct.

    Rationale: Increased anxiety is a possible side effect during the initial 4 – 6 weeks of taking sertraline. The client should continue to take the medication as prescribed and then evaluate its effect in a few weeks. The medication should not be suddenly discontinued without an order from the health care provider, and the nurse does not have the authority to change the client's dosage.

83. Numbers 1, 4, and 5 are correct.

    Rationale: Adverse effects of adenosine include nausea, chest pain, and facial flushing. The nurse should stop the infusion and monitor the client for abatement of symptoms. Adenosine has a half-life of 10 seconds, so symptoms should resolve shortly. A respiratory rate of 18 and heart rate of 97 are within normal limits and do not require any intervention.

84. Number 4 is correct.

    Rationale: The normal pH in adults ranges from 7.35 to 7.45. Albumin values range from 3.5 to 5.0 g/dL. Normal hemoglobin ranges from 12 to 16 g/dL for women and 14 to 18 g/dL for men. Normal potassium levels are 3.5 – 5.0 mEq/L. Potassium levels become elevated in burns due to disruption of the sodium-potassium pump, red blood cell hemolysis, and tissue damage.

85. Numbers 3, 4, and 5 are correct.

    Rationale: Males develop GBS slightly more often than females. The acute or initial period lasts from 1 to 4 weeks, beginning with the onset of symptoms and ending when no further deterioration occurs. GBS tends to be self-limiting with muscle weakness and temporary paralysis. Infections are commonly associated with GBS, with Campylobacter jejuni one of the more common bacterial infections.

86. Numbers 1, 3, 4, and 5 are correct.

    Rationale: Based on the confusion and drop in systolic blood pressure, the client may be becoming septic. The nurse should obtain blood cultures to determine if bacterial infection is triggering the response; this will also indicate which antibiotics would be effective. Fever can decrease oxygenation, so the client should be placed on oxygen. Antipyretics should be administered, and the nurse should follow up and recheck the temperature in 30 minutes or so to see if it is decreasing. The client should rest and avoid physical activity. There is no need to make the client NPO; fluids help with hydration and should be encouraged if the client can drink. Although the client may want a blanket if experiencing chills, the room temperature should be decreased and excess blankets removed.

87. Answer: one tablet.

    | 1 gr = 60 mg | Convert grains to milligrams. |

60 mg × 5	Multiply the quantity in milligrams by 5 (since 5 grains were ordered) to find the amount ordered in milligrams.
= 300 mg	
= **one tablet**	The quantity in milligrams is equal to one tablet: 300 mg.

88. Number 2 is correct.

Rationale: Humalog (lispro) is fast-acting insulin, with onset of action beginning 15 minutes after injection. Humalog peaks 30 – 90 minutes after administration, and during this peak time the client is most likely to experience a hypoglycemic reaction. It would be too early to check the client at 8:45 a.m., and checking the client at 11:30 a.m. or later is too late.

89. Number 4 is correct.

Rationale: Ototoxicity is a potential adverse reaction to gentamicin sulfate. Other adverse reactions include Stevens-Johnson syndrome, seizures, nephrotoxicity, and superinfection. Orthostatic hypotension, occult bleeding, and torsades de pointes are not known adverse reactions to gentamicin sulfate.

90. Numbers 2 and 3 are correct.

Rationale: Salmon is a cold-water fish that is rich in omega-3 fatty acids, a good fat that can help lower triglycerides. Grilling eliminates the need for oils or butter, which are high in saturated fat. Herbs offer a very low-calorie way to add flavor to grilled fish. An egg-white omelet eliminates the yolks, which contain the bulk of fat, and vegetables add flavor and nutrients. Animal-based foods are naturally higher in fat; therefore, vegetables such as spinach or red peppers are a better choice than cheese. Wheat toast is not a good choice since it is high in carbohydrates; too many carbohydrates convert into sugar which raises triglycerides. Although the jelly is sugar free, the high amount of carbohydrates in the whole wheat bread make it a poor choice. Natural honey is still very high in sugar, which should be avoided when trying to lower triglyceride levels. Plain grilled steak is not a good choice as it is an animal-based product that is high in fat. A four-ounce serving of sirloin contains about 16 grams of fat, 6 grams of which is saturated. The average person, especially a male, tends to eat far larger servings, which exponentially increases the amount of fat. Skinless poultry is a lower fat choice.

91. Numbers 3, 4, and 5 are correct.

Rationale: The medication regimen for tuberculosis may last up to 12 months, depending on the medications. Strict adherence is important to prevent a relapse. The client may return to most jobs after three sputum cultures are negative. Teaching the client about possible side effects and management of medication helps ensure compliance with treatment. The client should return to his previous activity level gradually, following the health care provider's recommendations. There is no need for the family to maintain respiratory isolation at home since they have already been exposed.

92. Number 3 is correct.

Rationale: Nail clubbing, night sweats, and fever are common symptoms of TB. Other symptoms may include weight loss, chills, and fatigue. People with TB may lose, not gain, weight.

93. Number 4 is correct.

Rationale: Sandimmune (Cyclosporine) is an immunosuppressive drug prescribed to prevent rejection in bone marrow or organ transplants. Etoposide and Cytarabine are anti-cancer chemotherapy drugs. Metoclopramide is an anti-nausea drug often prescribed for clients undergoing chemotherapy.

94. Answer:

1. stop the infusion and disconnect Ringer's lactate
2. scrub the catheter hub
3. attach the flush syringe and flush catheter with normal saline

    4. withdraw a blood sample and discard
    5. withdraw the blood sample for the lab

95. Number 3 is correct.

    Rationale: Clients near the end of life may lose interest in eating, and the nurse should respect the client's desire to make decisions about his treatment and care. In these cases, feeding tubes should be avoided, as should encouraging the client to eat any meals.

96. Number 2 is correct.

    Rationale: Plumbism, also known as lead poisoning, may occur if a child is exposed to lead paint. Living in a home built before 1976 may put children at risk, because paint manufactured before this date may contain lead. Signs and symptoms of lead poisoning in children include weight loss, developmental delay, learning disability, vomiting, and hearing loss. The most important factor in lead poisoning is exposure to lead dust and paint, not nutrition or tap water consumption. Phototherapy is prescribed to newborns with high levels of bilirubin, which can cause jaundice. Jaundice is not a known cause of lead poisoning.

97. Number 4 is correct.

    Rationale: Glossopharyngeal neuralgia is a condition caused by damage to cranial nerve IX (the glossopharyngeal nerve). Signs and symptoms may include episodes of pain in the throat, ears, tongue, and tonsils that can be triggered by swallowing or talking. Episodes of vertigo may be associated with vestibular neuritis, damage to cranial nerve VIII. Difficulty in moving the tongue is linked to damage to cranial nerve XII (hypoglossal nerve). Double vision is noted in abducens nerve palsy, damage to cranial nerve VI.

98. Numbers 1, 2, 3, and 4 are correct.

    Rationale: Social withdrawal, agitation, auditory hallucinations, and disorganized speech are all signs and symptoms of schizophrenia. Others include abnormal motor behavior, delusions, catatonia, inability to sleep, and feelings of apathy. Lack of attention to personal hygiene is not a symptom of schizophrenia.

99. Number 2 is correct.

    Rationale: Clients with cholecystitis have an inflamed gallbladder and should avoid high-fat foods. A low-potassium and low-phosphorus diet is associated with the renal diet followed by clients with kidney disease. Increased vitamin B 12 may be recommended for someone with pernicious anemia.

100. Number 4 is correct.

     Rationale: Mean arterial pressure (MAP) is the average arterial pressure during one cardiac cycle. It is calculated using a formula:

$MAP = \frac{(2 \times \text{diastolic pressure}) + \text{systolic pressure}}{3}$	Use the formula for MAP.
$(2 \times 84) + 132$ $= 300$	Calculate and solve.
$\frac{300}{3}$ $= 100 \text{ mmHg}$	

101. Number 1 is correct.

     Rationale: Tetracycline is an antibiotic prescribed for many bacterial infections. Patients should be instructed that this medication should be avoided in pregnancy, can cause photosensitivity, and cannot be taken with dairy products or other sources of calcium. Aluminum, iron, and zinc deactivate the medication, and tetracycline should not be taken with sources of these minerals, such as antacids.

102. Number 2 is correct.

Rationale: Purpura are reddish-purple non-blanching skin discolorations (sized 0.3cm – 1cm) caused by bleeding under the skin. Ecchymosis is a hematoma larger than 1 cm in size. Petechia is a small hematoma less than 3mm. A bruise is bleeding under the skin caused by trauma.

103. Number 2 is correct.

Rationale: The nursing priority is to administer oxygen in accordance with the airway, breathing, and circulation priority model. Once the client is receiving supplemental oxygen, the nurse can assess and further intervene.

104. Number 2 is correct.

Rationale: A client in restraints should be checked at least every 30 minutes for circulatory compromise. The restraints should be released every 2 hours to check skin integrity and range of motion.

105. Answer: 31 drops/min

total volume of solution/time in minutes	Use the formula.
$\dfrac{1{,}500\ \text{mL}}{720\ \text{min}}$ = 2.08 mL/min	Substitute and solve.
2.08 mL/min × drop factor	
2.08 mL/min × 15 drops/1 mL = 31.2 drops/min	
31 drops/min	Round to the nearest whole number.

106. Number 4 is correct.

Rationale: Agoraphobia is the fear of open spaces; these clients tend to stay indoors in a familiar space. Sociophobia refers to the fear of people or social situations. Anthropophobia is a related disorder that refers to the fear of being in the company of other people. The fear of strangers or foreigners is known as xenophobia.

107. Number 2 is correct.

Rationale: Flumazenil is given as an antagonist to benzodiazepines. Lorazepam and alprazolam are both benzodiazepines and would exacerbate the problem. Naloxone is given for opiate overdoses.

108. Number 4 is correct.

Rationale: Serotonin syndrome occurs if an excess amount of serotonin enters the central nervous system or peripheral nervous system. The classic clinical triad of abnormalities seen in serotonin syndrome includes cognitive, autonomic, and somatic effects.

109. Number 4 is correct.

Rationale: The patient has recently attempted suicide and is at a high risk of harming herself. She should not be left alone or assigned a roommate until she is no longer a risk to herself or others. A staff member should stay with the client at all times to keep the client safe.

110. Numbers 1, 3, and 5 are correct.

Rationale: A client with fluid volume excess may show decreased urinary output, jugular vein distention, and tachycardia. Other signs and symptoms include hypertension, bounding pulse, edema, and dyspnea.

111. Number 3 is correct.

Rationale: The BUN-to-creatinine ratio is used as a tool in determining kidney function: The ratio indicates if the levels are proportionate to each other. It is calculated by dividing BUN by creatinine.

18/0.7 = 25.7:1, which rounds to 26:1

112. Number 2 is correct.

Rationale: Clients at a higher risk for aspiration include those who have a nasogastric tube, those on mechanical ventilation, and those with a condition that leads to difficulty swallowing, such as dysphagia. Total parenteral nutrition has no effect on aspiration risk.

113. Number 4 is correct.

Rationale: Capsaicin, derived from chili peppers, is a topical pain relief ointment used for strains/sprains, arthritis, and muscle aches. Aloe gel is often used for burns and psoriasis. Zinc oxide and hydrocortisone are anti-itch ointments.

114. Number 3 is correct.

Rationale: As people age, they have greater difficulty distinguishing between blue and green, due to yellowing of the eye lens. They have less difficulty differentiating among the other colors mentioned.

115. Number 3 is correct.

Rationale: During the first 24 hours post-op following an ileostomy, expected drainage is between 1,500mL and 2,000 mL.

116. Numbers 2, 3, and 5 are correct.

Rationale: If the person vomits, saving the vomitus may help identify the substance ingested, especially in younger children. Quickly identifying the poisonous substance is key to intervention with an antidote. All homes with small children should post the number of the Poison Control Center near the telephone for quick access in an emergency, or the number should be programed into cell phones. Older adults may forget that they have already taken their medication or not be able to clearly read medication labels, which can lead to accidental overdose. Vomiting should never be induced unless instructed to do so by Poison Control. If the person needs to be transported to the hospital, emergency services should be called for an ambulance. The ambulance can get to the hospital quicker, and EMTs can start an IV and begin supportive treatment immediately. The nurse should never advise a client to drive quickly to the hospital, as this puts the client at risk for an accident.

117. Number 3 is correct.

Rationale: TB bacteria is spread through the air from one person to another. When a person breathes in TB bacteria, the bacteria can settle in the lungs and begin to grow. TB is not transmitted through blood, sharing a cup of coffee, or shaking hands with an infected person.

118. Number 3 is correct.

Rationale: The Center for Disease Control recommends the skin test be read 48 – 72 hours after administration. A test is considered positive if an induration of 5 – 15 millimeters is observed at the injection site. Results read after 72 hours are not accurate and another skin test needs to be conducted.

119. Number 2 is correct.

Rationale: Risk factors for colon cancer include being African American, being over 50, and having a past medical history of diabetes. Other risk factors include a personal or family history of colon cancer; a high-fat, low-fiber diet; a history of inflammatory intestinal disease; obesity; smoking; and a sedentary lifestyle.

120. Number 4 is correct.

Rationale: Normal urine specific gravity values fall between 1.000 and 1.030. An increased value over 1.035 indicates dehydration, which may be seen in a client who has been experiencing pronounced vomiting and diarrhea.

121. Numbers 1, 4, and 5 are correct.

Rationale: Clients with osteoarthritis should try to maintain a healthy weight; this has been shown to decrease joint pain and reduces stiffness. Using heat will help to ease stiffness, and moderate exercise three times a week is recommended. High-impact exercise should be avoided as it risks harming bone and tissue. Acetaminophen, not aspirin, is the first-choice drug to reduce osteoarthritis-related pain.

122. Number 2 is correct.

Rationale: Hepatitis B is transmitted via infectious blood, dirty needles, and sexual contact, and from mother to newborn. Hepatitis C is most commonly spread by infectious blood and needles. Contaminated food and water can transmit hepatitis A, while hepatitis E is transmitted only by contaminated water.

123. Number 4 is correct.

Rationale: A non-rebreather mask delivers the highest percentage of oxygen compared to a venturi mask, nasal cannula, or simple face mask. If the client does not improve with the non-rebreather mask, the physician is likely to intubate the client and place him on mechanical ventilation.

124. Numbers 1, 2, and 5 are correct.

Rationale: Clients with heat stroke have a body temperature of greater than 104°F. Tachycardia, hypotension, and tachypnea are other expected findings in heat stroke.

125. Numbers 1, 5, and 6 are correct.

Rationale: Late signs of increased ICP include seizures, severe headache, and nausea and vomiting (often projectile). Irritability, restlessness, and disorientation are early signs of increased ICP.

126. Number 4 is correct.

Rationale: An order with a trailing zero, or a zero that follows a decimal point, needs to be clarified by the physician. Here, the lorazepam (Ativan) 1.0 mg could be mistaken for 10 mg.

127. Number 2 is correct.

Rationale: An African American woman over the age of 65 is at highest risk for a CVA. Other risk factors include smoking, family history of stroke or heart attack, sedentary lifestyle, high cholesterol, and a history of atrial fibrillation.

128. Numbers 2, 3, and 4 are correct.

Rationale: Signs and symptoms of a transplanted kidney rejection include increased blood pressure, weight gain, and pain at transplant site. Other indications are decreased urinary output, elevation in creatinine level, fever, and sudden edema.

129. Number 1 is correct.

Rationale: Addison's disease is caused by the adrenal glands producing insufficient amounts of certain hormones. It requires lifelong medication therapy, and can lead to a life-threatening condition called Addisonian crisis. People with Addison's disease should not use salt substitutes. Clients with Addison's crave sodium in their diets and should be allowed salt. Salt substitutes are dangerous because they contain potassium; people with Addison's disease should limit dietary potassium.

130. Number 4 is correct.

Rationale: Because of a blunted immune response, elderly clients may not show many of the typical early signs and symptoms of pneumonia like chest pain, fever, and dyspnea. Instead, elderly clients may seem confused or have a change in mental status.

131. Number 1 is correct.

Rationale: Cases of genital herpes are not required to be reported to the CDC. Cases of chlamydia, hepatitis B, and gonorrhea must be reported, as well as chancroid, HIV, and syphilis.

132. Numbers 1, 2, 3, and 5 are correct.

Rationale: The nurse will educate the client on good sleep hygiene. Keeping the bedroom dark and quiet helps promote sleep. Rooms that are too light due to outside lights should be fitted with dark shades or curtains. Going to bed and getting up at the same time helps the body maintain a circadian rhythm. Sleeping in late on weekends can disrupt weekday sleep. Reading and other quiet activities help the client relax and prepare for sleep. Computers and TVs emit blue light, which stimulates the brain to stay alert. Despite common belief, alcohol does not help with sleep. It may make it easier to fall asleep initially, but later disrupts REM sleep, making it easier to wake. A heavy meal before bed stimulates the metabolism and can cause discomfort, leading to difficulty sleeping. Vigorous activity close to bedtime will stimulate the body, making sleep harder.

133. Number 3 is correct.

Rationale: Clients with pulmonary edema should be positioned upright with the legs dangling over the side of the bed to decrease venous return. Clients receiving an enema should be positioned on the left side in the Sims' position to allow the gravity flow of the solution to follow the direction of the colon. Client with lower limb amputations should have the affected limb supported but not elevated in order to prevent flexion contractures. Clients with a craniotomy should be positioned with the head of bed at a 30- to 45-degree angle to promote venous drainage from the head.

134. Number 4 is correct.

Rationale: Long-term use of corticosteroids has been associated with osteoporosis. It is also associated with hypertension, hyperglycemia, edema, weight gain, cataracts, and increased risk of infection.

135. Number 3 is correct.

Rationale: The priority after this procedure is monitoring the client for excessive bleeding. The nurse should observe the dressing for 24 hours for signs of bleeding or infection. It is not necessary to keep the client NPO after this procedure. Contact sports should be avoided for 48 hours. No further site care is required other than observing the dressing for 24 hours, unless signs of infection are noted.

136. Numbers 2, 4, and 5 are correct.

Rationale: Foul odor and purulent drainage should be reported, along with sudden increases in output. The T-tube should not be irrigated, clamped, or aspirated without an order. The tube should be clamped prior to meals. If nausea or vomiting occur, unclamp the tube. The drainage system should be kept below gallbladder level. The tube should not be removed without an order. The nurse should chart the amount, consistency, color, and odor of any drainage.

137. Number 3 is correct.

Rationale: The MMR vaccine is administered subcutaneously. It can be administered over the triceps using a 23- to 35-gauge, 5/8-inch needle. The skin should be pinched and the needle inserted at a 45-degree angle to avoid injecting into the muscle.

138. Number 2 is correct.

Rationale: Orthostatic hypotension is a condition in which one experiences low blood pressure when sitting or standing suddenly after lying down. The nurse should suggest the client wear support stockings, which will encourage venous return and prevent blood from pooling in the legs.

139. Numbers 2, 3, and 5 are correct.

Rationale: A cataract refers to the clouding of the eye lens. Signs and symptoms may include cloudy vision, double vision, diminished night vision, and halos seen around lights. Nausea and vomiting and severe eye pain are more typically associated with glaucoma.

140. Number 2 is correct.

Rationale: If possible, the nurse should utilize the hospital interpreter services. Using a certified interpreter is the most reliable method of communicating with a client who speaks another language. In addition, interpreters affiliated with a hospital specialize in medical and health terminology.

141. Number 4 is correct.

Rationale: Type IV hypersensitivity reactions are cell mediated and are delayed reactions. Examples of type IV hypersensitivity reactions include allergic contact dermatitis, Crohn's disease, and graft versus host disease. Others include type I diabetes mellitus, multiple sclerosis, and celiac disease. A penicillin allergy is a type I hypersensitivity reaction.

142. Number 3 is correct.

Rationale: Azoospermia (sperm count of zero) usually occurs 3 – 4 months after a vasectomy. Until a semen analysis is performed to confirm a sperm count of zero, a backup method of birth control should be used.

143. Number 4 is correct.

Rationale: Benztropine (Cogentin) is an anticholinergic sometimes prescribed to reduce extrapyramidal side effects caused by first generation antipsychotics such as Haldol. Flumazenil is used to treat benzodiazepine overdose. Donepezil is an acetylcholinesterase inhibitor commonly prescribed for clients diagnosed with Alzheimer's disease. Naloxone is an opioid antagonist.

144. Number 1 is correct.

Rationale: The nurse should fully assess the client before determining what action or intervention to take.

145. Number 1 is correct.

Rationale: The classic Cushing's triad includes increased blood pressure, irregular respirations, and decreased heart rate. This triad indicates an emergency situation of increasing intracranial pressure, usually leading to brain herniation or death if not immediately treated. Cardiac arrhythmia is not part of the Cushing reflex triad.

146. Answer:
1. sinoatrial node
2. atrioventricular node
3. bundle of His
4. bundle branches
5. Purkinje fibers

147. Number 3 is correct.

Rationale: A 3-in-1 TPN solution includes dextrose, amino acids, and lipids. TPN also may be prepared as a 2-in-1 solution, which only includes dextrose and amino acids, with lipids administered separately.

148. Number 1 is correct.

Rationale: The anticipated action of vasopressin administered during a cardiac arrest is to raise blood pressure. This is an antidiuretic drug, which works by reabsorbing water in the renal tubules.

149. Number 3 is correct.

Rationale: Due to many factors, older adults are at risk for malnutrition. Complications caused by malnutrition include an increased risk of falls due to weakness, poor wound healing, and an increased risk for infections. Malnutrition does not contribute to chronic heart failure; however, chronic heart failure does put a client at risk for malnutrition.

150. Number 4 is correct.

Rationale: Fungal infections such as Fusarium require treatment with antifungal medications such as Vfend. Combivir is an antiretroviral drug used to treat HIV-1 infections. It is not a cure but does help delay the process of the disease when taken in combination with other drugs. Famvir is an antiviral prescribed for the herpes zoster (shingles) virus. Cipro is a quinolone antibiotic.

151. Number 4 is correct.

Rationale: Modifiable risk factors are lifestyle changes a person can make in order to reduce their risk of developing a certain disease. A high-stress lifestyle, smoking, and obesity are all modifiable risk factors for CAD. Risk factors such as age, gender, race, and family history are nonmodifiable.

152. Number 1 is correct.

Rationale: BMI is a health screening tool calculated by considering an individual's height and weight. A BMI over 30 is considered obese. If BMI falls between 25 and 29.9, the individual is considered overweight. A BMI between 18.5 and 24.9 is considered a normal/healthy weight, and BMI under 18.5 is considered underweight.

153. Number 4 is correct.

Rationale: Pulmonary embolism is a possible risk of IV therapy. It is caused by air accidentally being pushed into a vein via an IV. If the air embolism travels to the lung, a dangerous pulmonary embolism can occur. Other signs and symptoms can include hypotension, confusion, stroke, and heart failure. The nurse would be alerted to the most likely cause based on her recent intervention. Septic shock and pneumothorax both have additional symptoms that develop over a longer period of time. While an allergic reaction to the medication given is possible, chest pain would be unlikely.

154. Number 1 is correct.

Rationale: Tunneling occurs when a wound spreads and travels to another break or opening in the skin. Undermining is less extensive than tunneling and would not create as large an area to the decubitis ulcer. Dehiscence is the separation and disruption of previously joined wound edges. In evisceration, wound edges separate and the intestines protrude.

155. Numbers 2, 3, 4, and 5 are correct.

Rationale: A client with measles should be placed under airborne precautions. The client should wear a mask when in the hallway and should enter through a separate entrance of the hospital to avoid the waiting/reception area. Any staff entering the client's room should wear a fit-tested N-95 respirator mask—put on prior to entering the room and removed upon exiting the room. In addition, any client under airborne precautions (tuberculosis, measles, varicella, and disseminated herpes zoster) should ideally be placed in an airborne infection isolation room.

156. Number 4 is correct.

Rationale: A pack year is one pack of cigarettes smoked daily for one year. This client smokes two packs per day. The calculation is 2 (packs per day) × 20 (years smoking) = 40 pack years. The other calculations are incorrect for this client.

157. Numbers 1, 2, 4, and 5 are correct.

Rationale: The health care provider should be consulted before receiving any vaccinations, and live vaccines should not be given. Avoiding aspirin and using electric razors and soft toothbrushes will help minimize the risk of bleeding. Mouth rinses may be prescribed for thrush and ulcers. Low-grade fever, sore throat, or chills indicate infection and should be reported to the health care provider.

158. Number 2 is correct.

Rationale: Clients age 65 – 85 are in the ego integrity versus despair stage. This is a time of reflection on life. Successful clients can look back with satisfaction, while unsuccessful clients may feel as if their lives were wasted. Young adults aged 19 – 34 years are in the intimacy versus isolation stage. Adolescents aged 12 – 18 years are in the identity versus role confusion stage. Adults aged 35 – 64 are in the generativity versus stagnation stage.

159. Number 1 is correct.

Rationale: Clients who take MAOI drugs should avoid foods with tyramine, which could trigger a hypertensive crisis. Tyramine can be found in aged cheeses, fermented meats, alcoholic beverages, pickled foods, chocolate, fava beans, and sauerkraut. These clients may still eat some dairy products. Foods with vitamin K might be avoided by clients prescribed blood thinners. Dietary fiber is important for healthy digestion and including it in the diet should be encouraged.

160. Number 2 is correct.

Rationale: The nursing priority is to obtain and determine baseline vitals, as well as to assess for abnormalities in blood pressure, respiration, and pulse rate, which may be signs of the body compensating for blood loss. The nurse can then prioritize care by talking with the client while taking vitals and ask about accident recall, assess the abdomen, and provide pain medication after assessing pain.

161. Number 1 is correct.

Rationale: Meniere's disease occurs when the pressure of the fluid in part of the inner ear gets too high. As a result, the client is at risk for injury related to altered mobility because of gait disturbance and vertigo. While hearing loss may occur, this does not result in disturbed body image, low self-esteem, or impaired skin integrity.

162. Number 3 is correct.

Rationale: Suicide, unintentional injuries, and homicide are the three main causes of death for college-age young adults. HIV is one of the top 10 causes of death in people ages 25 – 34. Cancer is the leading cause of death for people ages 45 – 64. Heart disease is the second-leading cause of death for people ages 45 – 64.

163. Numbers 2, 3, and 4 are correct.

Rationale: All evidence must be preserved and collected following a strict chain of custody in order to be admissible in court, should the client pursue legal action. Rape kits are available in the ED that utilize a standard format of what information and items to collect. Some EDs have SANE (sexual assault nurse examiner) nurses who perform forensic nursing functions with specialized training. Photographing injuries provides further evidence for the medical record. Reassuring the client that she did what was needed to survive offers comfort. Before beginning any assessments or treatments, the client's mental condition should be evaluated. If the client is in extreme distress, it may be necessary to delay certain treatments or provide medication per the health care provider. The nurse should remain with the client at all times, as the pelvic examination may be painful and/or trigger flashbacks. If possible, ask the client if she would prefer a female physician. Advising the client on clothing choices implies that the client is to blame for the assault and may make the client defensive or less compliant with treatment. The client should receive information on rape crisis groups or other forms of support and counseling once she is able to comprehend and process the information.

164. Number 1 is correct.

Rationale: Levothyroxine enhances the effects of warfarin, which could place patients at a higher risk for bleeding. A nurse should anticipate that the physician would evaluate the clotting time of the client more frequently and adjust the medication accordingly.

165. Number 1 is correct.

Rationale: Clients who have undergone a mastectomy should keep the affected arm slightly elevated in order to promote drainage and not impede circulation. A pillow generally allows the hand to remain higher than the elbow, which assists with lymphatic fluid drainage. The arm position in correlation with the heart is not important.

166. Number 4 is correct.

Rationale: The nurse should fully assess the client to determine the source and cause of the pain before attempting any interventions. Based on the findings of the assessment, he would then provide pain medication and contact the physician. The nurse could work with the client at a later time when the patient is comfortable to review guided imagery technique.

167. Number 3 is correct.

Rationale: It is the surgeon's responsibility to have the consent form signed, and it must be signed before she performs this procedure (protocol differs for emergency situations). If the form has not been signed, the nurse should go up the chain of command and report this to the nurse manager. The nurse manager would work with the surgeon and facility policy to determine the next course of action.

168. Number 4 is correct.

Rationale: The nurse should practice therapeutic communication by exploring the situation, allowing the client to verbalize her thoughts and feelings openly. The first three choices are not open-ended questions; some are judgmental and do not allow the client to express her feelings.

169. Number 4 is correct.

Rationale: The frontal lobe regulates intellectual functions, such as complex problem solving. The temporal lobe regulates memory, speech, and comprehension. The parietal lobe regulates reading ability, writing ability, and spatial relationships. The occipital lobe is responsible for vision function.

170. Number 2 is correct.

Rationale: Librium is commonly used with clients experiencing acute alcohol withdrawal to manage anxiety and withdrawal symptoms. Naloxone hydrochloride is given to reverse the effects of opioids. Disulfiram would be provided post acutely to help with ongoing alcohol abuse. Propofol is a sedative that is used during surgical anesthesia.

171. Number 2 and 3 are correct.

Rationale: The figure eight technique for bandaging helps to reduce edema by promoting venous return; it also minimizes discomfort. The bandage should be worn at all times, but should be removed completely and rewrapped several times each day. Proper bandaging ensures that the residual limb is shaped and molded. Activity is important in the postoperative period for prevention of blood clots and exposure to air is not harmful.

172. Numbers 1 and 2 are correct.

Rationale: Following an inguinal hernia repair, the nurse should encourage fluid intake to prevent constipation and straining during bowel movements. If the client cannot void, intermittent catheterization should be performed. Ice, not heat, should be applied to the scrotum to minimize swelling. The client should turn and deep breathe, but avoid coughing. The client should be encouraged to ambulate as soon as possible after surgery. Lifting more than 10 pounds should be avoided until approved by the health care provider.

173. Numbers 2, 4, and 6 are correct.

Rationale: An NG tube is placed to avoid complications from nausea, vomiting, and abdominal distention. IV fluids correct dehydration. Monitoring stools for bleeding is important because blood loss may lead to a drop in blood pressure or, in severe cases, progress to hypovolemic shock. A client in the acute phase of diverticular disease should have a low-fiber diet if she is able to eat. A high-fiber diet should be introduced gradually once the acute phase has resolved. Enemas are contraindicated because they cause an increase in intestinal motility. Coughing should be avoided because it increases intra-abdominal pressure.

174. Number 1 is correct.

Rationale: Patients with chronic kidney disease (CKD) can experience a buildup of magnesium. Magnesium is excreted by the kidneys, and decreased kidney function may lead to a dangerous level of magnesium in the body. Magnesium-based antacids, like Mylanta, should be avoided by CKD patients. Iron may be prescribed for anemia. Baby aspirin may be appropriate for other health conditions. Taking fish oil does not have any contraindications in patients with CKD.

175. Number 3 is correct.

Rationale: Clients who follow a dysphagia-pureed diet have difficulty swallowing and need foods that have been pureed or blended until smooth. Custard would be an acceptable choice. The other food choices would be too difficult to swallow and would put the client at risk for choking.

176. Number 3 is correct.

Rationale: Asking the client how many pillows she sleeps on evaluates the client for orthopnea, which is shortness of breath caused by lying down. The more pillows the client requires, the worse the orthopnea. This provides important information to the health care provider. Snoring partners, the amount of daily exercise the client gets, and eating heavy meals before bed also affect sleep; however, in the client with COPD, determining the extent of orthopnea will best help prescribe treatments.

177. Numbers 3, 4, 5, and 6 are correct.

Rationale: Listening to audio books or music can take the client's focus off the pain. Distraction is a useful tool to shift focus away from pain and also includes music therapy and art therapy when appropriate for the client. Splinting the sternum when coughing is one of the most important things post-CABG clients can do to increase their comfort. If the client engages in prayer, meditation, or other rituals at home, he should be encouraged to continue those practices in the hospital. This is respectful to the client and his beliefs and/or culture and allows him to have some measure of control on maintaining normal routines. The bed should be positioned so as to not increase pressure on the sternum. Hot or cold packs should not be used on the sternum, as this area is a fresh post-op site and should be kept clean. Also, the packs may place pressure on the sternum and cause more discomfort. Warm, not hot, heat packs may be used on the back to relieve aches from bed positioning if approved by the health care provider. Morphine is a pharmacological method of pain relief.

178. Number 2 is correct.

1.25 L NS × 1,000 = 1,250 mL	Convert the amount of saline in liters to milliliters.
1,250 mL/10 hrs **= 125 mL/hr**	To find the flow rate in milliliters per hour, divide the volume in milliliters by the time in hours.

179. Number 4 is correct.

Rationale: Signs of imminent death include fixed and dilated pupils, weak and rapid pulse, shallow respirations, and atonic muscles. Clenched muscles could be a sign that the patient is in pain and might need additional assessment. Steady, deep respirations and a slower pulse rate are a sign of a stable patient.

180. Number 4 is correct.

Rationale: Signs of Type 1 diabetes include polyphagia (increased hunger), polydipsia (increased thirst), and polyuria (increased urine output). While some of the answers in responses 1, 2, and 3 are correct, they are not all indicative of the specific signs of type 1 diabetes. Swollen lymph nodes, muscle weakness, bloating, ringing in the ears, and difficulty sleeping are associated with other medical diagnoses.

181. Number 4 is correct.

Rationale: Parathyroid hormone aids in the regulation of calcium and phosphorus levels in the body. The other hormones do not have a critical relation to calcium excretion.

182. Number 4 is correct.

Rationale: Calcium gluconate is given as an antidote to counteract magnesium sulfate toxicity. Magnesium sulfate toxicity is dangerous because it can cause respiratory depression and hypotension. Chlordiazepoxide (Librium) is used to assist patients in alcohol withdrawal. Naloxone (Narcan) is used in case of an opioid overdose. Vitamin K would be given to increase clotting.

183. Number 1 is correct.

Rationale: M0 refers to no distant metastasis being present; the cancer has not spread to the lymph nodes or other parts of the body. M1-4 indicates ascending degrees of metastatic involvement, including distant nodes. MX means metastasis cannot be evaluated.

184. Number 3 is correct.

Rationale: The priority nursing intervention is to flush the eye with normal saline for at least 10 minutes. After or during the irrigation, the nurse would address the chemical that was splashed into the eye and would potentially cover the eye with a sterile cloth. After treatment, vision testing would be appropriate.

185. Number 4 is correct.

Rationale: If a client experiences pain during passive ROM exercises, the nurse should stop and not force the joint movement; the client could become injured. The nurse would then assess the client's pain level and document. The physician could then make a decision on the future plan of care and whether modifications, medications, or a referral to physical therapy is appropriate.

186. Answer: 1.25 tablets

125 mcg/1000 = 0.125 mg levothyroxine (Synthroid)	Convert micrograms to milligrams.
0.125 mg/0.1 mg × 1 tablet **= 1.25 tablets**	Calculate and solve.

187. Number 3 is correct.

Rationale: Abdominal cramping and discomfort are possible if the enema flow rate is too rapid. The nurse should briefly stop the flow and restart at a slower rate. Squeezing the enema bag to increase the flow rate exacerbates client discomfort and could result in reflux or vomiting. A PRN pain medication should not be necessary at the proper flow rate.

187. Number 4 is correct.

Rationale: Foods high in B12 include eggs, lamb, beef, shellfish, some cheeses, seafood, and milk. While the other foods need not be avoided, diet should focus on consuming B12-rich foods.

188. Number 3 is correct.

Rationale: Oral potassium supplements can cause GI distress; they should be dissolved in a full glass of water or juice and taken close to mealtime, though the time of day does not matter. Taking them without food can cause additional GI distress. Potassium can be stored at room temperature.

189. Number 3 is correct.

Rationale: The most common cause of mitral valve stenosis is rheumatic heart disease caused by a past history of rheumatic fever. Infective endocarditis is another, less common, cause of mitral valve stenosis. Right-sided heart failure, hypercholesterolemia, and viral meningitis do not cause mitral valve stenosis.

190. Numbers 3, 4, and 5 are correct.

Rationale: Diabetes mellitus, obesity, and hypertension are all risk factors for developing glaucoma. Other risk factors include cardiovascular disease, uveitis, long-term use of steroids, family history, and being of East Asian or African descent. Asthma and pernicious anemia are not associated with risk factors for glaucoma.

191. Number 1 is correct.

Rationale: The normal electrolyte level of chloride is between 97 and 107 mEq/L. Hyperchloremia may be caused by kidney disease, diarrhea, and diuretic use. The other levels listed are within normal ranges.

192. Number 2 is correct.

Rationale: A client on mechanical ventilation may experience secretions that require suctioning. The nurse should watch for signs that the client needs to be suctioned, such as visible secretions, adventitious breath sounds, and restlessness. Increasing oxygen and lowering the head of the bed are not therapeutic interventions for the symptoms that the patient is experiencing. The rapid response team is not indicated unless the patient is in distress.

193. Number 4 is correct.

Rationale: An elevated temperature may indicate an underlying infection or illness, and the nurse should speak with the health care provider before continuing with the RBC transfusion.

194. Number 3 is correct.

Rationale: Metabolic (nonrespiratory) alkalosis is consistent with the stated values. The stated pH of 7.58 is alkalotic. The value of PaCO2, 48 mm Hg is within normal range indicating a nonrespiratory (metabolic) origin. The value of HCO3 of 44 mEq/L is indicative of metabolic alkalosis. A Base Excess of +13 mEq/L is consistent with severe metabolic alkalosis.

195. Number 1 is correct.

Rationale: A client with low platelet counts (thrombocytopenia) is at risk for bleeding, and the nurse should monitor for bruising, nosebleeds, blood in the urine or stool, and petechia. Neutropenic precautions would be utilized if the client had a low white blood cell count. Visiting hours do not need to be restricted. While adequate iron should be encouraged, it is not the best nursing intervention.

196. Number 2 is correct.

Rationale: The best practice to verifying NG tube placement is by aspirating gastric contents and checking the pH. If the pH is above 5.5, the placement is assumed to be correct and the nurse can continue with the feeding. While an X-ray is an accurate determination of testing NG tube placement, checking before each feeding is not feasible for practice. An air bolus can be used, but is not as effective as pH paper. Auscultation of bowel sounds is not effective as the client will have bowel sounds despite placement of the tube.

197. Number 3 is correct.

Rationale: The nurse will need to draw blood to monitor peak and trough levels of vancomycin in order to reduce the chance of side effects caused by toxicity. A low-residue diet and assistance with ambulation are unrelated to the vancomycin administration. Cardiac arrhythmia can be caused by antibiotics, but is not a common reaction.

198. Numbers 1, 5, and 6 are correct.

Rationale: Clients with delirium develop fever and other manifestations of delirium within 48 to 72 hours after the last drink. Disorientation and fluctuating levels of consciousness are common. Other signs in the delirium stage include anorexia and insomnia.

199. Number 4 is correct.

Rationale: In applying the nursing process, the most appropriate action is to assess the situation by interviewing the client. Recording suspicions in the medical record without further assessment would be premature. Obtaining information from the client, rather than his family, is most appropriate. Notifying the physician should occur after assessment.

200. Number 2 is correct.

Rationale: Tissue plasma activator (tPA) is used to dissolve clots in certain clients who have experienced a stroke or myocardial infarction. Blood in the stool or any other sign of bleeding (LOC changes, hypotension, and tachycardia) may indicate a hemorrhage and is an emergency situation. The other choices do not indicate an emergency situation that would be caused by the administration of tPA.

THREE: Practice Test Three

READ THE QUESTION, AND THEN CHOOSE THE MOST CORRECT ANSWER.

1. A nurse is asked to prepare a client for placement of a central venous catheter that will be inserted into the right jugular vein. The nurse asks the client to
   1. lie in a supine position with the head turned to the right.
   2. sit in a high-Fowler's position with the head turned to the left.
   3. lie in the Trendelenburg position with the head turned to the left.
   4. lie in a supine position with the head positioned straight.

2. A 46-year-old male has been placed under therapeutic hypothermic care after a myocardial infarction (MI). The nurse correctly explains to the family,
   1. "Therapeutic hypothermia increases the production of neurotransmitters in the brain."
   2. "Therapeutic hypothermia will repair damaged cardiac tissue."
   3. "Therapeutic hypothermia will help protect the brain from injury by slowing metabolism."
   4. "Therapeutic hypothermia will slow the heart rate to reduce likelihood of another MI."

3. An ICU nurse monitors a client recovering from a head injury. The client's intracranial pressure (ICP) has been between 15 and 19 mmHg throughout the shift. However, after the nurse suctions the client's endotracheal tube, the ICP jumps to 28 mmHg. It decreases a few minutes later to 20 mmHg. The best intervention by the nurse is to
   1. increase the rate of the sedative IV drip.
   2. chart the findings and continue to monitor the client.
   3. reposition the client.
   4. contact the physician.

4. A critically injured woman is rushed to the ER. She needs an immediate blood transfusion, and there is no time to cross-match blood type. The nurse anticipates the physician will call for
   1. 1 unit of AB positive blood.
   2. 1 unit of O positive blood.
   3. 1 unit of AB negative blood.
   4. 1 unit of O negative blood.

5. A client newly diagnosed with type 1 diabetes mellitus asks the nurse why it is important to rotate insulin injection sites. The nurse explains this is done to avoid
   1. tissue scarring.
   2. insulin resistance.
   3. localized edema.
   4. lipodystrophy.

6. A client is prescribed heparin 2,000 units SC q8 hours. The pharmacy sends heparin 5,000 units/mL. How many mL should the nurse administer every 24 hours?
   1. 0.4 mL/ day
   2. 0.8 mL/ day
   3. 1.2 mL/ day
   4. 1.4 mL/day

7. The nurse is teaching a group of premenopausal women how to conduct self-breast exams. The nurse should instruct the women to perform self-breast exams
   1. on the first day of the menstrual cycle.
   2. one week after the menstrual cycle.
   3. immediately after the menstrual cycle.
   4. on the first day of every month.

8. The nurse knows the best intervention for preventing a postoperative infection is
   1. wearing gown, gloves, and mask in the client's room.
   2. administering a prophylactic antibiotic.
   3. placing the client in a private room.
   4. following hand hygiene protocols.

9. A client in cardiac arrest shows to be in torsades de pointes, and magnesium sulfate is ordered STAT. The priority nursing intervention is
   1. monitor client for bradycardia and respiratory depression.
   2. prepare client for synchronized cardioversion.
   3. monitor client for tachycardia and hyperventilation.
   4. prepare client for Swan catheter.

10. A client with Graves' disease is brought to the ER with a suspected thyroid storm. The nurse expects to see what signs and symptoms?
    1. seizures, jaundice, irregular heartbeat, vomiting
    2. bradycardia, septic shock, polyuria
    3. increased cranial pressure, thready pulse, rash across chest
    4. poor muscle tone, dyspnea, cyanosis

11. Which treatment should be included in the immediate management of acute appendicitis?
    1. prevent fluid volume deficit
    2. administer antibiotic therapy
    3. reduce anxiety
    4. relieve pain

12. Medical management of a client with acute diverticulitis should include which treatment?
    1. increased fiber in diet
    2. administration of antibiotics
    3. pain medication administration
    4. liquid diet for 1 – 2 days

13. Which of the following is a metabolic, life-threatening adverse reaction to general anesthesia?
    1. hypothermia
    2. hyperthermia
    3. hypoglycemia
    4. hyperglycemia

14. A client diagnosed with Alzheimer's disease initiates the same conversation repeatedly, becomes aggressive when stressed, needs reminders to perform ADLs, and is easily lost in his neighborhood. This client is likely in what stage of Alzheimer's disease?
    1. pre-Alzheimer's
    2. early/mild
    3. moderate
    4. late to severe

15. The nurse is evaluating clients for risk of heparin-induced thrombocytopenia (HIT). Which client is at greatest risk for HIT, based on the nurse's assessment?
    1. a male client who just completed a 1-week course of heparin
    2. a male client taking enoxaparin for management of unstable angina
    3. a female client receiving heparin for postsurgical thromboprophylaxis
    4. a female client taking enoxaparin to prevent clots following a mild myocardial infarction

16. The nurse is caring for a client receiving total parenteral nutrition (TPN). During the assessment, the nurse notes absence of breath sounds on the right side, where the central catheter is placed. Which of the following does the nurse suspect is responsible for this abnormal assessment finding?
    1. air embolism
    2. fluid overload
    3. pneumothorax
    4. refeeding syndrome

17. The nurse is caring for a client who has an order for ceftriaxone IV. The client is awake and alert and has been taking PO medications and eating. The IV ceftriaxone is not available in the automatic medication dispenser. What should the nurse do next?
    1. hold the medication since the client is afebrile
    2. call the pharmacy to send up the missing IV medication
    3. obtain the PO ceftriaxone from the medication dispenser and administer it
    4. call the health care provider and see if the client can be switched over to oral ceftriaxone

18. An ICU nurse is caring for a client receiving total parenteral nutrition (TPN) via IV. The client's infusion ended 2 hours ago and the pharmacy has not yet sent another bag. The client is diaphoretic and tachycardic, and states he feels weak, dizzy, and fatigued. The nurse suspects
    1. dehydration.
    2. fluid volume overload.
    3. hyperglycemia.
    4. hypoglycemia.

19. A 22-year-old woman has just been diagnosed with myasthenia gravis. She asks the nurse what causes this disease. The most accurate response from the nurse is
    1. "This is a disease caused by a chromosomal defect in utero. It is a structural abnormality in the chromosome that causes nerve cells in your body to become inflamed and not function properly."
    2. "This is an autoimmune disease in which antibodies attack the muscles and muscle atrophy occurs. The muscles will become weak and begin to waste."
    3. "This is an autoimmune disease in which antibodies destroy acetylcholine at the neuromuscular junction. This prevents your muscles from contracting normally."
    4. "This is a hereditary condition caused by a recessive gene. It causes nervous tissue to be broken down, and damage occurs to the brain and spinal cord."

20. A client is admitted with inflammatory bowel syndrome (Crohn's disease). Which nursing measures would be included in the client's care plan? Select all that apply.
    1. high-fat diet
    2. lactulose therapy
    3. daily weight
    4. corticosteroids

21. A client is scheduled for a colonscopy. The nurse assists the client into which position?
    1. Sim's position
    2. supine position, with the head of the bed elevated 15 degrees
    3. left-side-lying position, knees to chest
    4. lithotomy position

22. A client comes into the dermatology office and shows the nurse a rash she is very concerned about. The nurse examines areas of skin on the elbows and scalp that are inflamed and covered with silvery-white scales. The nurse determines this is most likely
    1. scabies.
    2. plaque psoriasis.
    3. urticaria.
    4. contact dermatitis.

23. After a traumatic accident, the client must have his left arm amputated in an emergency procedure. When the client wakes from anesthesia and sees his arm has been amputated, he becomes extremely distressed. He cries uncontrollably and yells about how angry he is at the doctor. The best therapeutic action from the nurse is to
    1. close the door to the client's room and return to check on him periodically.
    2. sit quietly with the client until he calms down.
    3. explain to the client that he should not be angry because there was no other choice.
    4. call the hospital chaplain to come speak with the client.

24. A client with a past history of substance abuse and opioid addiction comes to the hospital after falling off a ladder. Upon assessment, the client reports his pain is a 9 out of 10 on the pain scale. The nurse should
    1. chart "The client states his pain is 9/10."
    2. chart "The client has a past history of addiction and is claiming he has severe pain."
    3. ask the client if his pain level is really as high as he states.
    4. report to the physician the client is likely seeking drugs.

25. A 22-year-old pregnant client is diagnosed with autoimmune hemolytic anemia. The nurse anticipates immediate treatment with

    1. IgA.
    2. IgG.
    3. IgE.
    4. IgD.

26. A client's serum sodium level is 113 mEq/L. The nurse would expect which findings upon assessment?

    1. headache, confusion, muscle weakness, fatigue
    2. hypertension, muscle cramps, respiratory depression
    3. cardiac arrhythmia, tetany, tachycardia
    4. confusion, nystagmus, tetany, hallucinations

27. A client with chronic kidney disease (CKD) is being evaluated by the transplant team. The client's glomerular filtration rate (GFR) is 14 mL/min. This places the client in which stage of CKD?

    1. stage 1
    2. stage 5
    3. stage 4
    4. stage 2

28. A client is admitted to the ED after complaining of acute chest pain radiating down the left arm. The client is diaphoretic and anxious, and has difficulty breathing. Which laboratory studies would the nurse anticipate?

    1. blood urea nitrogen (BUN)
    2. white blood cell count
    3. LDH
    4. myoglobin

29. A nurse is monitoring a client's intracranial pressure (ICP) after a motor vehicle accident. Upon checking the ICP, the nurse knows to contact the physician. What reading would warrant this action?

    1. 8 mm Hg
    2. 14 mm Hg
    3. 18 mm Hg
    4. 22 mm Hg

30. A client is prescribed diazepam (Valium) as needed to control the symptom of alcohol withdrawal. Which symptom may indicate the need for the nurse to administer phenytoin (Dilantin) to supplement the effect of Valium?
    1. disturbed heart rate
    2. hallucinations
    3. drowsiness
    4. seizures

31. The nurse is caring for a client who just had a laparoscopic appendectomy. The client tells the nurse that she does not want "drugs" for pain management, but prefers alternative therapy and/or complementary therapy. Which is the best response by the nurse?
    1. "I know of some herbs and supplements that you can take to manage the pain."
    2. "Tell me what works for you, and I will see what we can provide for your comfort."
    3. "We use real medicine here in the hospital, so I will bring you hydrocodone for pain when you need it."
    4. "Yoga always relaxes me. I will get you a foam mat from physical therapy so you can practice when you want."

32. A woman comes to a community health clinic and expresses concern she may have been exposed to HIV. The community nurse draws blood for an ELISA test, which comes back as positive. The nurse should
    1. ask the client to come into the clinic to tell her in person she is HIV positive.
    2. request the client come in and follow up with a Western blot test.
    3. explain to the client this shows she has been exposed to HIV, but does not have HIV.
    4. call and tell client that she is HIV positive.

33. A client confides in the nurse that a close friend recently died from pancreatic cancer. The client asks what the risk factors are for pancreatic cancer. The nurse should respond with
    1. "Being a female of Asian descent is linked to an increased risk of pancreatic cancer."
    2. "Drinking two or fewer alcoholic beverages per week is linked to an increased risk of pancreatic cancer."
    3. "Past history of acute pancreatitis before age 20 is linked to an increased risk of pancreatic cancer."
    4. "Cigarette smoking is linked to an increased risk for pancreatic cancer."

34. A triage nurse is reviewing messages from four clients. The nurse's priority is which client?
    1. 69-year-old male with cloudy urine and fever of 100.3°F
    2. 42-year-old female with pain in jaw and back that has become more intense in past 15 minutes
    3. 56-year-old female with hot flashes and inability to sleep the past four nights
    4. 10-year-old boy with a closed fracture of the tibia, who rates his pain level as 7 out of 10

35. A client prescribed furosemide (Lasix) should choose which meal for lunch?
    1. chicken breast, white rice, apple
    2. turkey sandwich on wheat bread, celery sticks, grapefruit
    3. egg salad, cooked carrots, strawberries
    4. baked salmon, spinach salad, banana

36. A client who has been taking Coumadin (warfarin) was stabbed in the upper arm. His prothrombin time is over twice the normal amount. The nurse anticipates an order for
    1. fresh frozen plasma
    2. whole blood
    3. platelets
    4. packed red blood cells

37. A client requires IV insulin. The pharmacy sends up a bag labeled 1,000 units of insulin in a 250 mL bag of 0.9% NaCl. The pump is set to infuse at 5 mL/hr. How much insulin does the client receive per hour?
    1. 20 units/hour
    2. 50 units/hour
    3. 25 units/hour
    4. 15 units/hour

38. After a train accident, the nurse is assigned to triage the injured. Based upon the triage protocol, which individual should be seen last?
    1. 66-year-old male with no visible injuries, but who is experiencing tachycardia and seems confused
    2. 16-year-old female with fixed, dilated pupils who is unresponsive and has clear fluid draining from right ear
    3. 25-year-old female with an abrasion to left eye and a swollen ankle, who is unable to put weight on right leg
    4. 80-year-old male with chest pains and shortness of breath

39. The priority nursing intervention for a client with sickle cell crisis is to
    1. administer pain medication.
    2. administer packed RBC.
    3. administer oxygen.
    4. administer IV fluids.

40. Which of the following statements regarding proper use of a cane is correct?

1. When standing, the cane should reach a height even with the natural waist.
2. When walking downstairs, the cane should be placed down on the step first, followed by the injured leg, and then the good leg.
3. The elbow should be straight when holding the cane.
4. The cane should be held in the hand of the same side that needs support.

41. The nurse is caring for a 42-year-old client who has a do not resuscitate (DNR) order on the chart. The client tells the nurse, "I've changed my mind about the DNR. I would like to cancel that and be given whatever care is needed to keep me alive." Which response by the nurse is correct?

1. "I will notify your health care provider right away."
2. "I'm glad to hear this. You shouldn't be a DNR at your age."
3. "Let me call your family and tell them you have changed your mind."
4. "You cannot change a DNR once it's on your chart. It is a legal document."

42. The nurse is developing a care plan for a client with hepatitis A. The nurse knows that the primary routes of transmission of this hepatitis virus are which of the following? Select all that apply.

1. sputum
2. blood
3. feces
4. contaminated food

43. The nurse is preparing to test a client who has the herpes virus. Which of the following tests should the nurse perform?

1. Rinne test
2. stress test
3. Tzanck test
4. patch test

44. The nurse is preparing to administer a unit of red blood cells (RBCs) to an anemic client. From starting the infusion (puncturing the blood pack) to completion, infusion of the pack should occur within which time period?

1. 8 hours
2. 6 hours
3. 4 hours
4. 2 hours

45. The nurse is caring for a client who suffers from post-traumatic stress disorder (PTSD) following the loss of her husband and children in an automobile accident while they were on a family vacation. Which interventions by the nurse are appropriate for this client? Select all that apply.
    1. assist the client to develop adequate coping techniques
    2. encourage the client to try different relaxation techniques
    3. listen to the client in a supportive and nonjudgmental manner
    4. allow the client a safe and secure environment to express her feelings
    5. encourage the client to avoid going out in public until she has worked through all the stages of grief

46. The nurse is teaching a client and her family about home care following a laryngectomy. Which statement by the client indicates a need for further teaching from the nurse?
    1. "I will purchase a Medic-Alert bracelet."
    2. "I can wear loose-fitting turtlenecks to cover the stoma."
    3. "I can resume water aerobics once my doctor says it is okay."
    4. "I have a lot of green houseplants year-round throughout my home."

47. The nurse is caring for a client in the cardiac unit and notices the client's rhythm changes from normal sinus rhythm to coarse ventricular fibrillation. Which is the priority nursing action?
    1. call a code blue
    2. check the client and check the leads
    3. initiate CPR while waiting on help to arrive
    4. prepare to start the client on a diltiazem (Cardizem) drip
    5. clear the room of unnecessary items to allow room for the crash cart and team

48. The nurse is working with a client in the psychiatric unit. The client has memory gaps, which she fills in with detailed fantasies that she believes to be true. The nurse understands that the client is exhibiting which type of abnormal thought process?

    _____

49. The nurse is caring for a client with bipolar disorder. The client has been manipulating some of the staff and other clients in order to get her way. Which actions by the nurse are appropriate in managing this client? Select all that apply.
    1. giving support when the client exhibits positive behaviors
    2. setting clear limits and communicating expected behaviors
    3. role playing with the client to demonstrate appropriate behaviors
    4. treating the client more like a friend in order to show respect for her as a person
    5. giving the client small gifts, such as extra dessert, in order to encourage appropriate behavior

50. The nurse is caring for an obese client who had a diagnostic laparotomy with midline incision one week ago. The client just called the nurse to report a "popping" sensation in the abdomen. Upon assessment, the nurse notes loops of bowel protruding through the incision. Which is the priority nursing action for this client?

    1. monitor vital signs
    2. stay with the client
    3. call for help and have the surgeon notified
    4. place the client in low Fowler's with the knees bent

51. Mix and Match: Match the nursing intervention to the location of injury to the portion of the client's brain.

Injured Brain Area	Nursing Intervention
1. frontal lobe	assist with ADL due to visual disturbances
2. temporal lobe	assist with walking
3. occipital lobe	monitor vital signs
4. brain stem	give simple instructions; reorient as needed
5. parietal lobe	provide simple, one-step instructions
6. cerebellum	speak clearly due to impaired hearing

52. The nurse is caring for a client scheduled to receive cyclopentolate HCl preoperatively. Which finding in the client's history would prompt the nurse to notify the health care provider?

    1. osteoporosis
    2. hypothyroidism
    3. renal insufficiency
    4. cardiac dysrhythmias

53. A client has orders for zoledronic acid (Reclast). Which lab value finding would prompt the nurse to notify the prescriber?

    1. ferritin level of 78 ng/mL
    2. magnesium level of 2.3 mEq/dL
    3. creatinine clearance of 29 mL/min
    4. platelet count of 135,000 cells/mcL

54. A nurse is caring for a client, diagnosed with Parkinson's disease, who scored as a high-risk fall candidate on the St. Thomas Risk Assessment Tool in Falling Elderly Inpatients. Which nursing interventions should the nurse implement? Select all that apply.

    1. provide the client with a call-light device
    2. keep the bed in the lowest position
    3. use a beveled floor mat at bedside
    4. implement a bed alarm

55. A nurse is preparing discharge instructions for a client with a below-the-knee amputation. Which instruction would be a priority?
    1. sterile wound management
    2. elevation of residual limb
    3. performing prescribed exercises
    4. reporting occurrence of phantom limb pain immediately

56. A client with a T5 spinal cord injury suddenly begins sweating profusely in the face and neck. Vital signs reveal sudden bradycardia and significant increase in blood pressure. Which is the priority nursing action?
    1. administer nitrate or nifedipine
    2. check the client for fecal impaction
    3. check the client for bladder distention
    4. place the bed in the high Fowler's position

57. The nurse is educating a client about MAOI and diet. Which dietary selection by the client indicates that the nurse's teaching was effective?
    1. egg-white omelet with a cup of yogurt
    2. baked chicken breast with green beans
    3. scrambled eggs with sausage and toast
    4. hot dog with sauerkraut, beans, and a fruit cup

58. The nurse is caring for a client who just returned from a total hip arthroplasty. A student nurse is helping provide care for this client. Which action by the student nurse requires intervention by the nurse?
    1. The student nurse floats the client's heels with a pillow.
    2. The student nurse positions the client with the legs adducted.
    3. The student nurse applies the sequential compression device (SCD) per orders.
    4. The student nurse encourages deep breathing and incentive spirometer use every 2 hours.

59. The nurse is caring for a client with stage 3 moderate chronic kidney disease. Which laboratory value would be expected for this client?
    1. GFR of 92 mL/min
    2. GFR of 63 mL/min
    3. GFR of 39 mL/min
    4. GFR of 16mL/min

60. The nurse is auscultating a client's breath sounds. Low-pitched grating and rubbing are noted on inhalation and exhalation. What will the nurse chart under assessment findings?

1. ronchi
2. stridor
3. friction rub
4. fine crackles

61. Which assessment finding would the nurse expect in a client with long-term venous insufficiency with the presence of a venous ulcer?

1. decreased or absent pedal pulses with cool or cold foot
2. the presence of stasis ulcers over the medial malleolus
3. skin atrophy and pallor with elevation of the affected leg
4. decreased circumference in the affected leg due to venous constriction

62. The nurse is preparing to remove a peripheral IV from a client. Which nursing action is the priority with this procedure?

1. checking for an intact catheter tip
2. washing the hands and donning gloves
3. charting the client's tolerance to the procedure
4. removing catheter slowly using the dominant hand
5. holding pressure on the site until hemostasis is achieved

63. The nurse has received shift report on the assigned client. Which client would the nurse anticipate to be at highest risk for skin breakdown?

1. an elderly client who is up to the chair for meals with assistance
2. a 24-year-old client with diabetes whose hemoglobin A1C is 6.4%
3. a client who is legally blind and lives independently, except for driving
4. a client with severe right-sided weakness from a stroke and residual peripheral neuropathy
5. a client who had a right pneumothorax and has a chest tube and can reposition independently

64. A nurse is preparing to lift a client up in bed. Which of the following should the nurse do to help avoid injuring his back?

1. keep his feet together
2. instruct the client to not help
3. tighten his stomach and leg muscles
4. elevate the head of the bed to about 30 degrees, if the client can tolerate it

65. The nurse is admitting a new client to the medical unit. When asked about advance directives, the client says, "I'm not really sure what that is, but I trust my doctor to do whatever he thinks I need." Which is the correct action by the nurse?
    1. tell the client not to worry about it, because the client can always add the advance directives later
    2. tell the client that she can pay her lawyer to draw one up and have a copy sent to the hospital
    3. explain what advance directives are and how they benefit the client, and offer to give the client a copy so she can read it and ask questions
    4. omit further discussion about advance directives, and chart that the client does not have one and refuses further information

66. An elderly adult has been admitted with a diagnosis of hypertension with a history of dementia. Which of the following nursing diagnoses has the highest priority for this client?
    1. ineffective coping
    2. activity intolerance
    3. ineffective tissue perfusion
    4. risk for injury

67. The nurse is caring for a client who has verbalized the desire to commit suicide. He has a detailed, concrete plan in place. The nurse places the client on suicide precautions, which include assigning the client a 24-hour sitter. The client becomes angry and refuses the sitter. Which action by the nurse is the most appropriate?
    1. place the client in soft wrist restraints
    2. have security sit outside the client's door
    3. assign a sitter despite the client's refusal
    4. allow the client to leave against medical advice (AMA)
    5. tell the client that a friend can come sit with him instead

68. The clinic nurse is seeing a client who suffers from caregiver strain due to caring for her elderly parents who have dementia and live with her. Which action by the nurse during the assessment is most important?
    1. ask the client about her support systems
    2. ask the client what she does for relaxation
    3. ask if her parents' insurance covers adult day care for them
    4. offer to give her a list of nursing homes to care for her parents

69. The nurse plans on administering a medication using the Z-track intramuscular technique. The nurse knows the following steps are required during the procedure. Select all that apply.
   1. Draw 0.2 – 0.5 cc of air after aspirating the prescribed medication.
   2. Use the vastus lateralis muscle.
   3. Replace the needle used for medication withdrawal with a new one prior to injection.
   4. Insert the needle at 45-degree angle.

70. The nurse is preparing to administer regular and NPH insulin to the client. He knows to do which of the following steps?
   1. insert air first into the regular insulin
   2. insert air first into the NPH insulin
   3. draw up regular insulin first
   4. draw up NPH insulin first

71. The nurse is preparing to perform a focused abdominal assessment on a client. Which is the correct order of this assessment?
   1. inspection, auscultation, palpation, percussion
   2. inspection, palpation, percussion, auscultation
   3. inspection, percussion, auscultation, palpation
   4. inspection, percussion, palpation, auscultation

72. The nurse is caring for a client who has just returned from the cardiac catheterization lab. Which complications of cardiac catheterization require immediate intervention by the nurse? Select all that apply.
   1. chest pain
   2. decreased appetite
   3. difficulty swallowing
   4. hematoma formation
   5. decreased pulses in the affected extremity

73. The nurse is preparing to administer the first dose of intravenous immunoglobulin (IVIG) to a 50-year-old female adult client admitted to the hospital with Guillain-Barre syndrome. Which nursing intervention is appropriate regarding administration?
   1. administer IVIG transfusion at a constant rate
   2. monitor vital signs within 15 minutes prior to administration and within 30 minutes after starting the infusion
   3. administer IVIG at room temperature
   4. should chills occur during the infusion, continue the infusion and provide the client with a blanket

74. The nurse reviews the chart of a client diagnosed with nephrotic syndrome and expects to note which finding associated with this diagnosis?
    1. lipiduria
    2. hypolipidemia
    3. hyperalbuminemia
    4. decreased coagulation

75. The nurse is caring for a client who presents with increased ammonia levels, elevated BUN, and altered mental status. Which medication would the nurse anticipate the health care provider ordering for this client?
    1. lactulose
    2. sucralfate
    3. lamotrigine
    4. gabapentin

76. The nurse is caring for a client with AIDS who is diagnosed with thrush. Which instruction should the nurse give to the client's caretaker, who will be administering nystatin (Mycostatin) oral solution?
    1. take the medication before meals
    2. take the medication after meals
    3. mix the medication with orange juice
    4. take the medication at bedtime

77. The nurse is caring for a client with a permanent tracheostomy who is able to eat. Which is the correct action by the nurse in managing this tube?
    1. if the tube must be capped, place the cap before deflating the cuff
    2. inflate the cuff and remove the inner cannula before capping the tube
    3. inflate the cuff (if the tube is not capped) for meals and 1 hour afterward to prevent aspiration
    4. deflate the cuff (if the tube is not capped) for meals and 1 hour afterward to prevent aspiration

78. The nurse is caring for a client who lives below the poverty level. While providing discharge teaching, the nurse notes that the client has received a prescription for warfarin (Coumadin) and will need to return to the clinic for regular lab work. Which of the following is most appropriate for the nurse to ask the client?
    1. "Which pharmacy do you use for your medications?"
    2. "Do you know when your next appointment is for lab work?"
    3. "Do you have a car or someone to take you to get your lab work done?"
    4. "Can you tell me the side effects that you should report to your physician?"

79. The nurse has received report on the day's assigned clients. Which of the following clients should the nurse see first?
    1. a client complaining of nausea and vomiting after eating breakfast
    2. a client complaining of itching and burning at the IV site while receiving normal saline
    3. a client who is post-op day 1 from a hernia repair with a pain level of 6 on a scale of 1 – 10
    4. a client who has been given the first dose of an antibiotic and complains of tingling in and around the mouth

80. The nurse is administering afternoon medications, which include an antihypertensive med and aspirin for pain relief. Which of the following should the nurse do first before administering the medications?
    1. match the client's date of birth and name on his wristband with the same information on the medication order
    2. ask the client his name and date of birth
    3. ask the client to confirm the medication ordered and compare this with the medication order
    4. match the client's name and room number with the medication order

81. The nurse is performing discharging instruction for a female client with cystitis. Which statement by the client indicates a need for further teaching?
    1. "I should void before and after intercourse."
    2. "I should wear loose-fitting cotton underwear."
    3. "I can continue using spermicide for birth control."
    4. "If I have burning when I urinate, I will contact my physician."

82. A client in the emergency department is complaining of abdominal pain after an episode of nausea and vomiting. Which statement by the client to the nurse necessitates prompt notification of the health care provider?
    1. "I started hurting when I got up this morning to go to work."
    2. "My grandmother had to have her appendix out many years ago."
    3. "I haven't eaten anything because I've been so nauseated and throwing up."
    4. "The pain is worse when I cough or move but feels better when I bend my right hip."

83. The physician orders an MRI of the spine with infusion for an adult female. Which of the following findings in the client's history should the nurse report to the physician?
    1. allergy to shellfish
    2. congestive heart failure (CHF)
    3. chronic cystitis
    4. metformin administered daily

84. The nurse is caring for a client with a history of cirrhosis of the liver. Lab values reveal rising ammonia levels. Which of the following actions should the nurse anticipate performing? Select all that apply.
    1. replace electric razor with a straight razor
    2. encourage frequent periods of rest
    3. instruct on a potassium-restricted diet
    4. monitor the client's mental status

85. The nurse is assessing a client with Graves' disease. Which assessment finding would the nurse expect in this client?
    1. bradycardia
    2. constipation
    3. exophthalmos
    4. recent weight gain

86. The nurse is preparing a client with acquired immunodeficiency syndrome (AIDS) for discharge home. Which of the following statements by the client indicates a need for further teaching by the nurse?
    1. "I do not need to limit my time in public places."
    2. "I may share food from serving dishes with others at a restaurant."
    3. "I may use public restrooms."
    4. "I may donate blood."

87. The nurse is visiting a client at home who is using a transdermal fentanyl patch. The nurse knows the client requires additional education based on which of the following statements?
    1. "I apply the patch when I have breakthrough pain."
    2. "I store my patches in a private location away from my grandchildren's reach."
    3. "I remove my old patch before applying a new one."
    4. "I enjoy orange juice for breakfast."

88. The nurse is caring for a client with compartment syndrome. The client's husband asks what causes the condition. Which of the following will the nurse share with the client's husband? Select all that apply.
    1. It can be present in severe burns.
    2. Most cases are caused by fractures.
    3. It can be caused by severe infiltration of IV fluids.
    4. It occurs with failure to ambulate after surgical procedures.
    5. Untreated high blood sugars are a contributing factor in some cases.

89. A client is prescribed heparin 5,000 units subcutaneously every 12 hours for deep vein thrombosis prophylaxis. The pharmacy dispenses a vial containing 10,000 units/1 ml. How many milliliter(s) of heparin should the nurse administer?

_____

90. A client with asthma has orders for terbutaline. Which finding in the medical history would the nurse be most concerned about?

1. diabetes
2. migraines
3. osteoarthritis
4. coronary artery disease

91. Mix and Match: Match the laboratory test to the abnormal value.

Laboratory Test	Abnormal Value
calcium	8.1 mg/L
pH	7.56
specific gravity	1.000
potassium	5.8
LDL	160 mg/dL
HDL	34 mg/dL

92. The nurse is caring for an elderly client who is 1 day post–hip replacement surgery. Which nursing interventions should be included on the care plan? Select all that apply.

1. apply compression stockings
2. ambulate with walker
3. encourage coughing and deep breathing every 2 hours
4. limit fluid intake

93. The nurse is caring for a client who has just returned from surgery for an ascending colostomy. The nurse plans to include reinforcement teaching for the client and spouse. Which statements should the nurse include in the teaching? Select all that apply.

1. The colostomy will begin functioning within 24 hours.
2. A large amount of bleeding may be present at the stoma site.
3. The first stools will be liquid and will gradually become more formed.
4. A healthy stoma is reddish-pink and moist and protrudes about 2 cm from the abdominal wall.

94. The nurse is caring for a client with multiple IV medications. Which of the following drugs are compatible?
    1. vancomycin and heparin
    2. nitroglycerin and dopamine
    3. sodium bicarbonate and dobutamine
    4. furosemide (Lasix) and ondansetron (Zofran)

95. The ED nurse has triaged a client who was in a severe motor vehicle accident. He is unconscious with fractures to the left femur and left humerus and ulna. CT also reveals a large amount of internal hemorrhaging. No identification was found on the client at the scene. What is the correct action by the nurse?
    1. prepare the client for emergency surgery
    2. try to obtain informed consent from a family member
    3. wait until the client is conscious, and then obtain the consent
    4. ask police to run the tag number so the client can be identified
    5. inform the health care provider that consent cannot be obtained at this time

96. The nurse is caring for an elderly client with a history of Alzheimer's and falls. The nurse understands which to be the priority nursing diagnosis for this client?
    1. risk for injury
    2. impaired skin integrity
    3. altered body image due to confusion
    4. impaired physical mobility due to dementia with Lewy bodies

97. The nurse is preparing to administer an antihypertensive and an anticoagulant to a client. Which should the nurse do first before administering the medication?
    1. verify the client's allergies
    2. verify the client's name and room number
    3. ask the client to state her name and date of birth
    4. scan the client's wristband and medication barcode
    5. verify the client's name, date of birth, and medical record number with the medication order

98. The nurse is teaching a 28-year-old male client about testicular cancer. Which statement by the client indicates understanding of the nurse's teaching?
    1. "Testicular cancer is one of the hardest cancers to treat and cure."
    2. "Testicular cancer is the most common cancer in men ages 25 – 35."
    3. "A lump larger than a quarter should be reported to my health care provider."
    4. "The best time to perform testicular self-examination is just after bathing because the scrotum is more relaxed."

99. The nurse is teaching a group of student nurses about principles of teaching. Which statement by a student nurse requires further instruction from the licensed nurse?
   1. "A client's living situation can affect his readiness and ability to learn."
   2. "The client's age and developmental stage must be considered when teaching clients."
   3. "Tactile or kinesthetic learners prefer to learn by watching a video or reading a handout."
   4. "I should allow clients to demonstrate their understanding of what they have learned and practice skills."
   5. "Some barriers to learning include financial resources, lack of support systems, and a low level of literacy."

100. The nurse is caring for a client who is a victim of domestic violence. Which of the following would the nurse expect to find in the client's social history? Select all that apply.
   1. The client is under 30 years old.
   2. The client is active in a local charity.
   3. The client has a history of child abuse.
   4. The client has been in past abusive relationships.
   5. The client is employed as a college professor.

101. The nurse discovers a hospice client has expired. The family members are assembled in the facility's waiting room. Which of the following statements by the nurse would be the most appropriate?
   1. "My condolences on the passing of your family member. You may visit him if you wish."
   2. "I will give you some time to spend with your loved one. Let me know if you need anything."
   3. "You should view your loved one as a way of saying farewell."
   4. "It would be best if you not view your loved one just yet."

102. The nurse is teaching a group of women at a community center about risk factors for spousal abuse. Which would the nurse identify as risk factors? Select all that apply.
   1. alcohol or drug use
   2. low income or poverty
   3. being over the age of 40
   4. a higher level of education
   5. having a large circle of friends
   6. pregnancy, especially if it is unplanned

CONTINUE

103. The nurse is teaching a group of student nurses about radiation therapy. Which would the nurse include in the teaching? Select all that apply.
    1. The dose is always more than the exposure.
    2. Clients receiving brachytherapy are radioactive.
    3. Clients receiving teletherapy are not radioactive.
    4. Beta particles are the most common type of radiation therapy.
    5. Bodily waste from a client receiving brachytherapy does not require special handling.

104. The nurse is caring for a client who has a lithium level of 2.2 mEq/L. Based on this lab value, what would the nurse anticipate to do in order to care for this client? Select all that apply.
    1. prepare to administer IV fluids
    2. notify the health care provider
    3. order a mechanical soft diet for the client
    4. administer the next dose of lithium when it is due
    5. observe the client for confusion and slurred speech

105. The nurse is caring for a client receiving hemodialysis. During hemodialysis, the client becomes anxious, experiencing tachypnea and hypotension. The nurse suspects which complication of hemodialysis?
    1. air embolism
    2. clotting of the graft site
    3. dialysis encephalopathy
    4. disequilibrium syndrome

106. The nurse is reviewing labs of a newly admitted client. Which lab result would prompt the nurse to contact the health care provider?
    1. ALT 33 units/L
    2. BNP 760 pg/mL
    3. WBC 10,450 mcL
    4. direct bilirubin 0.2 mg/dL

107. The nurse is caring for an adult client with a total bilirubin of 2.1 mg/dL. Which signs and symptoms would the nurse expect to find? Select all that apply.
    1. itchy skin
    2. nausea
    3. pale stools
    4. colorless urine
    5. none; this is a normal lab value

108. The nurse is preparing to extubate a client. Arrange in order of priority the actions that the nurse should take to perform this procedure.

    ___ hyperoxygenate the client
    ___ explain the procedure to the client
    ___ immediately instruct the client to cough
    ___ apply oxygen by nasal cannula or face mask
    ___ thoroughly suction the ET tube and the oral cavity
    ___ teach the client how to use an incentive spirometer every 2 hours
    ___ rapidly deflate the ET tube cuff and remove tube at peak inspiration
    ___ set up the prescribed oxygen delivery system and bring in equipment for emergency reintubation

109. The nurse is caring for a client who just returned from a right mastectomy. Which position does the nurse anticipate for the client?
    1. high Fowler's with the unaffected arm elevated on a pillow
    2. flat with the client positioned on the affected side or back
    3. semi-Fowler's with the affected arm supported on a pillow
    4. reverse Trendelenburg's with the arm on the affected side supported on a pillow

110. The nurse is caring for a client in the ICU who has an arterial line for hemodynamic monitoring. Which action will the nurse take in caring for this client?
    1. position the client with the transducer at the level of the right atrium
    2. position the client with the transducer at the level of the left ventricle
    3. position the client with the transducer at the level of the right clavicle
    4. position the client with the transducer at the level of the right ventricle

111. A 47-year-old client presents to the emergency department with severe hypotension, muscle weakness, fatigue, and vomiting. Labs reveal a potassium level of 6.1 mEq/L and a sodium level of 128 mEq/l. Which of the following should the nurse anticipate for this client?
    1. administration of IV spironolactone
    2. boluses of Lactated Ringer's to increase blood pressure
    3. administration of IV saline, dextrose, or hydrocortisone
    4. boluses of 0.45% normal saline with 40 mEq/L of potassium

112. The nurse is caring for a client who is on 2 L/minute of oxygen via nasal cannula. The nurse understands that this flow rate corresponds to which FiO2?
    1. 24% FiO2
    2. 28% FiO2
    3. 32% FiO2
    4. 36% FiO2

113. A nurse is providing pre-op teaching to a client who will be undergoing a coronary artery bypass graft. Which of the following should the nurse include in the teaching? Select all that apply.
    1. "Your medications will be changed after surgery."
    2. "You will be on strict bed rest for the first 48 hours."
    3. "You will be using a bedpan after surgery to urinate."
    4. "You will need to splint the chest incision when you cough or breathe deeply."
    5. "You will be on the ventilator after surgery and have one or more chest tubes."

114. The nurse is caring for a client with vitamin B12 deficiency anemia. Which physical assessment finding would the nurse expect to note in this client?
    1. glossitis
    2. paresthesias
    3. weakness and pallor
    4. dark purple or cyanotic skin on the face and mucous membranes

115. The nurse is caring for a client in the cardiac unit who has a systolic murmur. Which assessment finding would the nurse expect when auscultating this client's heart sounds?
    1. The murmur can be heard between S3 and S4.
    2. The murmur can be heard between S4 and S1.
    3. The murmur can be heard between S2 and S1.
    4. The murmur can be heard between S1 and S2.

116. A student nurse is precepting on the cardiac unit with the charge nurse. The charge nurse is educating the student about heart sounds and asks the student nurse to describe what causes the S1 sound. Which response by the student nurse reflects an understanding of cardiac sounds?
    1. "It is caused by the mitral and tricuspid valves closing."
    2. "It is caused by the mitral and pulmonic valves closing."
    3. "It is caused by the pulmonic and aortic valves closing."
    4. "It is caused by the aortic and tricuspid valves closing."

117. The nurse is seeing a client in the clinic who complains of a sore throat. The client asks for an antibiotic. How should the nurse respond? Select all that apply.
    1. "You can try gargling with warm saline to relieve the discomfort."
    2. "You should use a dehumidifier to dry out the air, which will soothe the throat."
    3. "Most sore throats are caused by viruses, which cannot be treated with antibiotics."
    4. "There are three or four antibiotics that we prescribe for a sore throat, so the doctor will decide which one you need."
    5. "You should increase your fluid intake. Drink lots of water and try warm soup to help with the discomfort."

118. A client with third- and fourth-degree burns is in the burn unit. The nurse understands that which of the following is true regarding fluid shift in burn clients?

    1. The fluid shift can cause hypokalemia and hypovolemia.
    2. Hemoconcentration increases blood flow and reduces blood viscosity.
    3. Excessive weight loss can occur during the first 12 hours post burn due to the fluid shift.
    4. Severe edema can occur in areas that were not burned, due to the leakage of electrolytes and fluids from the vascular space.

119. A client is 2 hours post-op for a right total knee replacement. Upon assessment by the nurse, which information requires notification of the doctor?

    1. hemoglobin is 10.2 grams per liter
    2. bleeding on the dressing of 2 cm
    3. oral temperature of 100.4°F
    4. complaint of pain at incision site

120. A client is brought to the ED following a drowning event. The nurse assigned to the client understands that which is true regarding drowning?

    1. Drowning in very cold water causes a worse outcome for the client than drowning in warmer water.
    2. Aspiration of both salt and fresh water increases surfactant in the lungs and leads to increased lung compliance.
    3. If possible, the cause of drowning should be determined in order to know if the client suffered a medical condition such as a seizure that requires follow-up treatment.
    4. Contaminants in the water such as microbes, mud, chemicals, and algae do not affect the degree of injury to the lungs.

121. The nurse is caring for a client in ICU diagnosed with rabies following a bite from an infected raccoon. The nurse understands which to be true regarding rabies? Select all that apply.

    1. The client should not be bathed, and no running water should be present within hearing of the client.
    2. Current treatment includes two doses of immunoglobulin and six doses of rabies vaccine over a period of 21 days.
    3. Nuchal rigidity, convulsions, and tonic or clonic muscle contractions can occur during the neurological phase.
    4. In the prodromal phase, the client can have irritability, extreme salivation, sore throat, fever, and hyperexcitability.
    5. During the neurological phase, the client may have aches and pains in different parts of the body, along with sensitivity to light.
    6. During the paralytic phase, the client becomes unconscious, has loss of bowel and urinary control, and has irregular or labored breathing.

122. The nurse is caring for a client who had a basilar artery stroke. The nurse would expect which signs and symptoms in this client?
    1. memory problems, visual hallucinations, visual deficits, hemisensory disturbances
    2. weakness in the foot and leg, sensory loss in the foot and leg, incontinence, ataxia, lack of spontaneity
    3. impaired consciousness, visual loss, bilateral sensory and motor dysfunction, and pupil abnormalities
    4. ataxia, contralateral facial weakness, contralateral hemiplegia, visual deficits, speech impairments, perceptual impairments

123. A client presents to the ED with complaints of sweating, heart palpitations, vertigo, and the urge to lay down shortly after eating. The nurse anticipates which diagnosis for this client?
    1. appendicitis
    2. cholecystitis
    3. ulcerative colitis
    4. dumping syndrome

124. The oncology nurse is assessing a client diagnosed with cancer of the tongue. Upon examination, which signs and symptoms would the nurse expect to find? Select all that apply.
    1. weight gain
    2. well-fitting dentures
    3. a black, hairy tongue
    4. difficulty swallowing
    5. a sore that bleeds or does not heal
    6. difficulty chewing or pain with chewing

125. The nurse is caring for a 52-year-old African American male newly diagnosed with hypertension. He has a history of chronic kidney disease and diabetes. The nurse would expect to see which medication order for this client?
    1. enalapril 5 mg PO QD
    2. enalapril 5 mg PO QD and amiloride 5 mg PO QD
    3. enalapril 5 mg PO QD and atenolol 50 mg PO QD
    4. enalapril 5 mg PO QD and amlodipine 2.5 mg PO QD

126. Which assessment finding in a client with chronic kidney disease indicates late-stage symptoms?
    1. shortness of breath
    2. oliguria
    3. tea-colored urine
    4. edema in lower extremities

127. The nurse is performing discharge teaching to a client diagnosed with chronic pancreatitis. Which statement by the client indicates an understanding of home management of the condition? Select all that apply.

    1. "I should avoid large, heavy meals."
    2. "I can have an occasional glass of red wine."
    3. "I can resume my daily jogging once I get home."
    4. "I should avoid smoking and caffeinated beverages."
    5. "I should add extra spices to my food to make it taste better."

128. The nurse is caring for a client with suspected connective tissue disease. Assessment findings include chronic back pain, weight loss, joint pain and itching, and visual disturbances. The nurse anticipates a diagnosis of which disorder for this client?

    1. Reiter syndrome
    2. Marfan syndrome
    3. ankylosing spondylitis
    4. systemic necrotizing vasculitis

129. The ED nurse has admitted a client who is homeless and was found unresponsive in the street during below freezing temperatures. The client is diagnosed with severe hypothermia. The nurse should implement which measures for this client? Select all that apply.

    1. apply a heating blanket
    2. obtain an oral temperature
    3. assess level of consciousness
    4. position in the supine position
    5. massage the extremities vigorously
    6. prepare to administer CPR if indicated

130. A client has arterial blood gases drawn. The results are as follows: pH, 7.58; PaCO2, 48 mm Hg; HCO3, 44 mEq/L, Base Excess, +13 mEq/L. Which condition is indicated?

    1. respiratory alkalosis
    2. respiratory acidosis
    3. metabolic alkalosis
    4. metabolic acidosis

131. The nurse is assessing a client with Parkinson's disease. Which sign of primary motor symptom involvement would the nurse expect to observe?

    1. resting tremor
    2. sleep disturbance
    3. constipation
    4. fatigue

132. A nurse is reviewing the laboratory reports prior to physician rounds. The serum calcium level of a client with hyperparathyroidism is 14.6 mg/dl. Which treatment should the nurse anticipate?

    1. corticosteroids
    2. renal dialysis
    3. calcitonin
    4. intravenous bisphosphonates

133. A nurse is employed on an oncology unit. A 62-year-old client is admitted for surgical treatment of a meningioma. The nurse would anticipate modifying the environment for which symptom?

    1. difficulty swallowing
    2. seizures
    3. poor concentration
    4. impaired mobility

134. A client presents to the emergency room with severe pain in the upper right abdomen. The client is nauseated and has a temperature of 102.2°F. Which nursing action would be a priority at this time?

    1. relieve pain
    2. obtain vital signs
    3. administer IV fluids
    4. prepare for surgery

135. The nurse is preparing to administer cefazolin to a client who is allergic to penicillin. The client states that penicillin causes him to itch and be slightly short of breath. Which response by the nurse is correct?

    1. administer the cefazolin as ordered
    2. call the pharmacy to substitute another medication
    3. hold the medication and notify the health care provider
    4. give the client diphenhydramine and then administer the cefazolin

136. The nurse is caring for a client who has shortness of breath, +2 pitting edema bilaterally of the lower extremities, crackles in the bases of the lungs, and a weight gain of 7 pounds in 1 week. The nurse administers furosemide 40 mg IV as ordered. Which would the nurse anticipate to indicate that the furosemide was effective? Select all that apply.

    1. pitting edema of +3
    2. pitting edema of +1
    3. less shortness of breath
    4. an increase in urine output of 250 mL/hr
    5. a decrease or absence of crackles in the lungs

137. The nurse is caring for a client with left-sided heart failure. Which assessment findings does the nurse anticipate for this client? Select all that apply.
    1. dyspnea
    2. engorged spleen
    3. dependent edema
    4. jugular vein distention
    5. weak peripheral pulses
    6. crackles or wheezes in the lungs

138. The nurse is providing teaching to a client newly diagnosed with type 2 diabetes. Which should the nurse include in her teaching?
    1. check the feet daily
    2. have eye examinations every 2 years
    3. use a heating pad to keep the feet warm
    4. take extra insulin before consuming sweets

139. The nurse is caring for a two-year-old client who presented to the ER with vomiting, currant jelly-like stools, and abdominal pain that causes the child to draw the knees up to the abdomen in a fetal position. Which interventions does the nurse anticipate for this client?
    1. assessing for respiratory distress
    2. orders for a soft diet as tolerated
    3. monitoring for a normal, brown stool
    4. preparing the client for a barium enema
    5. placement of a nasogastric (NG) tube
    6. monitoring for fever and changes in blood pressure

140. The nurse is assessing a client with Parkinson's disease. Which sign of primary motor symptom involvement would the nurse expect to observe?
    1. resting tremor
    2. sleep disturbance
    3. constipation
    4. fatigue

141. A nurse is reviewing the laboratory reports prior to physician rounds. The serum calcium level of a client with hyperparathyroidism is 14.6 mg/dl. Which treatment should the nurse anticipate?
    1. corticosteroids
    2. renal dialysis
    3. calcitonin
    4. intravenous bisphosphonates

142. The nurse is caring for a client with an infected leg wound. The client develops a fever of 102°F. Which action by the nurse is the priority for this client?

1. obtain a wound culture
2. administer acetaminophen
3. administer IV antibiotic as scheduled
4. perform the scheduled dressing change

143. A nurse must record daily liquid intake and output for a client with heart failure. The daily liquid intake includes 16 ounces of water, 12 ounces of apple juice, 1 pint of strawberry ice cream, and 0.75 L of normal saline IV. What would the nurse chart as daily intake in milliliters? Calculate and fill in the blank.

_____

144. The nurse is charting on his client, who had an open appendectomy the previous day. Which are appropriate nursing documentation entries? Select all that apply.

1. The client appeared anxious when several family members came to visit.
2. The client appeared angry when the health care provider changed her medications.
3. The client tolerated 80% of the lunch tray with no complaints of nausea or stomach cramping.
4. The abdominal dressing is clean, dry, and intact with a 3-cm area of light staining noted in the center.
5. The client ambulated 200 feet in the hall with a cane. No dyspnea or syncope noticed. Tolerated well.

145. A nurse is preparing a sterile field for a client who is having a central venous catheter placed for IV therapy. Which action reflects a break in the sterile field?

1. The nurse uses sterile gloves to place objects on the sterile field.
2. The nurse stays near the sterile field at all times without turning away from it.
3. The nurse removes a sterile syringe from the sterile field using clean gloves but does not touch the sterile field itself.
4. The nurse opens a syringe, carefully peeling the wrapper away from the syringe without touching it so that it can be removed by a clinician wearing sterile gloves.

146. The nurse is caring for a client who had an inguinal hernia repair. Which interventions by the nurse are appropriate for this client? Select all that apply.

1. encouraging fluid intake
2. relieving urinary retention
3. applying heat to the scrotum
4. teaching turning, coughing, and deep breathing
5. keeping the client on bed rest for the first 12 hours after surgery
6. teaching the client to avoid lifting more than 20 pounds until approved by the health care provider

147. The nurse is caring for a client with influenza. Which precautions would the nurse expect to be in place for this client?

1. contact
2. droplet
3. airborne
4. protective environment

148. The nurse is caring for a client with veno-occlusive disease. Which manifestations of this condition would the nurse expect to find? Select all that apply.

1. jaundice
2. weight loss
3. weight gain
4. right lower quadrant pain
5. enlargement of the spleen
6. right upper quadrant pain

149. The nurse is preparing to remove a client's abdominal stitches as ordered by the health care provider. Which is the correct action by the nurse?

1. clean the stitches with soap and water before removing
2. wash the hands and use gloves while removing the stitches
3. wash the hands and use sterile technique when removing the stitches
4. wear a gown, gloves, a mask, an eye shield, and shoe covers during the procedure

150. The ED nurse receives a client who is bleeding profusely from a gunshot wound. Which action by the nurse will best help this client avoid complications of extreme blood loss?

1. draw a type and match
2. administer type O blood
3. administer type AB+ blood
4. ask the family to donate blood

151. A 13-year-old female has been diagnosed with celiac disease. Which of the following dinner trays would be acceptable?

1. baked chicken breast, carrots, baked potato with cheese
2. turkey and cheese sandwich on wheat bread, cabbage slaw, apple slices
3. spaghetti with meatballs, Caesar salad, banana
4. pulled pork on flour tortillas, wild rice, black beans

152. The nurse is caring for a client admitted to ICU following a heart attack. The nurse notes on the chart that the client has named his spouse to make decisions regarding his care if he is unable to speak for himself. What is the name of the document the client has signed? Fill in the blank.

_____

153. The nurse is conducting a health fair at a local high school on reducing high-risk behaviors. Which teaching should the nurse include in the presentation? Select all that apply.

1. Always buckle up, even for a short trip.
2. Use approved bike helmets for bike riding.
3. Do not drive for one hour after drinking alcohol.
4. Condoms offer full protection against sexually transmitted infections.
5. Dive into untested waters with the hands fully extended over the head.

154. A student nurse overhears her instructor using the term pink puffer. The student knows this term refers to a client with which condition?

1. chronic bronchitis
2. chronic obstructive pulmonary disease (COPD)
3. emphysema
4. allergic asthma

155. A public health nurse works with a specific population. Many of the clients use herbal remedies at home. The nurse would express concern if which of the following clients reported using herbal remedies?

1. 13-year-old girl with a toothache
2. 42-year-old man with xerostomia
3. 59-year-old woman with nasopharyngitis
4. 20-year-old woman with psoriasis

156. According to Maslow's hierarchy of needs, "lack of prejudice" falls under which level of human need fulfillment?

1. love and belonging
2. self-actualization
3. safety
4. esteem

157. The client has a nitroprusside drip infusing at 0.3 mcg/kg/min. The concentration is 50 mg nitroprusside in 250 mL D5W. The client weighs 70 kg. What will the IV infusion rate be?

_____

In questions 158 – 161, identify each intramuscular injection site on the diagram using the corresponding letter.

158. deltoid muscle

159. ventrogluteal muscle

160. dorsogluteal muscle

161. vastus lateralis muscle

162. The nurse is caring for a client receiving TPN. The nurse understands that TPN management includes which of the following? Select all that apply.
  1. monitor daily weights and intake and output
  2. monitor serum electrolytes and glucose levels daily
  3. change IV tubing every 48 hours or per facility protocol
  4. change the IV site dressing every 24 hours or per facility protocol
  5. if TPN is unavailable, OK to give D10W or D20W until TPN becomes available

163. The nurse is preparing to hang a unit of blood on a client. The blood has been checked off with two RNs and the pre-infusion vitals recorded. The nurse is at the bedside monitoring the infusion. Shortly after beginning the infusion, the pump alarm sounds. The IV has infiltrated. No blood has yet reached the client. The client is a hard stick, and the nurse realizes that a line cannot be placed within the time frame to begin the infusion. Which action by the nurse is correct?
    1. return the blood and the tubing to the blood bank for storage until an IV can be placed
    2. place the blood bag and tubing in the medication refrigerator until an IV can be restarted
    3. cancel the order for blood and notify the health care provider that the client has no access
    4. wait until 30 minutes has passed while IV placement is attempted, and then waste the blood and chart it as expired
    5. return the blood to the blood bank and notify the next shift when they arrive that they need to start an IV and administer the blood

164. A student nurse is preparing to administer the client's first dose of tetracycline while the charge nurse observes. What statement by the student nurse prompts the charge nurse to provide further teaching? Select all that apply.
    1. "Tetracycline may be given with grapefruit juice."
    2. "After taking tetracycline, the client should wait two hours before eating."
    3. "It should be given with caution in clients with liver or renal dysfunction."
    4. "The client may have an antacid along with the tetracycline if it causes GI upset."
    5. "It should be taken on an empty stomach at least one hour before meals with a glass of milk."

165. The nurse has an order to give 500 mL of 0.45% NS over 12 hours. The IV set has a drop factor of 10. How many gtts/min should the client receive? Fill in the blank.

    _____

166. The nurse is assisting the health care provider to perform a renal biopsy. Which position should the nurse place the client in?
    1. in the semi-Fowler's position
    2. on the same side of the kidney to be biopsied
    3. on the side opposite of the kidney to be biopsied
    4. prone with a pillow under the shoulders and abdomen

167. The charge nurse in a cardiac ICU is precepting a student nurse. Which action by the student nurse requires immediate intervention by the charge nurse?

1. The student nurse stops the tube feeding to measure residual.
2. The student nurse lifts the urinary catheter bag up and over the client while turning her.
3. The student nurse scans the client armband and the medication barcode when administering medication.
4. The student nurse observes two other nurses verifying and administering blood to the client while the student nurse records the vital signs just prior to administration.

168. The client has an order for Claforan 665 mg. The directions say to reconstitute with 10 mL of bacteriostatic water to yield a concentration of 95 mg/mL. How many milliliters of solution should the nurse administer to give the dose of 665 mg?

_____

169. A new nurse has just completed orientation and is working on the medical unit. The new nurse is shadowing the charge nurse as they both care for a client with a potassium level of 6.3 mEq/L. Which action by the new nurse requires intervention by the charge nurse?

1. The nurse prepares to administer spironolactone (Aldactone) 25 mg PO.
2. The nurse delivers the client's morning meal tray for a low-potassium diet.
3. The nurse administers sodium polystyrene sulfonate (Kayexalate) 15 g PO.
4. The nurse teaches the client the importance of ambulating, coughing, and deep-breathing.

170. The nurse is precepting a student nurse who is helping to care for a client with a hip fracture. The client has Buck's traction applied. Which statement by the student nurse indicates a need for further explanation by the primary nurse?

1. "The weight on Buck's traction should be between 5 and 7 pounds."
2. "Buck's traction is a type of skeletal traction that helps in bone realignment."
3. "The weights should hang freely and be checked regularly for correct positioning."
4. "Diligent pin site care is crucial to prevent infection in clients with skeletal traction."

171. A client is receiving patient-controlled analgesia following surgery. Which statement by a family member indicates that the nurse needs to do further teaching?

1. "We will call you if the pump starts beeping."
2. "We will call you if she becomes oversedated."
3. "Nausea is not an allergic reaction to the medication."
4. "If she is asleep, we will press the button for her so she won't wake up in pain."

172. The nurse is observing a student nurse administer a client's medications via a nasogastric (NG) tube. The nurse understands that the student nurse needs further teach if the student nurse performs which action?

1. aspirates and checks the residual
2. places client in the semi-Fowler's position
3. verifies that the medications may be given via NG tube
4. stops the tube feeding before medication administration
5. flushes tubing with 15 – 30 cc of water after administering meds

173. The nurse is caring for a client who was admitted for chest pain. The client is oriented to person and place, but is often confused about the month of the year or what season it is. A family member tells the nurse, "I'd like for you to sign as a witness on my mother's living will, in case something happens to her and we need to make health care decisions for her." Which is the best response by the nurse?

1. "Let me have a copy so my attorney can look at it."
2. "My unit manager will need to come witness with me."
3. "Do you think your mother understands what is going on right now?"
4. "I'm sorry, but it is against policy for staff members to witness client forms."

174. A 19-year-old male with type 1 diabetes has the flu. The nurse expects what insulin changes may be required during the illness?

1. stopping all insulin
2. needing more insulin
3. needing less insulin
4. using the same amount of insulin

175. The nurse is doing hourly rounds when he finds a 73-year-old female client unconscious on the floor next to the bed. An incident report must be filled out. What is the best statement for the nurse to write on the incident report?

1. "Client fell out of bed at some point between 0700 and 0800."
2. "Client was found unresponsive on floor next to the bed."
3. "Client likely slipped on the floor and hit her head."
4. "Client attempted to ambulate without assistance and fell."

176. Raynaud's disease is most commonly found in

1. children under 10.
2. middle-aged males.
3. adults over the age of 65.
4. young women.

177. After a discharge, there is a private room available on the floor. The nurse should move which client to the private room?

1. a 28-year-old female with Cushing's disease
2. a 15-year-old male with pityriasis rosea
3. a 56-year-old male with diabetes mellitus
4. a 40-year-old male with heterochromia iridium

178. A nurse from the dialysis unit floats to the med-surg floor. He is doing afternoon rounds and medication administration. He brings a client her oral medications, but the client states, "What is this? Where is my yellow pill? This big white one is not mine." The best action from the nurse is to

1. take the medication out of the room and verify with the MAR and pharmacy.
2. explain to the client this is the correct prescribed medication she is ordered.
3. report to the nursing supervisor there has been a medication error.
4. explain to the client that sometimes medication comes from other manufacturers and the pills may look different.

179. A client diagnosed with hemophagocytic lymphohistiocytosis requires multiple blood transfusions. One of his family members wishes to donate blood. Which of the following conditions would DISQUALIFY someone from donating blood?

1. current medical condition of hyperthyroidism
2. new mother, 10 weeks postpartum
3. currently ill with common cold
4. past medical history of tuberculosis; completed treatment and recovered 3 years ago

180. The nurse is caring for a client who has a nasogastric tube for medication administration and tube feedings. How should the nurse care for the tube during her shift? Select all that apply.

1. flush tube every 4 hours with hot water to maintain patency
2. allow the feeding and tubing to hang until empty, up to 48 hours
3. maintain the head of bed in a high-Fowler's position during feedings
4. check residuals and replace them unless the amount is greater than 300 mL
5. check under the adhesive tape on the nose daily to assess for skin breakdown
6. assess the bowel sounds before feeding, and feed at half the rate if bowel sounds are absent

181. The nurse is caring for a group of clients in a medical/surgical unit. Which client does the nurse understand to be at highest risk for developing decubitus ulcers?

1. a 27-year-old client who fractured her arm playing volleyball
2. a 6-year-old client on pelvic skin traction for muscle spasms
3. a 42-year-old obese client with controlled atrial fibrillation who uses a wheelchair
4. a 70-year-old client with heart failure who uses a cane for ambulation in the room and hall

182. The nurse is reviewing a client's morning medication orders. Which of the following orders would prompt the nurse to call the health care provider for order clarification?
1. famotidine 20 mg PO BID
2. haloperidol 15 mg IM q4h prn
3. lithium carbonate 300 mg PO TID
4. amoxicillin 500 mg PO q12h × 7 days

183. A client with hypertension asks the nurse to explain how amlodipine besylate (Norvasc) lowers her blood pressure. The nurse gives which explanation to the client?
1. "It prevents calcium from entering the smooth muscle, which relaxes the blood vessels to lower heart rate and blood pressure."
2. "It is a diuretic that works by removing extra sodium and water from the body through the kidneys, which helps lower blood pressure."
3. "It causes the body to produce less angiotensin, which allows blood vessels to relax and open up, therefore reducing blood pressure."
4. "It lowers blood pressure by lowering the heart rate and the workload of the heart, and decreases the amount of blood pumped out of the heart."

184. The nurse is caring for a client who is taking bethanechol chloride (Urecholine) for neurogenic bladder. Which of the following does the nurse understand is correct concerning this medication?
1. This is the primary treatment for clients with a urinary obstruction.
2. If the client cannot swallow pills, the medication may be given by the IV or IM route.
3. Urecholine should be given with food to prevent nausea and vomiting.
4. Atropine sulfate should be readily available when a client receives this medication.

185. The nurse is caring for a client taking sulfonamides to treat a urinary tract infection. Which of the following should the nurse monitor for in this client? Select all that apply.
1. fever or sore throat
2. reddish-pink urine
3. side effects such as dyspnea, chest pains, chills, and cough
4. urinary output of 1200 mL daily to minimize the risk of renal damage
5. the need to decrease the dosage if the client takes warfarin sodium (Coumadin) or phenytoin (Dilantin)

186. The nurse is caring for a client with a staph infection. The client has orders for vancomycin 15 mg/kg per 12 hours. The client weighs 136 pounds. How much of this medication will the client receive every 12 hours?

_____

187. The nurse is caring for a client taking vancomycin. The nurse anticipates drawing a peak and trough on this client. Which statement regarding peak and trough levels is correct?
    1. The peak is drawn 1 hour after the infusion, and the trough is drawn right before the next scheduled dose.
    2. The peak is drawn 2 hours after the infusion, and the trough is drawn 1 hour before the next scheduled dose.
    3. The peak should be drawn immediately after infusion, and the trough is drawn right before the next scheduled dose.
    4. The peak should be drawn 30 minutes before the next scheduled dose, and the trough drawn immediately after the infusion.

188. The nurse is caring for a client diagnosed with tuberculosis. The physician plans to treat the client with a first-line medication. Which medication should the nurse prepare to administer?
    1. rifampin
    2. ciprofloxacin
    3. levofloxacin
    4. streptomycin

189. The nurse is caring for a client who complains of a headache with a pain level of 5 on a scale of 1 to 10. Which PRN pain medication order is most appropriate for the nurse to administer?
    1. morphine 2 mg IV q6h PRN
    2. aspirin 325 mg PO q6h PRN
    3. acetaminophen 650 mg PO q6h PRN
    4. nitroglycerin 0.4 mg sublingually every 5 minutes, up to 3 doses over 15 minutes

190. While preparing a client for a colonoscopy, the nurse would be correct to implement which interventions? Select all that apply.
    1. instruction on high fiber diet the day before the procedure
    2. instruction that a sedative will be administered before the procedure
    3. instruction not to eat or drink 6 – 12 hours before the procedure
    4. instruction not to eat or drink 18 hours before the procedure

191. A nurse is following the progress of a client being treated for hypothyroidism. Which findings indicate the client is experiencing side effects of the thyroid replacement therapy? Select all that apply.
    1. excessive sweating
    2. constipation
    3. inability to tolerate cold
    4. leg cramps

192. The nurse is preparing the client for surgery. The pre-op medication includes atropine sulfate 0.4 mg, meperidine (Demerol HCl) 50 mg, and promethazine hydrochloride (Phenergan) 25 mg IM. Which action should the nurse do first?
    1. make sure the surgical permit is signed
    2. ask the client to go to the bathroom
    3. explain the purpose of the medication to the client
    4. ask family members to exit the room

193. A nurse is preparing to administer IV Rocephin for infection to a client. The client has a central venous line infusing blood but no other IV access. The blood still has 30 minutes left to infuse. The Rocephin is due now. How should the nurse proceed?
    1. hold the Rocephin since it will be too late to give it after the blood completes infusing
    2. draw up the Rocephin in a syringe after reconstitution and inject it into the blood bag so it can infuse with the blood
    3. stop the blood, flush the line with 0.9% NS, administer the Rocephin, and then flush the line with the NS before restarting blood
    4. allow the blood to finish infusing before giving Rocephin; the Rocephin will be administered during an acceptable time frame for "on time" administration

194. The nurse is preparing to discharge a client with an ileal conduit done for treatment of bladder cancer. Which statement by the client indicates the need for further instruction?
    1. "I look forward to returning to my local health club to swim."
    2. "The local ostomy support group meets on Wednesday morning at 10 a.m."
    3. "My stoma should be cleaned daily with soap and water."
    4. "During the day I will wear a leg bag to collect my urine."

195. The nurse is caring for a client with a sacral wound. The wound is full thickness, measures 4 cm × 6 cm with irregular borders, and is covered by a layer of black collagen. Which is this wound stage?
    1. Stage I
    2. Stage II
    3. Stage III
    4. unstageable

196. Which diagnostic tool is most commonly used to determine the location of the myocardial damage?
    1. electrocardiogram (ECG)
    2. echocardiogram
    3. cardiac enzymes
    4. cardiac catheterization

197. A nurse is caring for a client in the immediate post–cardiac catheterization period. Which intervention should the nurse include in the client's care?

1. monitor vital signs every 30 minutes for the first 2 hours
2. assess the insertion site
3. maintain the client in a prone position
4. keep the client NPO for 2 hours

198. The nurse is preparing to administer metoprolol (Lopressor) to a new client. Which of the following actions by the nurse are correct? Select all that apply.

1. hold for a heart rate greater than 80 bpm
2. check the client's blood pressure and apical pulse
3. check the client's allergies before giving any medications
4. verify the client's identity using two patient identifiers
5. tell the client not to take the medication with grapefruit juice

199. The nurse is caring for clients on a medical-surgical floor. Which tasks related to pain management can be delegated to unlicensed assistive personnel (UAP)? Select all that apply.

1. assessing the pain level on a scale of 1 – 10
2. reminding clients to report pain immediately
3. reporting facial grimacing in unresponsive clients
4. asking clients directly, "Are you having any pain right now?"
5. giving acetaminophen (Tylenol) after the nurse obtains the medication but is interrupted to attend a code blue before she administers it

200. The nurse is precepting a student nurse on the medical-surgical unit. The student nurse is preparing to administer insulin. Which action by the student nurse calls for immediate intervention?

1. The student nurse verifies the insulin dose with another nurse.
2. The student nurse draws up regular insulin to be given intravenously.
3. The student nurse draws up intermediate-acting (NPH) insulin, and then regular insulin.
4. The student nurse draws up regular insulin, and then intermediate-acting (NPH) insulin.

PRACTICE TEST THREE ANSWER KEY

1. Number 3 is correct.

Rationale: The client should be placed in the Trendelenburg position with the head turned left. This position will reduce the risk of an air embolism and allow the physician best access to the vein. High-Fowler's places the patient at 90 degrees, Trendelenburg places the patient with the head lower than the body, and supine places the patient flat on the bed. These positions do not optimize central venous placement.

2. Number 3 is correct.

Rationale: Therapeutic hypothermia is used after an MI as a method to reduce injury to the brain. Hypothermia slows the brain's oxygen demand by lowering metabolism, and it reduces the production of free radicals and neurotransmitters.

3. Number 2 is correct.

Rationale: Intracranial pressure can increase with suctioning or repositioning the client, and a temporary jump in ICP is expected in these situations. If the ICP returns to normal, no further intervention is needed, and the nurse should chart the findings and continue to monitor the client.

4. Number 4 is correct.

Rationale: In an emergency situation, where there is no time to cross-match blood type, a client can be given a blood type O negative transfusion. O negative is considered a universal blood type and can be received by anyone. It is optimal for emergency situations. The other blood types could cause an ABO incompatibility reaction.

5. Number 4 is correct.

Rationale: Insulin lipodystrophy can occur if insulin is injected repeatedly into the same area of skin. This leads to formations of fat deposit that can cause unpredictable absorption of insulin at the site. While localized edema can occur at the injection site, this is not harmful and will quickly resolve. Tissue scarring will not occur in fatty tissue. Insulin resistance is a precursor to the development of type 2 diabetes.

6. Number 3 is correct.

Solution:

2,000 units × 1 mL/5,000 units = 0.4 mL	Find the milliliters of heparin 5,000 units/mL the client will require per dose.
0.4ml × 3 doses/day **= 1.2 mL/ day**	Multiply the volume of the dose by 3 to find the amount administered in 24 hours. (Administering a dose every 8 hours equals three doses in a 24-hour period.)

7. Number 3 is correct.

Rationale: Premenopausal women should conduct self-breast exams immediately after their menstrual cycle ends because this is the time the breasts are least tender. If a woman is prone to fibrocystic breast changes, they will be less pronounced immediately after menses.

8. Number 4 is correct.

Rationale: Hand washing is the most effective intervention for breaking the chain of infection. While barriers such as a gown, gloves, and mask might help in preventing transmission, hand washing is the first and most effective step to medical asepsis. Unless the patient is compromised or undergoing certain procedures, antibiotics are generally not indicated and may cause long-term resistance to antibiotics. A private room is not always feasible and hand washing is still indicated.

9. Number 1 is correct.

   Rationale: Magnesium sulfate is a CNS depressant and can cause marked bradycardia and respiratory depression. The nursing priority is to monitor the client's vital signs for CNS depression after this drug is administered. Tachycardia and hyperventilation are not side effects of magnesium sulfate. A Swan catheter and synchronized cardioversion are not indicated.

10. Number 1 is correct.

    Rationale: A thyroid storm is a life-threatening complication of hyperthyroidism seen in clients with Graves' disease. Signs and symptoms may include seizures, jaundice, irregular heartbeat, and vomiting. Agitation, dehydration, and heart failure may also be seen. The other answer groups are not specific to Graves' disease.

11. Number 4 is correct.

    Rationale: Relieving pain is the most immediate need for management. Preventing fluid volume deficit by infusion of IV fluids should occur once the client has experienced initial control of pain. Administration of antibiotic therapy will be important during the recovery phase. Reducing anxiety is important and will be partially addressed with the reduction of pain.

12. Number 2 is correct.

    Rationale: Acute diverticulitis results from inflammation of the diverticula, typically from an infection. As such, the priority treatment is administration of antibiotics to address the root cause of the condition. Gradually increasing fiber in the diet will occur during the recovery stage of the disease. Pain medication for residual pain would be a second management approach after initiation of antibiotic protocol. To promote rest of the intestinal tract, a liquid diet is advisable for an undeterminable time.

13. Number 2 is correct.

    Rationale: Malignant hyperthermia, not hypothermia, is a dangerous adverse reaction to certain drugs used in general anesthesia. Hypoglycemia and hyperglycemia could possibly be a concern if the patient has a diagnosis such as diabetes, but both would be addressed preoperatively.

14. Number 3 is correct.

    Rationale: Alzheimer's disease is a form of dementia that develops over time and gradually worsens. A client who initiates the same conversation repeatedly, displays aggression when stressed, and becomes easily lost in familiar places is showing signs consistent with the moderate stage of Alzheimer's disease. A client with pre-Alzheimer's would not have changes in function. Early and mild Alzheimer's is characterized by memory lapses but no changes in medical function that reflect dementia. Late to severe Alzheimer's is reflected by medical deficiencies such as incontinence, abnormal reflexes, and rigidity.

15. Number 3 is correct.

    Rationale: Increased risk factors for HIT include being female and heparin use as postsurgical thromboprophylaxis. HIT is more common in clients who have been on unfractionated heparin or who have used heparin for longer than 1 week. Enoxaparin is a low-molecular weight heparin, which carries a lower risk of developing HIT. It is often prescribed for clients with unstable angina to help increase blood flow through the heart.

16. Number 3 is correct.

    Rationale: A pneumothorax is one of the complications of TPN. It is caused by improper central catheter placement or by a catheter that has migrated. Absence of breath sounds on the affected side, chest or shoulder pain, tachycardia, cyanosis, and sudden shortness of breath are indications of pneumothorax.

The nurse should notify the health care provider and prepare the client for a portable chest X-ray. An air embolism is another complication of TPN. Signs and symptoms of air embolism include respiratory distress; a weak, rapid pulse; chest pain; dyspnea; hypotension; and a loud churning sound auscultated over the pericardium. Fluid overload would not present as absence of breath sounds; instead, expected findings include hypertension, bounding pulses, increased respiratory rate, distended veins in the hands and neck, and moist crackles. Signs of refeeding syndrome include arrhythmias, vomiting, shortness of breath, weakness, ataxia, and seizures. It occurs in severely malnourished clients who are undergoing nutritional replacement therapy.

17. Number 4 is correct.

    Rationale: If the client is eating and tolerating meals, the nurse should ask the health care provider if the client can take the medication in PO form. The oral form is more convenient for the client and lessens the need to repeatedly access the IV, which increases the risk of infection. If the health care provider declines to change the form of the medication, the nurse would then contact the pharmacy for the missing medication. The nurse should not hold medication without notifying the health care provider, nor should the nurse administer medication in a form different from what was ordered.

18. Number 4 is correct.

    Rationale: Total parenteral nutrition (TPN) is high in dextrose, and if it is suddenly stopped, the client can become hypoglycemic. The patient could also be dehydrated, but the priority would be blood glucose control.

19. Number 3 is correct.

    Rationale: Myasthenia gravis is an autoimmune disease in which antibodies destroy acetylcholine at the neuromuscular junction, causing muscles to be unable to contract normally. The muscles become weak and fatigued. While muscle wasting can occur in severe instances, it is not indicative of the condition. The brain and spinal cord are not damaged from myasthenia gravis.

20. Numbers 3 and 4 are correct.

    Rationale: Daily weight provides information about fluid balance and effectiveness of the therapy regime. Corticosteroids taken on a short-term basis are known to reduce the inflammation associated with Crohn's disease. A high-fat diet may exacerbate the diarrhea associated with Crohn's disease. Lactulose would promote peristalsis and would be contraindicated.

21. Number 4 is correct.

    Rationale: A colposcopy is a painless gynecological procedure, usually done after an abnormal pap smear. The client is placed in a lithotomy position, and a colposcope is used to view the cervix with a bright light. The other positions do not offer the best position to facilitate the medical procedure.

22. Number 2 is correct.

    Rationale: Plaque psoriasis is a noncontagious skin disorder in which plaquey areas of inflammation and silvery-white patches of skin develop on the knees, elbows, scalp, and back. Scabies present as a pimple-like rash. Urticaria is also known as hives and presents as red skin with areas of red itchy welts. Contact dermatitis causes skin to be red and inflamed without silvery-white scales.

23. Number 2 is correct.

    Rationale: The client is working through feelings of shock, anger, and sadness. The most therapeutic response from the nurse is to sit quietly with the client until he calms down. The nurse should not leave the client alone. The nurse can ask if the client would like to see a chaplain or a counselor but should not assume his wishes, as he did not ask to speak with the chaplain. The nurse should wait for the client to express his own feelings and not tell the client how to feel about the situation.

24. Number 1 is correct.

Rationale: Pain is subjective and is always what the client states. Therefore, the nurse should chart "The client states his pain is 9/10." If the client mentions that he has a history of addiction, the information can be charted. With prior opioid addiction, clients may experience pain more intensely. Pain management should not be withheld and levels should not be questioned.

25. Number 2 is correct.

Rationale: The client will likely require treatment with immunoglobulin G (IgG) because it is the only immunoglobulin treatment able to cross the placental barrier.

26. Number 1 is correct.

Rationale: Normal sodium levels in an adult are between 135 and 145 mEq/L. Signs and symptoms of hyponatremia may include headache, confusion, muscle weakness, and fatigue. Seizures, loss of appetite, and irritability may also occur. The other symptom groups do not all fit with symptoms of hyponatremia.

27. Number 2 is correct.

Rationale: Calculating glomerular filtration rate is the best way to determine kidney function. It is calculated with a formula that considers a client's age, gender, race, and serum creatinine level. A GFR < 15 mL/min indicates stage 5, end-stage CKD. These clients require dialysis or kidney transplant for survival. A GFR of 15 to 29 indicates stage 4 kidney disease, and preparation for dialysis or transplant is usually indicated. Stages 1 – 3 of kidney disease are less severe and can often be managed with medication and lifestyle changes.

28. Number 4 is correct.

Rationale: Myoglobin, a small hemeprotein, becomes abnormal within 1 – 2 hours of myocardial infarction (MI). BUN and white blood cell levels do not provide relevant information when an MI is suspected. LDH, lactate dehydrogenase, will begin to rise 2 – 5 days after an MI.

29. Number 4 is correct.

Rationale: In a healthy adult the ICP is 5 – 15 mm Hg. Any pressure greater than 20 mm Hg after a head injury is abnormal.

30. Number 4 is correct.

Rationale: Phenytoin (Dilantin) may be given to a person experiencing seizures while undergoing withdrawal from alcohol. For a disturbed heart rate, lidocaine (Xylocaine) may be given. For hallucinations, Haldol (haloperidol) may be given. For drowsiness, the nurse would lessen the dosage of diazepam.

31. Number 2 is correct.

Rationale: Asking clients what works for them shows respect for their practices and beliefs. Some low-risk therapies that the client might try include music therapy, meditation, prayer, and relaxation techniques. For mild pain, distraction may be helpful to remove the focus from the pain. Once the nurse knows the client's preferences, the health care provider can be consulted as to which therapies may be ordered. The nurse should not recommend any herbs or supplements for pain. This constitutes practicing medicine without a license. Any medication the client takes, including over-the-counter medicines or supplements, must be ordered by the provider. Some herbal mixtures or supplements can be toxic, and there is no consistent standard for such products. The client has had anesthesia for the procedure, therefore increasing the risk of an interaction between anesthesia and an unknown substance. Telling the client that they only use "real" medicine in the hospital shows a lack of respect for the client and her beliefs and is insulting. The nurse should not insist on opioids or other medications if the client states that she does not want to take them. While yoga may help relieve stress and pain, a client who is newly post-op will not be able to perform such activities. The nurse is also pushing his own agenda by telling the client what works for him. The focus is on therapies that help the client, not the nurse.

32. Number 2 is correct.

    Rationale: The ELISA test is often the first test used for HIV screening. It can detect antibodies to HIV, and DNA/RNA of HIV in the blood. If the ELISA test is positive, further testing must be done, such as the Western blot test. Although false positives are rare, one positive ELISA test is not diagnostic of HIV. Because of possible HIPAA violation and the severity of the diagnosis, discussing HIV test results over the phone should not be done.

33. Number 4 is correct.

    Rationale: Smokers are two to three times more likely than nonsmokers to develop pancreatic cancer, and smoking is considered a major risk factor for developing the disease. Other risk factors include African American race, obesity, familial history, PMH of certain cancers (breast, lung, bladder, etc.), chronic pancreatitis, liver cirrhosis, and diabetes. Alcohol abuse is linked to an increased risk of pancreatic cancer; however two or fewer alcoholic beverages a week is considered social alcohol consumption.

34. Number 2 is correct.

    Rationale: The nurse should prioritize by first assessing for risks to airway, breathing, or circulation. The woman reporting jaw and back pain may be experiencing a myocardial infarction, which is a priority situation. While all of the other situations should be addressed, they should be triaged appropriately as they are not emergencies.

35. Number 4 is correct.

    Rationale: A client taking furosemide (Lasix) is at risk for hypokalemia, because this medication is a (potassium wasting) loop diuretic. Salmon, spinach, and bananas are all foods high in potassium. While the other foods are not harmful, they are not the most beneficial for replacing potassium in the body.

36. Number 1 is correct.

    Rationale: Prothrombin time is a measure of the clotting tendency of the blood. Since warfarin is an anticoagulant, this client is at an increased risk for hemorrhage. Clients who are taking warfarin and are in an emergency situation where they are actively bleeding can be given fresh frozen plasma to quickly reverse the effects of warfarin and reach homeostasis. Red blood cell transfusions are utilized to treat hemorrhage. Platelets are used to prevent hemorrhage in patients with thrombocytopenia or platelet function defects.

37. Number 1 is correct.

    Solution:

$\dfrac{1{,}000 \text{ units}}{250 \text{ mL}} = \dfrac{4 \text{ units}}{\text{mL}}$	Find the number of units of insulin per milliliter.
4 units/mL × 5 mL/hr = **20 units/hr**	Multiply the number of units per milliliter by the milliliters per hour to find the number of units administered per hour.

38. Number 2 is correct.

    Rationale: The 16-year-old female is not likely to survive her injuries. Fixed, dilated pupils, unresponsiveness, and probable severe head trauma are indicators of a very poor prognosis. Clients who are not expected to survive, even with treatment and intervention, are not the triage priority. Triage should prioritize critical clients who have a chance of survival if treated quickly, and then should see clients with less serious injuries.

39. Number 4 is correct.

Rationale: All of the interventions listed are important during a sickle cell crisis; however, administering IV fluids is the priority. Hydration can stop the sickling process of the blood cells by causing hemodilution.

40. Number 2 is correct.

Rationale: A cane can offer stability and balance to clients who have minor injuries, pain, or weakness. The proper order for coming down the stairs is to place the cane down on the step first, then step with the injured leg, and then step down with the good leg. The cane should reach a height even with the wrist, and the elbow should be slightly bent when holding the cane. Additionally, the cane should be held opposite of the side that requires support.

41. Number 1 is correct.

Rationale: Clients have the right to change DNR orders or advance directives whenever they choose. It is important to notify the health care provider immediately so that the DNR order may be rescinded. Response 2 is inappropriate because the nurse is expressing her opinion about what the client should do. Response 3 is inappropriate because the client is of legal age and has rights protected under HIPAA to make her own decisions regarding care. Response 4 is incorrect because although a DNR is a legal document, the client retains the right at any time to change her mind regarding treatment.

42. Numbers 3 and 4 are correct.

Rationale: Hepatitis A is transmitted when an uninfected person ingests food or water that is contaminated with the feces of an infected person. Hepatitis C is transmitted through blood. Hepatitis B is transmitted through various body fluids, including sputum.

43. Number 3 is correct.

Rationale: The Tzanck test will determine the presence of cells from the herpes virus. The stress test assesses cardiac response to increased workload. The Rinne test compares bone conduction to air conduction in the ears. The patch test identifies the cause of allergic contact sensitization.

44. Number 3 is correct.

Rationale: Transfusion rates for a unit of RBCs should occur within 4 hours. The 2-hour infusion would be appropriate for a client experiencing an emergency situation. The 6-hour and 8-hour infusion rates are too long.

45. Numbers 1, 2, 3, and 4 are correct.

Rationale: There are several nursing interventions to help the client suffering from PTSD. Most clients will require a combination of different techniques to maximize coping skills. Every client is different, and some clients will try many techniques before finding what works best for them. The nurse should help the client develop adequate coping techniques and practice using a variety of techniques. The client should also be encouraged to try relaxation techniques. Listening to the client in a supportive and nonjudgmental manner paves the way for therapeutic communication and offers a safe environment for the client. A client who does not feel as if the environment is safe and secure is less likely to express her feelings and may delay her progress. There is no need for the client to wait until she has worked through all the stages of grief before going out in public; doing so may delay healing and keeps the client from attending to the necessary duties of everyday life, such as working, shopping for food, and keeping physician appointments.

46. Number 3 is correct.

Rationale: Swimming should be avoided and care should be taken when shaving or showering. A Medic-Alert bracelet is useful in life-threatening situations. Loose-fitting, high-neck sweaters and shirts may be worn to cover the stoma or tracheostomy tube. Green houseplants help increase humidity. Clients may also increase the humidity by using saline in the stoma as ordered, sitting pans of water around the house, or using a humidifier. Low humidity may make it more difficult to breathe and cause crusting around the stoma.

47. Number 2 is correct.

    Rationale: The priority with any dysrhythmia is to check the client and the leads first to ensure that the client is truly having a rhythm change. Improperly placed or loose leads can mimic dysrhythmias; coughing or movement can create artifacts. Ventricular fibrillation is a life-threatening emergency; once the client is checked, the nurse should immediately call a code and initiate CPR when the backboard arrives. While waiting on the crash cart, the client should be positioned flat with the rails down for access. If the client is not intubated, pull the bed away from the wall for the anesthetist. The room should be cleared of furniture or other items that will crowd the room. Diltiazem is given in cases of supraventricular tachycardia and is not part of the ACLS protocol for treatment of ventricular fibrillation. Drugs are given only after shocking the client to stabilize the rhythm and improve cardiac output.

48. The correct response confabulation.

    Rationale: Clients experiencing confabulation may fill in memory gaps with elaborate, detailed fantasies which they believe to be true. They are not intentionally trying to deceive others; their fantasies are often based on old memories.

49. Numbers 1, 2, and 3 are correct.

    Rationale: The nurse can best manage the behavior of the client by showing support when the client exhibits positive behaviors. The nurse should set clear, enforceable limits and communicate expectations to the client. The client should also be informed of consequences of not complying. Role playing demonstrates appropriate behaviors to the client and allows her to practice best responses before a situation arises. Treating the client more like a friend is inappropriate; the nurse should maintain a professional relationship with the client and not try to be her friend. This only confuses the client; it also makes the situation worse for other staff members and can lead to infighting among staff. Giving small gifts to encourage desired behavior is a form of bribery. The nurse should not try to bribe or manipulate the client, nor should the nurse accept gifts from the client. Consistent treatment by all staff members gives the client a stable and safe environment in which to work on her behavior.

50. Number 3 is correct.

    Rationale: This client is experiencing wound evisceration, which is an emergency. The first priority is to call for help and have the surgeon notified. While waiting on another nurse to bring needed supplies, the nurse stays with the client and positions him in a low Fowler's with the knees bent to prevent tension on the incision. Monitor vital signs as soon as equipment is available. The wound should be covered with a sterile normal saline dressing and kept moist. After the surgeon arrives, the client is prepared for surgery if ordered.

51. Answers:

Injured Brain Area	Nursing Intervention
1. frontal lobe	give simple instructions; reorient as needed
2. temporal lobe	speak clearly due to impaired hearing
3. occipital lobe	assist with ADL due to visual disturbances
4. brain stem	monitor vital signs
5. parietal lobe	provide simple, one-step instructions
6. cerebellum	assist with walking

52. Number 4 is correct.

Rationale: Cyclopentolate HCl is a mydriatic medication used to dilate the pupils preoperatively and for eye examinations. Use of mydriatics is contraindicated in clients with cardiac dysrhythmias, as this increases the risk of serious side effects such as tachycardia and hypertension due to systemic absorption. This can lead to stroke, myocardial infarction, and cardiac ischemia, especially in the elderly or those with pre-existing myocardial disease. Osteoporosis, hypothyroidism, and renal insufficiency are not conditions that would contraindicate use of mydriatics.

53. Number 3 is correct.

Rationale: Reclast is contraindicated in clients with a creatinine clearance less than 35 mL/min. The other lab values are within normal range and do not affect administration of this medication.

54. Numbers 2, 3, and 4 are correct.

Rationale: Keeping the bed in the lowest position reduces the impact if the client falls from the bed. Special flooring provides a cushioned surface that reduces impact. A bed alarm will notify staff if the client moves from the bed. Providing a call-light device to a client with Parkinson's is ineffective as the client's ability to use the device is impaired because of fine motor movement limitation.

55. Number 3 is correct.

Rationale: The nurse should advise the client to exercise as instructed to prevent contracture formation. Aseptic dressing wound management is acceptable. Elevation of the residual limb should be avoided to prevent contracture formation. As phantom limb pain is common, reporting on an imminent basis is unnecessary.

56. Number 4 is correct.

Rationale: This client is experiencing autonomic dysreflexia, which requires immediate treatment to prevent hypertensive stroke. Placing the client in the high Fowler's position reduces blood pressure by promoting gravitational pooling of blood in the lower extremities. The nurse should notify the health care provider immediately and assess for the cause. Bladder distention and fecal impaction are common causes; if the client has a urinary catheter in place, the nurse should check for kinks in the tubing. If indicated, preparation to catheterize the client should begin immediately. Nitrate or nifedipine are the most common drugs used for treatment.

57. Number 2 is correct.

Rationale: A baked chicken breast with green beans is an acceptable diet choice for the client on MAOI. Clients on MAOI should avoid all foods containing tyramine, which can cause hypertensive crisis. Yogurt, sausage, and sauerkraut are high in tyramine.

58. Number 2 is correct.

Rationale: The client should be positioned with the legs abducted using a pillow or splint. Floating the client's heels is appropriate to prevent skin breakdown. Application of SCDs reduces the risk of venous thromboembolism. Deep breathing and incentive spirometer use help prevent respiratory complications.

59. Number 3 is correct.

Rationale: The client with a glomerular filtration rate (GFR) of 92 mL/min has a normal value but may have physical findings or genetic traits that indicate stage 1 kidney disease. A GFR of 63 mL/min indicates stage 2, or mild chronic kidney disease (CKD). A GFR of 39 mL/min is consistent with stage 3, or moderate CKD. A GFR of 16 mL/min indicates stage 5, end-stage kidney disease.

60. Number 3 is correct.

Rationale: Low-pitched grating and rubbing is indicative of friction rub. Rhonchi are either low-pitched, continuous rattling sounds (sonorous) or high-pitched and continuous (sibilant) sounds. Stridor occurs on inspiration and is loud, high-pitched crowing that can be heard without a stethoscope. Fine crackles are brief and high pitched.

61. Number 2 is correct.

Rationale: Stasis ulcers often form as a result of edema or minor injury to the leg. They occur more often medially than laterally over the malleolus of the affected limb. Decreased or absent pulses with cool or cold feet is a finding of arterial ulcers. Skin atrophy and pallor with elevation are another indication of arterial ulcers. Edema is often present due to valvular damage from the backup of blood and venous hypertension.

62. Number 2 is correct.

Rationale: Before touching the client, the nurse should wash her hands and don gloves for protection from blood or other body fluids. While all of the other steps are part of the procedure, safety against blood-borne pathogens is the priority.

63. Number 4 is correct.

Rationale: A client with severe weakness on one side will have difficulty turning and repositioning without assistance and will require turning and skin assessment every 2 hours. Neuropathy affects the client's ability to feel pain and causes damage to the skin to be less apparent to the client. An elderly client who can get up with assistance has more mobility than one with weakness and neuropathy. Younger clients tend to be at lower risk of skin breakdown, and although this client has diabetes, his hemoglobin A1C reflects well-controlled blood sugars. Being blind is not necessarily a risk factor for skin breakdown, especially in the client who is able to live independently. Although the client with the chest tube may have diminished mobility, the ability to reposition independently minimizes the risk of skin breakdown from lying in one position too long.

64. Number 3 is correct.

Rationale: Engaging the core (stomach) and leg muscles provides the safest traction for moving a client in bed. Feet should be shoulder width apart. The client should be instructed to help as much as possible. The head of the bed should be flat, if the client can tolerate it.

65. Number 3 is correct.

Rationale: The Patient Self-Determination Act of 1990 requires that all clients of health care facilities be informed of their right to refuse care or specify their wishes should they become unable to speak for themselves. Giving the client a copy to read allows the nurse to answer questions and explain that the client may choose which interventions she does or does not want. For example, a client may refuse to be on a ventilator but will accept tube feedings for nutrition. If the client fills out the advance directives, it should be witnessed by two nonfamily members or other neutral parties and placed on the client's chart. While the directives can be added later, the nurse should not tell the client not to worry about it. The directives may be forgotten, and should an emergency arise, the client will not have as much autonomy in her care. Advance directives do not need to go through a lawyer in most cases, and waiting to have them drawn up and sent causes unnecessary delays for the client. The nurse should never simply drop the discussion and chart that the client refused them. The nurse is duty bound to make the client fully aware of all of her rights. It is important to avoid any actions that may endanger a client or lead to potential legal action.

66. Number 4 is correct.

Rationale: Older adults with dementia are at risk for injury due to increased risk for falls. They may not recognize their limitations given the ineffective tissue perfusion that occurs with hypertension. Ineffective coping, activity intolerance, and ineffective tissue perfusion would not be the highest priority.

67. Number 3 is correct.

Rationale: The nurse should assign a sitter, because keeping the client safe after he has verbalized a suicide plan is more important than the client's right to refuse care. Placing the client in restraints does not guarantee his safety and may escalate the situation. If the client manages to get out of the restraints, he might hang himself with them. Having security sit outside the door does not provide direct observation of the client and uses up a limited resource of the facility. Allowing the client to leave AMA leaves the nurse and the facility vulnerable to legal action if the client commits suicide after leaving. Having a friend come sit does not guarantee safety; the friend may provide him with the means to commit suicide, such as bringing drugs for him to overdose on.

68. Number 1 is correct.

The most important information for the nurse to find out is what support systems the client has available. The nurse must remember that this information is key in order to know how to approach the client and how to plan care. If the client has few or no support systems, the priority is to help her find resources to help her. Asking the client what she does for relaxation is little help if she has no support system. Asking about her parents' insurance coverage for adult day care may be an option to explore down the road, but it takes a back seat to determining the client's support systems. Offering a list of nursing homes is not appropriate at this time and does not offer timely help with her situation. Once the nurse understands the client's support systems, she can make appropriate decisions on where to proceed next.

69. Numbers 1 and 3 are correct.

Rationale: Withdrawing air after aspirating the prescribed medication creates an air-lock to seal in the medication once injected. The needle used for medication is replaced with a new one prior to injection so no drug is on the outside of the needle shaft. The ventrogluteal muscle is used for Z-track injection. The needle is inserted at a 90-degree angle.

70. Numbers 2 and 3 are correct answers.

Rationale: Air is inserted first into the cloudy insulin (NPH) followed by insertion of air into the regular insulin. Regular (clear) insulin is drawn up first followed by cloudy insulin (NPH).

71. Number 1 is correct.

Rationale: The correct order is inspection, auscultation, palpation, percussion. Abdominal assessment varies slightly from other assessments in that auscultation is performed before palpation or percussion in order to avoid changing the intensity and frequency of bowel sounds.

72. Numbers 1, 3, 4, and 5 are correct.

Rationale: Chest pain, hematoma formation, and decreased pulses are signs of cardiac ischemia. The nurse should call the Rapid Response Team or health care provider immediately. Difficulty swallowing may indicate possible stroke. A decreased appetite is not a complication of cardiac catheterization and does not require emergent care.

73. Number 3 is correct.

Rationale: IVIG is stored under refrigeration yet should be administered at room temperature, typically within 30 minutes of removal from cold storage. The IVIG infusion rate is slow at first and increased gradually every 15 to 30 minutes as tolerated by the client until the maximum infusion rate may be administered. Vital signs should be monitored 15 minutes prior to administration, 15 minutes after initiation of infusion, and at every rate change. Chills, considered an adverse reaction to IVIG, warrant stopping the infusion.

74. Number 1 is correct.

Rationale: Lipiduria is a key feature of nephrotic syndrome. Other key findings include hyperlipidemia, hypoalbuminemia, and increased coagulation.

75. Number 1 is correct.

Rationale: Lactulose is a laxative given to lower ammonia levels in clients with hepatic encephalopathy. Elevated BUN indicates a dysfunction in the body's ability to convert protein to nitrogen; this coupled with elevated ammonia levels would present as confusion. Sucralfate is an anti-ulcer medication used in the management of GI ulcers. Lamotrigine is an antiepileptic medication used to control seizures. Gabapentin is an anticonvulsant and mood stabilizer.

76. Number 2 is correct.

Rationale: Oral thrush (candidiasis) occurs when the fungus Candida albicans accumulates on the lining of the mouth. While more likely to occur in babies, this condition also appears in persons with a suppressed immune system. The medication should be swished in the mouth, then either spit out or swallowed. To make the best contact with the oral mucosa, the medication should be taken after meals. The solution should not be diluted with other liquids. The standard frequency of nystatin is four times a day.

77. Number 3 is correct.

Rationale: Inflating the cuff (if the tube is not capped) during meals and for 1 hour afterward prevents aspiration. The client should sit up for all meals. When capping the tube, the cuff is first deflated and the inner cannula removed prior to capping in order to avoid blocking the airway. The cuff is not inflated prior to capping. The cuff must be inflated for meals.

78. Number 4 is correct.

Rationale: Warfarin is a high-alert drug and clients should know which side effects to report to their physician. Bloody, black, or tarry stools; pink urine; or excessive bleeding should be reported immediately. Which pharmacy the client uses is not as important as knowing which side effects to report. Knowing the next lab appointment is important but not as important as knowing the side effects of warfarin. Clients must undergo regular laboratory testing to ensure that the warfarin is at a therapeutic level. Clients living at poverty level often lack reliable transportation to return to clinics for follow-up lab work. The nurse should ensure that the client has transportation for lab work to prevent the risk of bleeding. If the client expresses doubt about being able to return for labs, the nurse should notify the health care provider and ask for a social worker consult. The social worker may know of free transportation for low-income individuals or be able to provide a bus or cab voucher. Nurses collaborate with other disciplines to ensure the best care for the client. The nurse is often the only one that the client confides in regarding obstacles to care.

79. Number 4 is correct.

Rationale: The client experiencing tingling in and around the mouth may be having an allergic reaction to the antibiotic. The nurse should immediately assess the client's airway and breathing, as the client is at risk for the tongue swelling and blocking the airway. The other clients may be seen after assessing the client for an allergic reaction. While it is important to address the other clients' needs quickly, the nurse always addresses potentially life-threatening situations first.

80. Number 1 is correct.

Rationale: The 2016 Hospital National Patient Safety Goals by the Joint Commission on Accreditation of Hospitals states that at least two ways to identify patients are needed to promote patient safety. Asking the client to state his name and date of birth is only one form of identification. Asking the client to confirm the medication ordered and comparing this with the medication order are not two viable means of identifiers. The room number is not used as a client identifier.

81. Number 3 is correct.

Rationale: Spermicides can increase the risk of cystitis and another form of birth control should be used if possible. Voiding before and after intercourse minimizes the risk of bacteria being introduced into the urethra. Loose-fitting cotton underwear helps prevent irritation to the area. Burning upon urination may indicate another infection and should be assessed by the health care provider for diagnosis and treatment.

82. Number 4 is correct.

Rationale: Abdominal pain that increases with cough or movement and is relieved by bending the right hip or knees indicates perforation and peritonitis. Untreated peritonitis can be life-threatening. Pain is a common finding in appendicitis and other inflammatory bowel problems. Family history can play a part in the risk of abdominal alterations. Nausea and vomiting are common findings.

83. Number 4 is correct.

Rationale: Metformin within 48 hours of a contrast study can result in lactic acidosis. The physician will need to withhold Metformin on the day of contrast administration and for an additional 48 hours; instead, use another hypoglycemic agent during this period. Allergy to shellfish is not a contraindication to the use of a contrast dye nor is CHF or chronic cystitis.

84. Numbers 2 and 4 are correct.

Rationale: Due to diffuse destruction of hepatic cells with cirrhosis of the liver, the client will experience fatigue and need frequent rest periods throughout the day. An inability of the liver to filter toxins can lead to hepatic encephalopathy making assessment of the client's mental status imperative. Due to impaired clotting function, clients need safety measures implemented such as replacing a straight shaving razor with an electric one. Sodium rather than potassium should be restricted with cirrhosis of the liver.

85. Number 3 is correct.

Rationale: Exophthalmos, or a "startled" look, is caused by edema in the extraocular muscles. Clients may report difficulty in focusing, dry eyes, or photophobia. Graves' disease causes tachycardia, not bradycardia. The client may report an increase in bowel movements. Unplanned weight loss is also common.

86. Number 4 is correct.

Rationale: The human immunodeficiency virus (HIV), which causes AIDS, is concentrated mostly in blood and semen. The client should not donate blood. Someone with HIV does not need to limit time in public places. As HIV is not transmitted by sharing food, there are no restrictions on this activity. Use of public restrooms by persons with HIV is an acceptable practice.

87. Number 1 is correct.

Rationale: A transdermal patch of fentanyl is to be worn continuously to provide round-the-clock pain relief. A potent opioid analgesic, fentanyl needs to be stored in a safe location where others may not access the drug. Orange juice may be ingested while on fentanyl; however, grapefruit juice should be avoided as it increases the effect of the drug.

88. Numbers 1, 2, and 3 are correct.

Rationale: Severe burns can lead to compartment syndrome because edema increases pressure in the compartments, which house muscles, nerves, and blood vessels. Fractures are present in 75% of all cases of compartment syndrome. Severe infiltration of IV fluids also increases compartment pressure due to edema surrounding the area of infiltration. Failure to ambulate after surgery is not a cause of compartment syndrome. Blood sugar levels do not affect compartments.

89. Answer: The nurse should administer 0.5 mL of heparin.

Rationale:

10,000 units/1 mL = 5,000 units/X	Set up a proportion (dose on hand/quantity on hand = dose desired/X)
10,000 units × X = 5,000 units × 1 mL	Calculate.
X = 5,000 units × 1 mL/10,000 units	Solve for X.
X = 0.5 mL	

90. Number 4 is correct.

Rationale: Terbutaline is contraindicated with coronary artery disease. It may increase blood glucose levels and should be used with caution in diabetes. Migraines and osteoarthritis are not contraindications for this medication.

91. Answers:

Laboratory Test	Normal Value
calcium	8.5 – 10.9 mg/L (serum)
pH	7.35 – 7.45 (arterial blood gases)
specific gravity	1.010 – 1.030 (urine)
potassium	3.5 – 5.1
LDL	Less than 100 mg/dL (serum)
HDL	40 – 59 mg/dL (serum)

92. Numbers 1, 2, and 3 are correct.

Rationale: Applying compression stockings will assist in preventing a deep vein thrombosis. Ambulation post-surgery with a walker is done to prevent complications of immobility. Coughing and deep breathing will facilitate oxygenation of the body after receiving anesthesia. Fluid intake need not be restricted post-op and may be encouraged depending on the client's medical history.

93. Numbers 3 and 4 are correct.

Rationale: The first stools are liquid and gradually become more formed. The healthy stoma is reddish-pink and moist and protrudes about 2 cm from the abdominal wall. Only a small amount of bleeding should be present at the stoma site. The colostomy will begin functioning in 2 to 3 days.

94. Number 2 is correct.

Rationale: Nitroglycerin and dopamine are compatible. The other drug combinations listed are not compatible.

95. Number 1 is correct.

Rationale: In an emergency situation where the client is suffering a potentially life-threatening event, it is not necessary to obtain consent. Trying to obtain consent from a family member wastes valuable time, since the client's identity is unknown. The client may not gain consciousness, so waiting until he can be roused is not the correct action. Asking the police to run the tag number wastes precious time that the client needs to be prepped for surgery, and is not a feasible option. Informing the health care provider that consent cannot be obtained does not apply in an emergency situation. The client is at high risk for death from internal bleeding.

96. Number 1 is correct.

Rationale: The priority nursing diagnosis is risk for injury. Client safety is always the priority, especially with a client who has a history of falls and Alzheimer's or confusion. Impaired skin integrity is an important nursing diagnosis but is not the priority for this client. There is nothing to indicate that this client has altered body image; risk for injury would take priority over altered body image. Impaired physical mobility due to dementia with Lewy bodies is a medical diagnosis, not a nursing diagnosis.

97. Number 5 is correct.

Rationale: The nurse should verify the client's identity by comparing the name, date of birth, and medical record number on the armband with the medication order. The 2012 National Patient Safety Goals require using at least two identifiers to avoid medication errors. Verifying the client's allergies should be done after correctly identify the client. Verifying the client's name and room number is not as accurate. Asking the client to state her name and date of birth is not reliable in persons with altered mental status or in a nonresponsive client. Scanning the wristband and barcode should be done only after the two identifiers are completed, just prior to administering the medications.

98. Number 4 is correct.

Rationale: The best time to perform testicular self-examination is just after bathing because the scrotum is more relaxed. Testicular cancer is one of the most curable cancers. It is most common in men ages 15 to 35. Any lump or swelling regardless of size should be reported to the health care provider.

99. Number 3 is correct.

Rationale: Clients who are tactile or kinesthetic learners prefer to learn by touching and doing. If they are learning how to administer insulin injections, they learn better by holding the syringe in their hand as opposed to simply watching a video or reading a handout. A client's living situation can affect his readiness and ability to learn. A client who has visual deficits will have a harder time reading a medication bottle and may be embarrassed about verbalizing his needs. The age and developmental stage must be considered; teaching a school-age child is much different from teaching a grown adult. Clients should be allowed to demonstrate their understanding of teaching, ask questions, and practice skills if necessary. There are many barriers to learning, including financial resources, lack of support systems, and a low level of literacy.

100. Numbers 1, 3, and 4 are correct.

Rationale: Risk factors for domestic violence include being under age 30 and growing up in a home where child and spousal abuse occurred. Victims tend to have multiple abusive relationships over their lifetime. Many abusers severely restrict the victim's movement, so social isolation from friends and family is common. If the client is employed, she typically works in a low-paying field or goes through multiple jobs. Economic factors such as low income and lack of education are common in domestic violence, although it can occur in any environment.

101. Number 1 is correct.

Rationale: In response 1, the nurse expresses sympathy, acknowledges the family's loss, and leaves the decision to view their loved one with the family. The second and third responses assume the family wants to view their loved one. In the last response, the nurse makes the decision about the family viewing the body.

102. Numbers 1, 2, and 6 are correct.

Rationale: Risk factors for spousal abuse include alcohol or drug use by either partner and low income or living at the poverty level. An unplanned pregnancy may trigger violence in the spouse, especially if the couple has any of the other risk factors. The more risk factors a couple has, the greater the potential for abuse. The risk is greater for those under the age of 30. A higher level of education lessens the risk of abuse, but does not guarantee it will not occur. Having a large circle of friends is less risky than being socially isolated from friends or family. Many abusers control their spouses by keeping them from family and friends and limiting their freedom. The nurse must understand that simply living at a low income level or having less education does not automatically mean that the relationship is abusive, because abuse can occur in any environment for any number of reasons.

103. Numbers 2 and 3 are correct.

Rationale: Clients undergoing brachytherapy have radioactive isotopes inside the body and are radioactive and potentially hazardous to others. Their bodily wastes are radioactive and require special handling until the isotope is completely eliminated from the body. Teletherapy uses a source of radiation outside the body; therefore, these clients are not radioactive. The dose is always less than the exposure because of energy loss on the way to the target tissue. Gamma rays are most commonly used for radiation due to their ability to deeply penetrate tissues.

104. Numbers 1, 2, and 5 are correct.

Rationale: Lithium has a narrow therapeutic range of 0.6 to 1.2 mEq/L. A level of 2.2 mEq/L indicates moderate toxicity. The nurse should notify the health care provider immediately, as severe toxicity can cause tonic-clonic seizures, coma, or death. Treatment typically involves administering IV fluids to dilute the concentration of the medication, holding the medication, and possible hemodialysis in severe cases. The client may exhibit signs of toxicity such as confusion, slurred speech, and severe diarrhea. A mechanical soft diet will not treat the toxicity. The nurse would hold the next dose and prepare to draw lab work, including lithium and electrolyte levels, BUN and creatinine, and a CBC.

105. Number 1 is correct.

Rationale: This client is exhibiting signs of an air embolism, which is a complication of hemodialysis. The nurse should stop the dialysis immediately and turn the client on the left side in the Trendelenburg's position. The health care provider should be notified immediately. The nurse should administer oxygen and assess vital signs and pulse oximetry. Positioning the client in this manner helps to trap the air in the right side of the heart so it cannot travel to the lungs. Clotting at the graft site would be present when there is no thrill to palpate or a bruit to auscultate. A clotted graft site would not produce this client's signs. Dialysis encephalopathy is caused by aluminum toxicity from dialysate water that contains aluminum. Signs include mental cloudiness, speech disturbances, bone pain, and seizures. Disequilibrium syndrome is characterized by nausea and vomiting, headache, hypertension, muscle cramps, and confusion.

106. Number 2 is correct.

Rationale: BNP, or B-type natriuretic peptide, is a hormone released by the heart in response to pressure changes within the heart. It is used to gauge the severity of congestive heart failure. A normal range in a client with heart failure is 0 to 100 pg/mL. A BNP of 760 pg/mL indicates severe heart failure. ALT (alanine aminotransferase) tests liver enzymes. The normal range of ALT is 7 – 56 units per liter, so a value of 33 units/L is within normal limits. WBC (white blood cell) count normally ranges from 4,500 to 11,000 mcL, so a value of 10,450 is within normal limits. Direct bilirubin is a by-product of RBC breakdown. Normal lab values for direct bilirubin range from 0 to 0.3 mg/dL, so a value of 0.2 mg/dL falls within normal limits.

107. Numbers 1, 2, and 3 are correct.

Rationale: This is an elevated total bilirubin level. Signs and symptoms include itchy skin, nausea, and pale stools. Dark urine, not colorless urine, would be present. Normal total bilirubin levels range from 0.3 to 1.9 mg/dL.

108. The correct order is:

1. hyperoxygenate the client
2. explain the procedure to the client
3. immediately instruct the client to cough

4. apply oxygen by nasal cannula or face mask
5. thoroughly suction the ET tube and the oral cavity
6. teach the client how to use an incentive spirometer every 2 hours
7. rapidly deflate the ET tube cuff and remove tube at peak inspiration
8. set up the prescribed oxygen delivery system and bring in equipment for emergency reintubation

Rationale: Explaining the procedure to the client first helps minimize fear. Equipment should be set up before performing the procedure. Hyperoxygenation should be performed before suctioning to avoid dropping the client's oxygen saturation levels. Deflating the tube cuff aids in removal and prevents injury to client. Coughing helps clear any remaining secretions. The nurse should apply oxygen to the client and ensure it is in place before teaching. The client should demonstrate use of incentive spirometer to verify proper technique and lower risk of respiratory complications.

109. Number 3 is correct.

Rationale: Following a mastectomy, the client should be positioned with the head of the bed at 30 degrees or more, with a pillow supporting the arm on the affected side to allow lymphatic fluid return. The other options describe either incorrect bed positioning or incorrect placement of the pillow.

110. Number 1 is correct.

Rationale: The transducer must be at the level of the right atrium in order to accurately measure arterial blood pressure and other hemodynamic pressures. Options 2, 3, and 4 are incorrect positions for the transducer and will not give accurate results.

111. Number 3 is correct.

Rationale: This client is experiencing acute adrenal insufficiency, or Addisonian crisis. This is a life-threatening event if left untreated. Treatment consists of IV saline, dextrose, or hydrocortisone. IV spironolactone would not be given, since it is a potassium-sparing diuretic. Boluses of normal saline or dextrose 5% in normal saline are the fluids of choice to deliver medications and restore fluid balance. Since the client is hyperkalemic, fluids containing potassium would not be given. Also, potassium is never given as a bolus due to the risk of cardiac dysrhythmias.

112. Number 2 is correct.

Rationale: Oxygen delivery at 2 L/minute via nasal cannula is equivalent to 28% FiO2. A flow rate of 1 L/minute is equal to 24% FiO2. A flow rate of 3 L/minute is equal to 32% FiO2. A flow rate of 4 L/minute is equivalent to 36% FiO2.

113. Numbers 1, 4, and 5 are correct.

Rationale: The client will be on different medications following surgery. The nurse should demonstrate to the client how to splint the incision when coughing or breathing deeply to minimize pain and lessen pressure on the incision site. After surgery, the client will be on the ventilator and have one or more chest tubes. The client will be encouraged to ambulate as early as possible to prevent complications from pneumonia. The client will have a urinary catheter following surgery and will not need to void in a bedpan.

114. Number 1 is correct.

Rationale: Glossitis, or a smooth tongue, is a sign of vitamin B12 deficiency anemia. Inflammation causes the tongue to appear smooth. Paresthesias are found in pernicious anemia. Weakness and pallor are found in iron deficiency anemia. Dark purple or cyanotic skin on the face and mucous membranes are signs of polycythemia vera.

115. Number 4 is correct.

    Rationale: A systolic murmur occurs between the S1 and S2 heart sounds. A diastolic murmur will be heard between S2 and S1. Options 1 and 2 are incorrect for hearing a systolic murmur. A murmur can occur during any phase of the cardiac cycle.

116. Number 1 is correct.

    Rationale: The mitral and tricuspid valves produce the S1 sound when they close. Option 3 describes the action that produces the S2 sound. Options 2 and 4 do not describe the mechanism of the S1 heart sound.

117. Numbers 1, 3, and 5 are correct.

    Rationale: Gargling with warm saline can decrease discomfort caused by a sore throat. Many people think that an antibiotic is what they need for a sore throat, when most sore throats are actually caused by a virus. Antibiotics are ineffective on viruses. Overuse of antibiotics for sore throats can lead to antibiotic resistance. Increased fluid intake with water and warm beverages or soups can help with the pain. A humidifier should be used to add moisture to the air. The doctor will not prescribe an antibiotic if it is determined that the client's sore throat is caused by a virus.

118. Number 4 is correct.

    Rationale: Severe edema can occur in areas that were not burned, due to the leakage of electrolytes and fluids from the vascular space. The fluid shift causes hyperkalemia and hypovolemia. Hemoconcentration is caused by vascular dehydration, which increases blood viscosity. Excessive weight gain can occur during the first 12 hours following the burn and may continue for 24 – 36 hours due to the fluid shift.

119. Number 1 is correct.

    Rationale: Anemia is a prime concern after a total knee replacement. A hemoglobin level of 10.2 g/L is low (normal is 13.5 – 17.5 for men, 12.0 – 15.5 for women) and might require a blood transfusion. Bleeding on the dressing of 2 cm is not of concern. Circle, date, and time the bleeding initially and monitor closely for changes. Recheck the temperature in 30 minutes; if above 100.6, report finding to the doctor. Complaint of pain at the incision site is routine, and pain medication should be administered as prescribed.

120. Number 3 is correct.

    Rationale: A medical condition such as a seizure or stroke may have been the underlying cause of the drowning event and would require further treatment once the client's respiratory status is stabilized. Drowning in very cold water appears to have a protective effect by causing a reduction in cardiac output and reducing the cerebral metabolic rate, even with prolonged arrest. Aspiration of both salt and fresh water decreases surfactant to the lungs and leads to decreased lung compliance. Contaminants in the water such as microbes, mud, chemicals, and algae may play a significant role in how much damage to the lungs is sustained.

121. Numbers 1, 3, 4, and 6 are correct.

    Rationale: Rabies causes encephalitis, which causes paralysis and difficulty swallowing water. This manifests as an apparent fear of water, which can cause the client to become adversely irritated when he or she sees water or hears running water. Nuchal rigidity, convulsions, and tonic or clonic muscle contractions can occur during the neurological phase. In the prodromal phase, the client can have irritability, extreme salivation, sore throat, fever, and hyperexcitability. During the paralytic phase, the client becomes unconscious, has loss of bowel and urinary control, and has irregular or labored breathing. Current treatment includes one dose of immunoglobulin and five doses of rabies vaccine over a period of 28 days. Aches and pains in different parts of the body and light sensitivity occur during the prodromal phase.

122. Number 3 is correct.

Rationale: Impaired consciousness, visual loss, bilateral sensory and motor dysfunction, and pupil abnormalities are seen with basilar artery strokes. Memory problems, visual hallucinations, visual deficits, and hemisensory disturbances occur with posterior cerebral artery strokes. Weakness in the foot and leg, sensory loss in the foot and leg, incontinence, ataxia, and lack of spontaneity occurs with anterior cerebral artery strokes. Ataxia, contralateral facial weakness, contralateral hemiplegia, visual deficits, speech impairments, and perceptual impairments occur with middle cerebral artery strokes.

123. Number 4 is correct.

Rationale: Dumping syndrome signs and symptoms include sweating, heart palpitations, vertigo, and the urge to lay down shortly after eating. Onset of symptoms occurs within 5 to 30 minutes after eating. Signs and symptoms of appendicitis include rebound tenderness and abdominal rigidity, pain in the lower right quadrant, nausea and vomiting, and low-grade fever. Cholecystitis manifests with pain to the right upper quadrant that radiates to the right scapula, Murphy's sign, belching, indigestion, and nausea and vomiting. Signs and symptoms of ulcerative colitis include abdominal cramping and tenderness, severe diarrhea that may present with mucus and blood, weight loss, anorexia, and malaise.

124. Numbers 4, 5, and 6 are correct.

Rationale: Cancer of the tongue causes difficulty swallowing due to enlarged lymph nodes in the neck. Sores that bleed or do not heal over time are another sign of tongue cancer. Chewing may be difficult or painful for clients with cancer of the tongue. Weight loss, not weight gain, can occur due to difficulty chewing and swallowing. Poor-fitting dentures or loose teeth are another sign. A black, hairy tongue is caused by overgrowth of yeast and bacteria and is a benign condition unrelated to cancer of the tongue.

125. Number 4 is correct.

Rationale: ACE inhibitors alone are less effective in African American clients unless they are combined with a calcium channel blocker or a thiazide diuretic. Therefore, the client would not be given an ACE inhibitor by itself. Amiloride can cause hyperkalemia in clients with impaired renal function, especially if given in conjunction with ACE inhibitors. Atenolol can increase the incidence of diabetes and mask symptoms of hypoglycemia, as well as delay recovery from hypoglycemic episodes.

126. Number 2 is correct.

Rationale: Oliguria, the production of an abnormally small amount of urine, is indicative of stage 5 chronic kidney disease. Symptoms of stage 3 chronic kidney disease include shortness of breath, tea-colored urine, and edema in the lower extremities.

127. Numbers 1 and 4 are correct.

Rationale: Home management of chronic pancreatitis includes eating small meals throughout the day and avoiding heavy meals. Nicotine and caffeine can worsen symptoms. Alcohol contributes to flare-ups and should be avoided. The client should rest frequently until full strength has returned and the health care provider has approved of vigorous activity. Spicy foods stimulate the GI tract and should be avoided. Bland, high-protein, low-fat, and moderate-carbohydrate meals and snacks are the best for the client.

128. Number 3 is correct.

Rationale: Chronic back pain, weight loss, joint pain and itching, and visual disturbances describe signs and symptoms of ankylosing spondylitis. Reiter syndrome is characterized by burning upon urination, joint pain, and eye infection with pain, redness, and drainage. Marfan syndrome presents with excessive height, elongated hands and feet, scoliosis, and cardiovascular problems. Signs and symptoms of systemic necrotizing vasculitis include peripheral arterial disease with severe pain and necrosis of fingers or toes, kidney or heart failure, and stroke-like symptoms.

129. Numbers 3, 4, and 6 are correct.

Rationale: The client's level of consciousness must be assessed as part of a standard admission assessment, as it will determine treatments needed. The client is placed supine to avoid orthostatic alterations in blood pressure due to cardiac instability. The client should be handled gently to prevent ventricular fibrillation. The nurse should administer CPR if the client does not have spontaneous circulation. Heating blankets are contraindicated in severe hypothermia; the treatment of choice is extracorporeal rewarming via cardiopulmonary bypass or hemodialysis. A rectal temperature is the most accurate in the hypothermic client. Massaging the extremities may injure frostbitten extremities and should not be performed.

130. Number 3 is correct.

Rationale: Metabolic (nonrespiratory) alkalosis is consistent with the stated values. The stated pH of 7.58 is alkalotic. The value of PaCO2, 48 mm Hg is within normal range indicating a nonrespiratory (metabolic) origin. The value of HCO3 of 44 mEq/L is indicative of metabolic alkalosis. A Base Excess of +13 mEq/L is consistent with severe metabolic alkalosis.

131. Number 1 is correct.

Rationale: A resting tremor is a primary motor symptom of Parkinson's disease seen in either the hand or the foot on one side of the body. Sleep disturbance, constipation, and fatigue are nonmotor symptoms of Parkinson's disease.

132. Number 4 is correct.

Rationale: The normal serum calcium level is 8.5 – 10.2 mg/dL, making the client's results extremely high (hypercalcemia). The condition typically results from hyperparathyroidism. The priority treatment of choice is intravenous bisphosphonates. Calcitonin is the secondary medical treatment of choice followed by corticosteroids. Renal dialysis is not considered an acceptable treatment.

133. Number 2 is correct.

Rationale: Seizures are associated with meningiomas along with headache, weakness in an arm or leg, and personality changes. Other stated symptoms are not seen with this type of cancer.

134. Number 2 is correct.

Rationale: Assessment of the client is a priority in the nursing process; therefore, obtaining vital signs would be a priority. The nurse must assess before performing interventions such as relief of pain, administration of IV fluids, and preparation for surgery.

135. Number 3 is correct.

Rationale: Cefazolin can cause a reaction in clients allergic to penicillin. The nurse should hold the medication and notify the health care provider. Administering the cefazolin is likely to trigger another allergic reaction, which potentially may worsen. The pharmacy cannot change health care provider orders. The nurse should consult the health care provider before giving diphenhydramine in order to give the cefazolin, as the provider will more than likely order another medication from a different drug family.

136. Numbers 2, 4, and 5 are correct.

Rationale: Furosemide increases urine output, which removes excess fluid from the body. Pitting edema of +1 indicates an improvement due to the fluid loss. Urine output of 250 mL/hr is an expected finding in this client. Crackles in the lungs should be decreased or absent. Pitting edema of +3 indicates an increase in edema. Shortness of breath should be resolved, not merely decreased.

137. Numbers 1, 5, and 6 are correct.

Rationale: Left-side heart failure manifestations include dyspnea, weak peripheral pulses, and crackles or wheezes in the lungs. Left-sided heart failure causes pulmonary congestion and decreased cardiac output. Right-sided heart failure causes systemic congestion, leading to an engorged spleen, dependent edema, and jugular vein distention.

138. Number 1 is correct.

Rationale: Diabetics should check the feet daily for injury since diabetes causes a loss of sensation in the feet over time. A cut that goes unnoticed may become infected and progress to amputation. Eye examinations should be done on a yearly basis. Heating pads should be avoided on the feet due to the risk of injury caused by loss of sensation. The client should be encouraged to adhere to a diabetic diet and not to take extra insulin just to be able to eat off-limits food.

139. Numbers 1, 3, 5, and 6 are correct.

Rationale: This client is exhibiting signs of intussusception. The nurse should monitor for and report respiratory distress immediately. Respiratory distress can be caused by pressing the knees up to the abdomen. Passage of a normal, brown stool indicates reduction of the intussusception. An NG tube is placed to decompress the stomach. Fever and changes in blood pressure can indicate perforation and shock. The client should be kept NPO until the intussusception is resolved. A barium enema is contraindicated for any client at risk of bowel perforation.

140. Number 1 is correct.

Rationale: A resting tremor is a primary motor symptom of Parkinson's disease seen in either the hand or the foot on one side of the body. Sleep disturbance, constipation, and fatigue are nonmotor symptoms of Parkinson's disease.

141. Number 4 is correct.

Rationale: The normal serum calcium level is 8.5 – 10.2 mg/dL, making the client's results extremely high (hypercalcemia). The condition typically results from hyperparathyroidism. The priority treatment of choice is intravenous bisphosphonates. Calcitonin is the secondary medical treatment of choice followed by corticosteroids. Renal dialysis is not considered an acceptable treatment.

142. Number 3 is correct.

Rationale: Administering the IV antibiotic is the priority because it will treat the infection that is causing the fever. Giving an antipyretic should follow the IV antibiotic. Since the client has scheduled antibiotics, a wound culture is not necessary. The dressing change is important but should be performed after the antibiotic is administered.

143. Answer: 2,090 mL

Solution:

1. Find how many milliliters of solids (ice cream) the patient consumed.	1 pt. ice cream = 500 mL ice cream	Convert pints to milliliters.
2. Find how many milliliters of fluids (water and apple juice) the patient consumed.	16 oz. of water + 12 oz. of juice = 28 oz. fluids (total)	Find the total amount of fluids consumed.
	1 oz. = 30 mL	Convert ounces to milliliters.
	= 28 oz. × 30 = 840 mL of fluids consumed	Find the total amount of fluids consumed in milliliters.

3. Find how many milliliters of saline IV the patient consumed.	1 L = 1,000mL	Convert liters to mL.
	0.75L saline IV × 1,000 = 750 mL saline IV consumed	Find the total amount of saline IV consumed in milliliters.
4. Combine the amount of solids, fluids, and saline IV (in milliliters) consumed to find the patient's total daily intake.	500 mL ice cream + 840 mL fluids + 750 mL saline IV = **2,090 mL**	Add the totals (in mL) of solids, fluids, and saline IV.

144. Numbers 3, 4, and 5 are correct.

Rationale: Charting should always contain only objective facts regarding what the nurse sees, hears, or feels. Noting that the client tolerated 80% of the lunch tray with no complaints of nausea or stomach cramping is an objective observation. It is important to note how well the client tolerated the meal. If the client complained of nausea while eating, this observation would be noted, preferably in the client's own words, such as "I started to get nauseated when I tried to eat." The observation about the abdominal dressing is factual and objective, noting the size of the area of light staining. When a client ambulates in the hall, it is important to chart the distance, whether assistive devices were used, and how well the client tolerated it. The nurse states that no dyspnea or syncope was noted. Statements that the client appeared anxious when family came to visit infers that the client was anxious due to the family's visit. This is presumptive on the nurse's part, as the client could be appearing anxious from unvoiced thoughts. Likewise, the nurse makes it sound as if the client is angry because her medications were changed, when there is no evidence that this is the case. The nurse should avoid charting that a client "appears" to have a certain type of reaction to an event, and chart only those objective facts without speculation.

145. Number 3 is correct.

Rationale: Although the nurse does not touch the sterile field with the clean gloves, there is still contamination because clean gloves were used to remove a sterile object. The syringe is now contaminated, and the close proximity of the clean gloves to the sterile field poses a transmission risk. Any time there is even a suspicion of contamination, the sterile field must be reestablished. Options 1, 2, and 4 reflect safe practice for sterile technique.

146. Numbers 1 and 2 are correct.

Rationale: Following an inguinal hernia repair, the nurse should encourage fluid intake to prevent constipation and straining during bowel movements. If the client cannot void, intermittent catheterization should be performed. Ice, not heat, should be applied to the scrotum to minimize swelling. The client should turn and deep breathe, but avoid coughing. The client should be encouraged to ambulate as soon as possible after surgery. Lifting more than 10 pounds should be avoided until approved by the health care provider.

147. Number 2 is correct.

Rationale: Droplet precautions focus on diseases that are spread by large droplets (greater than 5 microns) expelled into the air and by being within 3 feet of a client. Contact precautions are used for direct and indirect contact with clients and their environments. Airborne precautions are used with diseases that are transmitted by droplets smaller than 5 microns. These smaller droplets remain in the air longer and necessitate the use of an N95 respirator. These clients require a negative pressure or negative airflow room. Protective environments focus on a very limited client population that require a room with positive airflow greater than 12 exchanges per hour through HEPA filters.

148. Numbers 1, 3, and 6 are correct.

Rationale: Veno-occlusive disease is the blockage of blood vessels in the liver and is a complication of bone marrow transplant, also known as hematopoietic stem cell transplant. Manifestations include jaundice, weight gain, and right upper quadrant pain. Liver enlargement is another sign of veno-occlusive disease.

149. Number 3 is correct.

Rationale: Removing stitches is a sterile procedure. The nurse should wash her hands and use sterile technique when removing stitches. Soap and water is not sufficient for cleaning the stitches prior to removal. Washing the hands and using regular gloves is not sterile. The sterile field must be maintained during the procedure, which contraindicates the use of regular gloves. It is not necessary to wear a gown, a mask, gloves, an eye shield, and shoe covers unless the client is on contact precautions. Nothing in this question indicates that the client is on contact precautions.

150. Number 2 is correct.

Rationale: In an emergency situation, type O blood can be given because it is the universal donor. There is not enough time to draw a type and match before the client bleeds out. Type AB+ blood is the universal recipient. There is not enough time to ask the family to donate blood for the client.

151. Number 1 is correct.

Rationale: Clients with celiac disease must follow a strict gluten-free diet. Chicken, carrots, potatoes, and cheese are gluten free and acceptable food choices for this client. Wheat bread, regular spaghetti, and flour tortillas all contain gluten. Any croutons in the Caesar salad would have gluten, too, if they are made from regular bread.

152. (Correct response: Health care Power of Attorney)

Rationale: A Health care Power of Attorney is the document that names a specific person to be in charge of making health care decisions for the client if he is unable to communicate. This differs from a living will, which states which treatments the client wants to have or does not want to have.

153. Numbers 1 and 2 are correct.

Rationale: Unintentional injuries are the leading cause of death for teenagers. Wearing seatbelts, even on short trips, and using approved helmets when bike riding can help prevent injuries. One hour after the last drink of alcohol is not a safe window for driving, especially when multiple drinks have been consumed. Condoms are not 100 percent effective against sexually transmitted infections, even when used correctly. Abstinence is the only method guaranteed to avoid sexually transmitted infections. Never dive into untested waters, even with the arms over the head to "break" the fall. If the bottom of a body of water is not visible, it should not be considered safe for diving.

154. Number 3 is correct.

Rationale: Pink puffer is used to describe a client with emphysema based on the symptoms, which include increased CO_2 retention, minimal cyanosis, pursed-lip breathing, dyspnea anxiety, and a barrel chest. Blue bloater is used to describe a client with chronic bronchitis, based on the symptoms of dusky color due to cyanosis, recurrent cough with sputum, hypoxia, increased respiratory rate, and respiratory acidosis. Asthma and COPD do not carry the same symptoms.

155. Number 1 is correct.

Rationale: The nurse would express concern if a child with a toothache was using herbal remedies. A toothache can indicate a problem and should be evaluated by a dentist for more comprehensive treatment. There is no objection to adults using herbal remedies for xerostomia (dry mouth), nasopharyngitis (common cold), or psoriasis.

156. Number 2 is correct.

Rationale: In Maslow's hierarchy of needs, the highest level of fulfillment is self-actualization, which includes morality, creativity, problem-solving, spontaneity, acceptance of facts, and lack of prejudice.

Esteem follows as the next need and presents as the human desire to be accepted and valued by others. Love and belonging and safety follow esteem on the hierarchy of needs pyramid.

157. The infusion rate is 7mL/hr.

$\dfrac{\text{ordered amount of drug} \times \text{weight in kg} \times 60 \text{ (min per hr)}}{\text{drug concentration}}$ = mL/hr	Solve using the formula.
$\dfrac{50 \text{ mg nitroprusside}}{250 \text{ mL D5W}}$ = 0.2 mg/mL	Find dose per milliliters
0.2×1000 = 200 mcg/mL	Convert milligrams to micrograms.
$\dfrac{0.3 \text{ (ordered amount)} \times 70 \text{ kg} \times 60 \text{ min}}{200 \text{ mcg/mL}}$	Input into formula and solve.
$\dfrac{1260}{200}$ = 6.3 mL/hr	
= 7 mL/hr	Round up to find the IV infusion rate.

158. Answer: B

159. Answer: C

160. Answer: D

161. Answer: A

162. Numbers 1, 2, and 5 are correct.

Rationale: TPN tubing should be changed every 24 hours or per facility protocol. IV site dressing changes should be performed every 48 to 72 hours or per facility protocol.

163. Number 1 is correct.

Rationale: Before blood is picked up, the nurse should check the IV for good blood return and verify that it is working. This saves time and is more efficient than picking up the blood first. Blood must be administered within 30 minutes of the time it leaves the blood bank. This does not leave a lot of time to restart an IV if needed. If the nurse determines that the blood cannot be started within the guidelines, the blood should be returned to the blood bank before it is spiked for administration. Once blood is spiked, there is potential for contamination. The blood should never be placed in the medication refrigerator on the unit; it must be returned to the blood bank. The nurse should not cancel the order and notify the provider that there is no access. All reasonable attempts must be made to restart the IV. If the client appears to need a PICC or other central line due to being a difficult stick, the nurse can notify the health care provider, but should not cancel an order for blood. The blood has been ordered for a reason. Blood should never be wasted. Once it is apparent that time is an issue, the blood should be returned to the blood bank before the last minute. Delaying administration and telling the next shift to start an IV is inappropriate. Blood is too important to delay to another shift, and the nurse has the duty to complete orders given on her shift. The client needing blood should never be without an IV for a long period of time, in case other fluids or emergency resuscitation is needed.

164. Numbers 4 and 5 are correct.

Rationale: Antacids interfere with absorption of tetracycline, along with food, milk, and milk products. Aluminum, calcium, and magnesium decrease absorption of the drug. It may be taken on an empty stomach with another liquid besides milk. Grapefruit juice does not interfere with tetracycline, which should be given on an empty stomach at least one hour before meals or two hours afterward. Tetracycline should be given with caution in clients with renal or liver dysfunction, and blood panels should be monitored.

165. The client should receive 7 gtts/min.

$\dfrac{\text{volume (mL)} \times \text{drop factor (gtts)}}{\text{time (min)}}$ = flow rate in gtts/min	Solve using the formula.
$12 \times 60 = 720$ min	Convert hours to minutes.
$\dfrac{500 \text{ mL} \times 10 \text{ gtts}}{720 \text{ min}}$	Input into formula and solve.
$\dfrac{5{,}000}{720} = 6.94$	
= **7 gtts/min**	Round up to find gtts/min.

166. Number 4 is correct.

Rationale: Clients having a renal mass removed should be placed in a prone position with a pillow under the shoulders and abdomen. Options 1, 2, and 3 are incorrect positions for this procedure.

167. Number 2 is correct.

Rationale: Lifting the urinary catheter bag above the client's bladder allows backflow of urine and increases the risk of a urinary tract infection. The bag should be passed around the end of the bed, not up and over the client. Stopping a tube feeding to check residual is a correct action. Scanning the armband and medication prior to administration is the correct and safe technique to ensure client safety. Recording vital signs and observing other nurses in the blood administration process is educational for the student nurse and demonstrates proper procedure for blood administration.

168. 7 mL

$\dfrac{665 \text{ mg}}{95 \text{ mg/mL}} = 7$	Divide 665 mg of Claforan by 95 mg/mL.
7×1 mL	Multiply the quotient, 7, by 1 mL.
= **7 mL**	Solve.

169. Number 1 is correct.

Rationale: Spironolactone is a potassium-sparing diuretic, which is inappropriate for this client. Furosemide (Lasix) is a better choice for this client, because it helps remove excess potassium. Delivering a low-potassium meal tray is an appropriate action. Sodium polystyrene sulfonate (Kayexalate) helps remove excess potassium from the body, and is often prescribed for clients who have elevated potassium levels. All clients should be ambulating, coughing, and deep-breathing as their condition permits.

170. Number 2 is correct.

Rationale: Buck's traction is a type of skin traction used mainly to reduce painful muscle spasms. A Velcro boot is placed around the affected limb, with the weights attached via a single pulley and the leg elevated. The weight range for skin traction is from 5 to 7 pounds. Using a heavier weight increases the risk of severe skin irritation. Skeletal traction uses heavier weights (15 – 30 pounds) and surgical screws that attach directly to the bone. The weights should hang freely and not be moved unless ordered by the health care provider. Pin site care should be done regularly and the skin checked for signs of infection such as redness, swelling, or pus.

171. Number 4 is correct.

Rationale: No one other than the client should press the button to deliver medication, in order to avoid oversedation. Remind the family to report if anyone other than the client administers a dose. The family should call if the pump starts beeping or the client becomes oversedated. Nausea is not an allergic reaction.

172. Number 2 is correct.

Rationale: The client should be in the high-Fowler's position when administering medications by NG tube to prevent aspiration. Before administration, the nurse must aspirate and check the residual, and then return it to the stomach. Not all medications may be given via NG tube. Extended release and enteric coated medications may not be given via this route. If tube feeding is in place, it must be stopped before giving medications. Following medication administration, the tubing should be flushed with 15 – 30 cc of water, or as per facility protocol.

173. Number 4 is correct.

Rationale: It is never in the nurse's best interest to sign legal documents with clients that are not part of the admissions or informed consent process. The nurse knows the client is not fully oriented to person, place, and time; therefore, the nurse is not acting in the best interest of the client as a client advocate. The nurse may also face disciplinary action from the state board of nursing, or could become involved in a legal case if anything happens to the patient. Most facilities would not allow nurses to sign as a witness on these types of documents. Asking for a copy of the document implies that the nurse will witness it, which is incorrect. Having a copy of the document in the nurse's possession away from the facility would be a HIPAA violation. The unit manager may not serve as a witness in this situation. Asking the daughter if the client is aware of what is going on incorrectly implies that the nurse might sign the document. The nurse has the clinical training and expertise to determine when a client is not fully oriented—not a family member.

174. Number 2 is correct.

Rationale: The client will likely require more insulin during his illness because the body produces more glucose while fighting infection. The client's blood sugar should be closely monitored.

175. Number 2 is correct.

Rationale: The incident report should include only factual information, nothing that adds to the story, makes assumptions, or speculates as to what occurred. If the nurse did not witness the other scenarios, he should not allege or assume they occurred.

176. Number 4 is correct.

Rationale: Raynaud's disease is a disorder in which the blood vessels in the fingers and toes contract when the client is cold or stressed, causing temporary discoloration and pain. It is most common in young adult females.

177. Number 1 is correct.

Rationale: Cushing's disease is a disorder in which there is an increased secretion of adrenocorticotropic hormone, which leads to immunosuppression. An immunosuppressed client should be placed in a private room if possible. Pityriasis rosea is a bothersome, but usually harmless, skin rash. It is not contagious. Patients with diabetes mellitus normally need not be isolated. Heterochromia iridium, or multicolored irises, is almost always harmless and requires no treatment.

178. Number 1 is correct.

Rationale: Many clients recognize their daily medications, and the nurse should be concerned if the client states the medication is different from what she usually takes. The nurse should not administer the medication until he verifies the order. There may indeed have been a medication error, so the nurse should not tell the client the medication is correct. The nurse should not report that there has been a medication error before verifying with the MAR and pharmacy, because there may not be an error at all. While it may be helpful to explain to the client that medications can vary in appearance even if they are the same substance, in this situation the nurse should verify the medication before making any assumptions.

179. Number 3 is correct.

Rationale: Someone with current symptoms of a common cold or the flu cannot donate blood. A potential donor must be free of cold or flu symptoms on the day of donation. Those with hyperthyroidism, new mothers, and people who are at least 3 years recovered from tuberculosis after completing treatment are eligible to donate blood.

180. Numbers 3 and 5 are correct.

Rationale: In order to prevent aspiration, the head of the bed should be in a high-Fowler's position whenever feedings are infusing. The tape on the nose should be removed daily and the skin assessed for breakdown; the tape should then be replaced, using care not to move the tube. The tube should be flushed every 4 hours using tepid water, not hot. Using hot water can cause discomfort and possibly burn the client. Tubing and feedings must be changed every 24 hours, even if there is still feeding left in order to prevent bacterial growth. Residuals should be replaced unless the amount is greater than 250 mL. In that case, discard the extra and consider slowing the feeding rate using the health care provider's guidelines. If no bowel sounds are present, hold the feeding and contact the health care provider.

181. Number 2 is correct.

Rationale: The client in pelvic traction is on bed rest wearing a traction belt around the pelvis. This client is the most immobile of the clients listed. The client who fractured her arm playing volleyball is able to get up and easily change positions, even with an arm brace. The client who uses a wheelchair is able to be out of the bed. The client who uses a cane for ambulation is walking in the room and hall and is active. The client's condition, medical diagnosis, and treatment plan—not age—determine how great the risk is for developing decubitus ulcers. The greater the immobility, the greater the risk.

182. Number 2 is correct.

Rationale: The typical dosage for haloperidol is 2 – 5 mg IM. This dose is three times the normal dose and should be questioned by the nurse. Options 1, 3, and 4 reflect average dosing ranges for those medications.

183. Number 1 is correct.

Rationale: Norvasc is a calcium channel blocker. Calcium causes the heart to beat stronger and harder, so by blocking it, the blood pressure is lowered. Option 2 describes the action of diuretics, such as furosemide. Option 3 describes ACE (angiotensin-converting enzyme) inhibitors, such as lisinopril. Option 4 describes the action of beta-blockers, such as metoprolol tartrate.

184. Number 4 is correct.

Rationale: Atropine sulfate is the antidote for Urecholine, which can cause transient complete heart block. Urecholine is contraindicated in clients with urinary obstructions or strictures. It should never be given by IV or IM routes. It should be given on an empty stomach to decrease the risk of nausea and vomiting.

185. Numbers 1, 4, and 5 are correct.

Rationale: The nurse should monitor for fever or sore throat, as sulfonamides can cause leukopenia, hemolytic anemia, thrombocytopenia, and agranulocytosis. If the client develops a fever or sore throat, the health care provider should be notified. The client should drink 8 – 10 glasses of water daily to maintain daily urinary output of 1200 mL to minimize the risk of renal damage. If the client takes warfarin sodium, phenytoin, or oral hypoglycemics, it may be necessary to reduce the dosage of the medication: sulfonamides potentiate the effects of those drugs. Sulfonamides can cause the urine to turn dark brown or red when taken with some combination sulfonamide medications. Dyspnea, chest pains, chills, and cough are side effects of urinary tract antiseptics such as Macrodantin and Macrobid.

186. Answer: The client will receive 930 mg of vancomycin every 12 hours.

$\frac{136 \text{ lbs}}{2.2 \text{ kg}}$	Convert pounds to kilograms.
= 61.8 kg = 62 kg.	Round up to find patient's weight in kilograms.
15 mg × 62 kg	Multiply milligrams of vancomycin by client's weight in kilograms.
= **930 mg**	Solve for dose per 12 hours.

187. Number 1 is correct.

    Rationale: Drugs requiring peak and trough levels, such as vancomycin, require precise timing in order to obtain accurate results. The peak dose should be drawn 1 – 2 hours after infusion, when drug levels are at their highest. Troughs are drawn when the drug is at its lowest level, which is right before the next dose is due. Options 2, 3, and 4 reflect inaccurate draw times.

188. Number 1 is correct.

    Rationale: Rifampin is one of the first-line agents for tuberculosis. Ciprofloxacin, levofloxacin, and streptomycin are second-line medications for tuberculosis.

189. Number 3 is correct.

    Rationale: Acetaminophen is commonly given to relieve mild headache pain, and this is a typical dose. Morphine is an opioid and would not be the first choice, due to the risk of dependency and/or abuse. It may also make the client drowsy, which increases the risk of falls. Aspirin increases the risk of bleeding, especially at doses greater than 81 mg, so this would not be a first choice. Nitroglycerin is given for angina pain, not headaches.

190. Numbers 2 and 3 are correct.

    Rationale: Before the procedure a sedative will be administered. The typical pre-procedure diet is low fiber or clear liquids only for one to three days prior to the procedure. Clients should not eat or drink 6 – 12 hours pre-procedure.

191. Numbers 1 and 4 are correct.

    Rationale: Excessive sweating and leg cramps are side effects of thyroid replacement therapy. Diarrhea rather than constipation is a side effect of thyroid replacement therapy. Inability to tolerate heat rather than cold is a side effect as well.

192. Number 1 is correct.

    Rationale: The surgical permit must be signed before a preoperative medication is administered. Other actions follow this initial step in this sequence: 2, 3, and 4.

193. Number 4 is correct.

    Rationale: Blood must be given within a certain time frame, and delaying the administration may cause the blood to expire. Most facilities allow a 30-minute to 1-hour time frame for "on time" medication administration. Option 1 is incorrect because a 30-minute delay will not be too late. Option 2 is incorrect because IV medications are never given in tubing that is infusing blood, blood products, or TPN. Option

3 is incorrect because it involves stopping blood and infusing medication through the same tubing as the blood.

194. Number 1 is correct.

Rationale: During the initial postoperative period after an ileal conduit, the client should not swim due to the risk of infection. Attendance at an ostomy support group will help the client deal with altered body image. Cleaning the stoma with soap and water will help reduce chance of infection. Wearing a leg bag during the day to collect urine allows the client to return to a normal lifestyle. At night, a larger urine collection bag will be needed.

195. Number 4 is correct.

Rationale: A full-thickness wound covered with black collagen, known as eschar, is unstageable. Wounds covered in eschar or slough cannot be staged because the full depth of the wound is not visible.

196. Number 1 is correct.

Rationale: The ECG is most commonly used to initially determine the location of myocardial damage. An echocardiogram is used to view myocardial wall function after an MI has been diagnosed. Cardiac enzymes will aid in diagnosing an MI but not the location. While not performed initially, cardiac catheterization determines coronary artery disease and would suggest the location of myocardial damage.

197. Number 2 is correct.

Rationale: Assessment of the insertion site for bleeding is a priority. Should bleeding occur, additional compression may be needed. Vital signs are monitored every 15 minutes for 2 hours after the procedure, every 30 minutes during the next 2 hours, and then every hour for 2 hours. The head of the bed may be elevated up to 30 degrees. Clients post-catheterization may eat and drink as tolerated.

198. Numbers 2, 3, and 4 are correct.

Rationale: Before giving metoprolol, the nurse should check the blood pressure and apical pulse. If the apical pulse is less than 60, the nurse should hold the medication and contact the health care provider. The nurse should always check for allergies before administering any medications. Joint Commission safety guidelines require that at least two patient identifiers are used before administering medications. The client's name, date of birth, and medical record number on the bracelet should match the chart. The nurse would not hold metoprolol for a heart rate greater than 80 bpm. There are no indications that grapefruit juice should be avoided when taking this medication.

199. Numbers 2, 3, and 4 are correct.

Rationale: Asking clients if they currently have any pain and reminding clients to report pain are within the scope of practice for the UAP. The UAP may also report facial grimacing to the nurse, who can then assess the pain. Assessing pain using the pain scale should be done by the nurse, as assessment is a nursing action. No medications, even over-the-counter ones, may be given by anyone other than the licensed nurse. If the nurse is interrupted for an emergency, another nurse may administer the medication after assessing the client's pain and checking the chart for any allergies, if facility protocols permit this. The nurse is ultimately responsible for the task that has been delegated.

200. Number 3 is correct.

Rationale: If both regular and intermediate-acting (NPH) insulins are ordered for a client, the regular insulin should be drawn up first to prevent contamination with the intermediate-acting (NPH) insulin. Insulin is a high-alert drug that requires two nurses to verify the dosage. Regular insulin is the only type that may be given intravenously.

www.ingramcontent.com/pod-product-compliance
Lightning Source LLC
Chambersburg PA
CBHW081153290426
44108CB00018B/2535